AMONG PAPUAN HEADHUNTERS

AMS PRESS
NEW YORK

WABUDA GIRLS IN DANCING DRESSES.
The head ornaments are Bird of Paradise plumes and are extraordinarily beautiful.

AMONG PAPUAN HEADHUNTERS

AN ACCOUNT OF THE MANNERS & CUSTOMS OF THE OLD FLY RIVER HEADHUNTERS, WITH A DESCRIPTION OF THE SECRETS OF THE INITIATION CEREMONIES DIVULGED BY THOSE WHO HAVE PASSED THROUGH ALL THE DIFFERENT ORDERS OF THE CRAFT, BY ONE WHO HAS SPENT MANY YEARS IN THEIR MIDST

BY
E. BAXTER RILEY, F.R.A.I.

WITH 50 ILLUSTRATIONS & 2 MAPS

Philadelphia
J. B. Lippincott Company
1925

Library of Congress Cataloging in Publication Data

Riley, E. Baxter.
  Among Papuan headhunters.

  Reprint. Originally published: Philadelphia:
Lippincott, 1925.
  Includes index.
  1. Kiwai (Papuan people) I. Title.
DU740.42.R54 1982   306'.0899912   75-35155
ISBN 0-404-14170-6

Reprinted from the edition of 1925, Philadelphia. Trim size has been slightly altered. Original trim: 13.2 × 21.2. cm.

MANUFACTURED
IN THE UNITED STATES OF AMERICA

CONTENTS

CHAPTER I
The Fly River & its Peoples 17

CHAPTER II
The Kiwai Child 28

CHAPTER III
Youths & Maidens 38

CHAPTER IV
Kiwai Women 52

CHAPTER V
Widows 66

CHAPTER VI
Kiwai Men 76

CHAPTER VII
Gardening 92

CHAPTER VIII
Canoes & Canoe-Makers 108

CHAPTER IX
Turtle Fishing 118

CHAPTER X
Dugong Fishing 128

CHAPTER XI
Games & Amusements 142

CHAPTER XII
Indoor & Outdoor Games 150

Contents

CHAPTER XIII
Death & Burial 165

CHAPTER XIV
The *Kaikai Oboro* 175

CHAPTER XV
Muguru, or First Initiation Ceremonies . . 189

CHAPTER XVI
Yam Muguru, or Second & Third Initiation Ceremonies 201

CHAPTER XVII
The *Gamabibi Muguru* 208

CHAPTER XVIII
The *Mimia Abere* 219

CHAPTER XIX
The *Uruba Muguru* 234

CHAPTER XX
The *Taera* Ceremonies 241

CHAPTER XXI
The *Gaera* Ceremony 253

CHAPTER XXII
Headhunters on the Warpath 261

CHAPTER XXIII
Sorcery 276

CHAPTER XXIV
Kiwai Ideas of the Spirit World . . . 290

CHAPTER XXV
Psychology of Native Dancing 299

Index 313

LIST OF ILLUSTRATIONS

Wabuda Girls in Dancing Dresses	*Frontispiece*
	PAGE
Women making Sago (3)	32
Boys going fishing by Torchlight	40
Boys shooting with Small Bows & Grass Arrows	40
Marks used in the *Wete* Ceremony	43
Framework for Vegetables and Fruit	44
Dori Head-dress	45
Scraping a Coco-Nut	56
Cooking the Evening Meal	56
On the Way to the Gardens	56
Economy in Dress	64
Widowers of Daware, Fly River	72
Suwami Widows	72
Two Goaribari Natives	80
Native Dancers	80
Caps worn by Gaima Natives	80
Framework of a Hut in course of erection	84
Plan of *Darimo*	86
How the Bow of a Canoe is built	96
A Double Outrigger Canoe with Platform	96
A Canoe manned by Ten Men on the Fly River	112

List of Illustrations

	PAGE
A Canoe & Children	112
A Decorated Canoe	112
A Double Outrigger Sailing Canoe	120
The *Agu*, upon which Turtle Shells are placed	127
Ready to Strike	128
Native Harpoon, or *Wapo*	129
Native Drawings of Dugong Fishing	130, 131, 133, 135, 136, 140
Mosibo or *Tea Koroio*	145
The Game of Water	156
A Gogobe Head-dress	176
A Fly River Native with Cassowary-Feather Head-dress	176
Dead Body drying on a Platform	176
Horiomu, or Sacred Dancing Ground	180
Men seated in the Shape of a Bull-Roarer	204
The *Yam Muguru*	206
A Dancer's Dress for the *Oromo rubi oboro*	208
Boy blowing a Conch Shell	216
Knives used for severing the Head from the Body	232
The Gora	232
Bamu River Native	232
A Dancer at the Ceremony in Memory of the Dead	232
Plan of War Dance	268
Old Head Knife & Carrier	272
Drying a Head	272

Maps

Sketch Map of Daru District	99
Map of Papua or New Guinea	313

THE FLY RIVER  ITS PEOPLES

AMONG PAPUAN HEADHUNTERS

CHAPTER I

THE FLY RIVER & ITS PEOPLES

BY glancing at the map the reader will see that the Fly river, which is over six hundred miles long, flows in a winding course through the western division of Papua. Some readers may possibly ask two questions: What is Papua and where is it? Papua, then, is a large island lying north-east of Australia, and, like ancient Gaul, is divided into three parts: Dutch New Guinea; Papua, formerly known as British New Guinea; and the Mandated Territory, which once belonged to Germany and is now administered by the Commonwealth of Australia.

The source of the river is in the region of Mounts Donaldson (2000 feet) and Blucher (5000 feet). The approximate position of the latter is in latitude 5° south, and longitude 142° east. The position of the former is some miles to the north-west of Mount Blucher.

Sir William MacGregor made the following interesting calculation; he says in his report: " Opportunity was also taken to estimate as accurately as possible the quantity of water coming down the Fly river, at a spot just beyond the tidal influence and at a time when the stream was probably about an average volume. The average depth straight across from our camp to the opposite bank was found to be

39 feet; the average current at the rate of 3·25 miles an hour; and the width of the river 600 yards. Our estimate of the quantity of water coming down in twenty-four hours was, in round numbers, 180,000,000,000 gallons. To put it in a simpler form and to make the significance of these figures more comprehensible, it may be stated that the Fly river sends down fresh water enough to supply the present population of the globe with 60 gallons a day a head. The volume of water was far from being clear, but on the contrary contained a considerable quantity of mud" (1890 Report, pp. 49-50).

This estimate was made, approximately, some 176 miles from the mouth of the river, and, interesting though it may be, does not convey the slightest notion of what the river is like in the tidal regions, where numerous streams flow into it, swelling its already large volume of water; nor of the bore at spring tides which commerces between the island of Gebaro and the left bank of the river; nor of the estuary with its fifty-mile-wide mouth which is open to the Coral Sea; nor of the delta with its many islands, mud-flats and sand-banks; nor of the raging seas experienced there.

I am indebted to Captain Harrold P. Reynolds, whose knowledge of the lower regions of the Fly is unsurpassed, for the accompanying sketch of the estuary and delta, which he has prepared at my request. He has been good enough to mark the sand-banks in dotted ink. It will readily be admitted by anyone looking at this sketch that navigation in the Fly river and its estuary is not without its difficulties and dangers, even in the very best of weather (*vide* p. 99).

The Seasons.—Roughly speaking, there are only two

The Fly River & its Peoples

seasons in the year: the south-east or windy season, which lasts some seven months, from June to the end of December; and the north-west or rainy season, which is of five months' duration, January to the end of May. In the south-east season the two worst months are July and August, when the winds are very strong and at times terrific. Huge waves, rushing before the wind into the delta from the open sea, dash violently against the sand-banks (which are miles long) in tempestuous fury, making the waters of the estuary a seething sea of ugly breakers and boiling surf. The scene is most impressive, grand, even fascinating, to the mere onlooker, but not so to the person who is in charge of a ten or fifteen ton vessel. I would rather cross the Bay of Biscay or the Gulf of Lyons in a gale (in a great comfortable ocean liner, of course) than I would beat down the Fly (in a small boat) from Iasa to Toro Pass, only fifteen miles, when the tide is running out against the wind.

Each season has its advantages and its disadvantages. In the south-east we have strong winds and horrible seas, but no mosquitoes to worry about on board ship; whilst in the north-west we have flat calms, stifling heat, fierce squalls, heavy thunderstorms with vivid lightning, swarms of houseflies in the daytime and greater swarms of mosquitoes at night.

A night in a large steamer cabin during heavy rain when all the ports are closed and the ship battened down is far from pleasant, but a night in a small fourteen-ton vessel during a heavy thunderstorm, with all ventilation stopped and hundreds of mosquitoes in the cabin, together with the suffocating heat, can perhaps be better imagined than described. I have spent some horrible nights and anxious times in the day in the Fly estuary in both seasons of the year, but on the whole I think the worst have been in the north-west. I will give one illustration. I was once travelling from Samari to Toro Pass. When we left there was hardly a breath of wind and the omens looked most favourable for a good passage. Though the tide was against the launch, she did very well. We had got only just about half-way across when we were struck by a terrible squall from the north-west which sprang up quite suddenly. The rain was so heavy that we could not see where we were going. We were between two sand-banks and there was another a distance ahead of us. There was nothing for it but to anchor. We did so, and paid out fifteen fathoms of chain. There were only two fathoms of water. I gave a cast of the lead and to my surprise found that the ship was drifting. We paid out more chain and let a second anchor go. Still we drifted towards a sand-bank which was not more than half-a-mile away. I then ordered the engine to be put full speed ahead and by this means we held on for two hours, when the squall died as suddenly as it had sprung up. We managed to get to a safe anchorage in Toro Pass just as the sun went down. What an awful time we had! I spent the whole of those long hours burning insect powder in the cabin to keep the mosquitoes out, but even by this means did not succeed in doing so. I tried to rest under the mosquito curtain very scantily clad, but that was far worse than the stifling atmosphere outside the net, plus the smoke of the fire, the odour of the incense and the tormenting mosquitoes put together. I have spent many such nights, but never from choice.

At low spring tides the river presents a most depressing appearance; the mud-flats and sand-banks are all bare, whilst all along the muddy banks of the stream are piles of debris left by the receding tide. In the north-west, large trees, nipa palms and driftwood float down the river in great quantities. These nipa palms, with their long leaves standing straight up out of the water, often present a very strange and curious appearance. When seen at a great distance (the visibility is much greater in the north-west than in the south-east) they resemble ships with their sails set. It is not often that the members of a Papuan crew on the Fly make a mistake of this kind, but only a short time ago when coming down the river two members of my crew reported a top-masted schooner on the horizon. Upon looking at the object through the marine glasses I concluded that the boys were correct. It was not until we had travelled several miles towards the supposed vessel that we discovered the object to be a large nipa palm drifting up the river towards us. These floating nipa palms do not have such an appearance in the south-east season.

The scenery on the Fly river cannot, by any stretch of the imagination, be called impressive. There is absolutely nothing to excite the emotion of admiration except the large quantities of mud. The numerous islands, all low and swampy, are for the most part covered with mangrove, nipa palms and other short, stumpy trees. On some islands large numbers of coco-nut and sago palms flourish, which may be seen from the deck of a ship. These may be interesting on a first visit, but become very monotonous after a few days in the river. The most depressing feature is the mud.

It is everywhere. One cannot get away from it even though one decides to remain on board the ship, for then it is always before one's eyes.

I will relate an amusing experience which occurred a few years ago when landing at Iasa, which is the most abominable place to go ashore at in the Fly river at low water.

It was during the north-west season, and a strong spring ebb-tide had almost spent itself when we anchored the boat about a mile and a half from the beach. It was the lowest tide I had ever seen in the river. On this occasion I had a very distinguished guest with me, a man of very pronounced aldermanic proportions. I told him that it was necessary for me to go ashore at once, and then politely suggested that he should remain on board for a time until the tide had flooded sufficiently to allow of his coming ashore in the dinghy, and also to save him from having to walk through the sea of mud staring us in the face. His Yorkshire blood was up in a moment. He scorned the idea of remaining aboard. We therefore left the ship together in the dinghy with two boys as crew, and went as far as we could through the muddy water until our progress was stopped by the boat grounding on the bottom. Minus shoes and socks, with pants rolled up over the knees, we got out of the dinghy and commenced our journey to the beach, which was about three-quarters of a mile away. At first the mud was only ankle-deep and we made good progress; soon, however, the mud was over our calves. At this point my guest requested the help of the two boys who had come in the dinghy with us; both went to his assistance, one taking his right arm and the other his left. We had not gone very far when my friend struck a very bad patch of glutinous mud which was well over his knees. He could go no farther. He was unable to withdraw either leg from the sticky substance, even with the aid of his two assistants. I was most fortunate in missing the patch where he got stuck. A party of natives ashore, seeing our difficulty, launched a *peere* (that is, the half of a canoe which has been split in two) on the appalling expanse of mud and dragged it along to the place where we were anchored. The distressed passenger was safely extricated from the mud (which the natives dug away with their hands) and placed amidships in the half-canoe, which was only about an inch above the mud, except at the ends, which were curved upwards. A dozen strong men pulled the craft through the mud to the beach and the passenger had a smooth, if somewhat uncomfortable, trip ashore. I managed to walk the whole distance, but had to obtain the help of two natives. My friend was awfully good over the whole business. Fearing that I should be distressed on account of his misfortune, he tried to console me with the kind assurance that he had thoroughly enjoyed himself and would not have missed the experience for worlds.

The amount of denudation going on all round the river is tremendous. New islands are in process of formation and old ones are being washed away. The native communities are continually having to rebuild their villages farther back from the banks of the river. With the exception of the village of Parama, there is not a single one in the delta occupying the same site as when I first came into this part of the country; some sites have been changed three or four times during that period.

Animals.—The Fly river district, and in fact the whole of Papua, is, like the neighbouring continent of Australia, singularly destitute of quadrupeds. We have the orange-coloured dog, the wild pig, the wallaby or small kangaroo, the cuscus or ring-tailed opossum, the rat, the hedgehog, the bandicoot, and other small animals.

Of reptiles we have the crocodile and many kinds of snakes. Of birds there are a great number: the cassowary, wild geese, ducks, pelicans, blue, white and goura pigeons (the last-named have beautiful plumes on the top of their heads), parrots, black and white cockatoos, parakeets, birds of paradise and a host of others. One of these birds, named Kapia, which has a red beak, no native will kill or eat. Legend says that it carried fire from Manawete to Iasa, hence its red beak. This is one of the origins of fire on Kiwai Island, from whence all other places obtained it.

Salt-water fish and sharks are plentiful in the estuary. Thirty miles from the mouth of the river fresh-water fish are found. The flesh of these is soft and not at all good eating for Europeans.

Sword-fish are well known. I have in my possession the sword of one which measures 3 feet 10 inches long. This was caught at Domori, sixty miles from the river mouth. Fresh-water turtle, with their round, hard shells, are numerous. Along the coast to the west sea-turtle and dugong are plentiful in their respective seasons. The methods of capture will be explained in detail in other chapters.

Pests.—Pests abound in the district; their name is legion: centipedes, frogs, fleas, mosquitoes, crickets,

The Fly River & its Peoples

cockroaches, house-flies, sand-flies, moths, scorpions, white ants, and a host of others.

If any European desires to have his or her clothing beautifully cellularized without cost, let such a one put the garments away in a drawer, box or wardrobe unprotected and in a very short time a wonderful transformation will take place. The said articles will be full of holes and completely ruined. This may, however, be prevented by wrapping the garments in unbleached calico. What moths are to clothing white ants are to timber.

Sand-flies and mosquitoes are perhaps the greatest abominations. I am now writing under a mosquito curtain in bed and there are swarms of mosquitoes buzzing round with the usual musical accompaniment. The very worst spot I know for mosquitoes is a village eight miles from Daru, named Katatai. It is the most depressing place I have ever slept in, or rather tried to sleep in. I spent two days and a night there once and took every meal under the curtain, and even then there were scores inside the net. The native community are now living on a sand-bank (on which they have erected houses), on account of the hordes of mosquitoes. It is impossible to live ashore in the north-west season, even though they have smoke fires inside and under their houses.

The People.—The natives inhabiting the islands in the Fly estuary are called Kiwai. This term includes those living on both banks of the river for a distance of some thirty miles from the mouth, and also those residing in a few coastal villages extending forty miles to the west. The people vary much in language, manners, customs and character. They are energetic, industrious, shy, suspicious, revengeful and very vindictive. They never forgive or forget an injury until the account has been squared.

Forty years ago they were fierce headhunters, an occupation which has not yet been abandoned in the higher regions of the river. Only a few of the old Kiwai headhunters are living to-day. For a distance of eighty miles from the mouth of the river this practice has not been indulged in for many years past.

Some of the people are very hospitable, especially those of Sumai and Auti, two villages on Kiwai Island. (The former have recently gone to live on the right bank of the river on account of the land washing away.) The natives of these two places were at one time the most fierce and terrible of all the headhunters in the district. During the last twenty years I have often visited these people, and on almost every occasion they have supplied my crew with cooked food during our stay in their midst. The first time I went to Auti I received a large portion of sago, bananas and other native vegetables, along with the hind leg of a dog, cooked to a turn on a hot wood fire. I did not partake of this delicacy, but took it aboard my ship. It disappeared later on, and my crew were very much upset when they discovered that it had mysteriously vanished. I had no idea at the time that some of them had cast covetous eyes upon it. Of the coastal natives Tureture and Mawata are very hospitable when they have a plentiful supply of food on hand.

The coastal natives are clever, much more so than the river folks, and have greater initiative. All are lacking in the sense of decorative art compared with what is found among other native communities. Some of their old drums were

The Fly River & its Peoples

shaped at one end like the mouth of a crocodile and lightly chipped round the edges. As far as I know, the Wabuda people, and those to the east of Wabuda, are the only ones who have decorated paddle-heads. I have seen obscene posts in the houses at Wabuda which were well carved. Apart from these I have not seen any decorative art about any of their houses. The Mawata, Tureture and other coastal villages show no little ingenuity in making dancing dresses and ornaments.

Both men and women act as sorcerers. I have known many of the former but have not met any of the latter, some of whom are supposed to have great skill in black and white magic.

Their folk-lore is amazing and shows great powers of imagination. I once sat from nine-thirty P.M. till twelve P.M. without speaking a single word, listening to an old man relating one of their legends. I took notes for two hours, but had to give it up as the mass of details was so absolutely bewildering that I gave up the attempt to record the story. At midnight I suggested a rest, but have not had the heart to listen to the other half of the legend.

The imagination or creative power of the native mind is seen at its best in their magic ritual and in their ideas of the spirit world. Some of these, along with their manners and customs, will be dealt with in the following pages.

CHAPTER II

THE KIWAI CHILD

IN the Fly river district children are born in various places, sometimes in the house, as on Kiwai Island, sometimes under the house, or in the open on the sea beach, or in some secluded place in the woods not far from the village. No feast is made to celebrate the arrival of a newly born baby. After the mother has recovered her strength she obtains as much food from her garden as possible, and is assisted by the relatives of her husband, who supply quantities of vegetables, so that a fairly large stock is accumulated. This is presented, just as it came from the gardens, and uncooked, to the women who attended the mother during her confinement. The relatives of the mother do not in any way contribute to this present of food. No man is permitted to partake of it; were one to do so it is believed that he will be stricken with paralysis. Only women and children may eat it.

The naming of a child is somewhat complicated. Four or five names are often given to one person. The father and his elder brother generally give the offspring one name. This must be the name of one of their own clan. Each clan has its own names, and no person may take a name for his own child which belongs to another clan. A concrete illustration will perhaps make the case more intelligible. A man named Adagi of the Doriomu clan married a woman,

The Kiwai Child

Bugido, of the Merewadai clan. They had a son. The father and uncle gave him the name of their own grandfather, Hariba. The mother's people gave him two names, Wageru and Madua. An old woman, a friend of the family, named him Waiba. The father also gave another name, Murau. Thus the boy has five different names, and the persons who gave them generally address him by the name they themselves gave him. Now the two names Wageru and Madua, which were given by the mother's relatives, must be returned to the clan from whence they came. This is done in the following manner. In after years, when the boy with five names has grown into manhood, he hears that a child is born in his mother's clan, so will visit the particular house and bestow the name Wageru upon the new arrival; to another newly born baby he will give the name Madua, thus returning the names and squaring the account.

The Kiwai child is not so fortunate as to be the happy possessor of a comfortable perambulator or push-car. Such things would be practically useless on the Fly river district on account of the uneven tracks used as roads and the large quantities of mud. Each child, however, is provided with an excellent substitute for the above methods of travel, and that is a special contrivance which serves the purpose of perambulator as well as that of a cradle. This is made from the long acute leaflets which spring from the midrib of the coco-nut leaf, and is named *neteru* (Mawata, *sisa*). It is really a basket of interlaced leaflets, two feet or more in length, and eighteen inches broad; all round the rim of the basket a dried leaf of the pandanus-tree is laid and bent over; this is securely tied with string made from the *warakara* tree. The rim is thus strengthened, and greater stability imparted to the basket. Two native-made belts are passed under the basket and looped over the open part. These belts are about nine inches apart, and are interwoven into both sides of the basket. The looped parts of the belt are used as handles, and are so conveniently long that they can be slipped over the arm on to the shoulder. This enables the mother to tuck her baby and basket under her arm without fear of its falling to the ground in case of accident or some unforeseen emergency. A small *tiro* mat is placed inside the basket, which is called *tiro bare* ; this serves as a kind of sheet upon which the child lies ; a larger piece of *tiro* mat (*soboro*) is wrapped on the outside of the basket in bad weather to keep out rain and wind ; two or three pieces of a banana leaf are laid at one end of the basket and serve as a pillow, whilst another small piece of mat is used as a covering for the child's body and as a protection against the hot sun and rain.

This style of perambulator and cradle combined is perhaps the most simple that the human mind could conceive, and it is certainly very easy to manipulate. Nineteen out of every twenty married white men would be able to take a baby out of this cradle without endangering its life, whereas only one (possibly) in a thousand could remove a baby from the cradle used in the Port Moresby district without suffocating the infant. The difficulty with the latter is that mere man never knows which end should come out first, the head or feet. It is perhaps unfortunate that these primitive yet most serviceable cradles appear to be rapidly going out of fashion, and nowadays pieces of cotton print replace them.

The Kiwai Child

The babies are carried about in these baskets, which can be hung up on the branch of a tree whilst the mother is at work in the garden. When the baby is carried under the arm it is called *arategere*; when carried on the top of a bundle on the back it is named *karamitiai*.

When a child is two or three months old it undergoes a small surgical operation, which is performed by the mother's brother, generally the elder brother of her family. The mother takes a piece of *warakara* string or twine, raises the child's hand towards the shoulder, ties one end of the string round the wrist, then passes the twine across the infant's shoulder blades and ties the other hand in a similar position. The child cannot use or move its hands. It is then put in the cradle for the night. On the following day the operation takes place. The uncle procures an instrument, *barane*, which is a thin bone from the lower extremity of the leg of a wallaby, sharpened at one end on a stone. The mother holds the infant and the uncle then makes a small hole in the septum of its nose. A piece of string two or three inches long is passed through the hole, and a knot tied at each end so that it cannot be withdrawn should the baby by any chance get its hands free. The string remains until the hole is healed, the hands being kept tied up in the meantime. When the string is removed a chip of wood about the thickness of a match (*tere iopu*) is inserted, which enlarges the hole. This is again substituted by a thicker piece, and so on until the hole in the adult nose will admit a piece of shell an inch in diameter. Sometimes a bit of leaf from a pandanus-tree is rolled up and put in the hole as an ornament. When a boy becomes a youth he has a nose-stick four or five inches long, or a shell, crescent-shaped like half a pig's tusk, named *nii* (Mawata, *wodi muti*). This, however, is not till the initiation ceremony. The piercing of the nose is called *wodi karo*. Sometimes a feast is made when the septum of the child is considered satisfactory.

Piercing the Ears.—A second operation takes place when the child is about two years of age, when its ears are pierced. The lobe or lower part of the ear is first operated upon with the same instrument that was used for the nose. Before this takes place the half of a coco-nut shell is half filled with milk taken from a woman's breast. This is placed upon a pile of food which has been collected. In Mawata a number of small bones from a fish named *bira* are placed in the milk, and remain there until they are needed. The milk may be taken from any woman in the village, and the operation may be performed by any man. The child is then brought forward and firmly held by strong hands. It may shriek and struggle, but no one hesitates or flinches from the task. The operator now comes along and places his fingers in the milk, then rubs the lobe and the outer rim of the ear, the helix, with the milky fingers. The object of this is to soften the tough areolar and adipose tissue, so that the pain may not be great. The lobe is then pierced, and one of the fish-bones inserted in the hole. On the Fly river bones are not used, but the thorns from the sago-tree, called *dou oro*.

The external prominent rim of the ear is next punctured in a dozen or more holes. I have counted the holes in an old man's ears and there were sixteen in each one. A piece of twine (*sosogoro*) is inserted in each puncture. Both ears are operated on at one sitting. These do not become very much

SAGO MAKING.

Observe the trough which is formed of the bark of the Sago Palm, in which the pith of the palm is kneaded in water and filtered through coconut fibre.

The Kiwai Child

larger, though I have seen some large enough to admit a lead pencil. The most important puncture is that made in the lobe; this is enlarged by inserting a horseshoe-shaped piece of wood, named *uu* (Mawata, *gua-gua*), which drags down the lobe until it almost reaches the shoulder, or actually does so. When the ear reaches the shoulder it is called *sageu* or *hageu*.

Fresh human milk is constantly sprinkled on the child's ears for several days until the soreness has vanished. The mother usually pays great attention to this method of alleviating the pain of her little one. The main object in piercing both the nose and ears is to decorate or make the child look smart and pretty. In olden times if a child's nose and ears were not pierced such a one would be called *obere mere*, a bush child, or, worse still, a *tumu boromo*, a bush pig. This method of piercing the child's ears is rapidly dying out.

When a boy or girl reached the age of about twelve or thirteen years the inner side of the looped lobe was cut with an ipa shell, or with a thin reed which was sharpened for the purpose. The ear then reached down on to the chest and was called *atari*. The place where the ear was cut is called *odowaro*.

If a man's wife dies another man comes along and cuts off the long lobe (*atari*) of the husband, also the *waro* or long hair. If a husband dies the wife's lobe is severed. If a married daughter dies and the mother's and father's ears have not been already severed, the father performs the operation on his own ears, or calls in a friend to oblige, whilst another woman does the same office for the ears of the mother. The same regulation applies in the case of the death of an unmarried child. The part of the ear which is cut off is buried with the remains of the offspring. On the island of Kiwai, if a husband died the wife put her finger in the large hole in the septum of the nose and wrenched it clean open. This statement was first made to me by Awani of Iasa and has been confirmed by several others. Along the coast this was not practised.

The Child's Education.—In olden times the Kiwai child was not taught to read, as there were no books or written language, and no schools. Yet the children received an education which fitted them for the life which lay before them. Some of them are very clever, and at an early age have an extensive knowledge of natural history which is not a little surprising. Every child is a trained observer of things pertaining to the material world. There is not a bird in the district whose name a boy does not know, or whose note, call or whistle he does not recognize. He can imitate their cries with great skill. He knows their habits and what kinds of food they eat. He is skilful at trapping and shooting them with toy bows and grass arrows. If he is walking through the forest and hears a noise in the long grass he can generally diagnose the cause, and say whether it was made by a pig, cassowary, wallaby, snake or man. When walking on a road where footprints of animals or men are discovered, a boy can form a good idea as to the time when they were made. He knows the names and much of the nature of all the creeping things of the forest; the names of all the economic plants, and what can be made from them. He is taught fishing, and knows the names of every fish caught in the waters round about his home. He learns in infancy to paddle and manage a canoe, and if he lives on the coast he is generally a good swimmer. He is taught how to shoot and fight, and how to stalk an enemy. When receiving instruction in the last-named the crocodile is the illustration used to impress upon the young mind the necessity of taking cover and being very watchful, cautious and ever on the alert to take advantage of any good opportunity which may present itself. In all these things every boy receives instruction, but the greatest stress is laid upon the absolute necessity of making good gardens. I have often asked both men and boys on what subject did their parents lay most stress, and in every case I have received the same answer—namely, the garden. Every child, boy and girl, is told that unless they make good gardens, with fences, and attend to the weeding and cultivation of the same, they will go hungry. Whatever else a boy or girl may neglect, they are taught not to neglect that which provides the means of existence. This idea is instilled into the child's mind not by precept alone, but by the living example of both father and mother.

Girls do not get exactly the same education as the boys. They are, however, instructed in all domestic duties which will fall to their lot to perform in after life: gardening, fishing, cooking, the making of baskets, mats, dyes, and their own dresses or grass petticoats. They are extremely clever at making " cat's-cradles," as also are some of the boys. They romp and play just like other children all the world over.

The formative period of a child's life, which ought to be the happiest, brightest and most sunny part of its existence, is unfortunately, in the vast majority of cases, made the most unhappy, sad and fearful. The cause of this unfortunate state of affairs is the mythology which the children hear repeated time after time until every detail is fixed in the brain. Just imagine the effect upon a child's mind when it is told that there is an evil spirit in every nook and corner, a goblin in every tree in the bush and forest; that there are huge monsters prowling about the roads and in the river and sea, ever ready to eat or swallow them, and that the spirits of the dead are prowling round night and day to catch and make them sick. There is, however, an object in relating these weird stories to them in their childhood. It is said that this is done deliberately to scare and terrify the children so that they will be more obedient to their parents. The thought that there are horrible, ugly and wicked creatures lurking in the forest, roads, rivers, the sea and other places keeps a child from going away from its mother's or father's side and wandering abroad when it has been forbidden to do so. Fear keeps the children near their parents when they are working in the gardens. As they dare not wander round, greater thought and attention is given to the cultivation of the gardens by the boys and girls than would otherwise be the case, and their parents get more help out of them in consequence of the concentration of thought. The parents are relieved of much anxiety by knowing that their children will not attempt to go, unaccompanied, very far from home. Such are the native reasons for imparting these wretched stories of the tribe to the young children.

In the good old days it was the custom for the women to take all the babies out into the rain during the north-west season of the year and to place a leaf upon the head of each one. The wind was allowed to blow the leaf away, and when this took place the child was considered to be in no danger of contracting any illness in the years to come. I asked my informant what the effect would be if the wind did not blow the leaf off. He said that this was only practised when the wind was very strong, and that the ceremony would not be attempted at all if there was not a good wind blowing.

The women teach the girls to dance. An old man is engaged to drum for the practices and, at the conclusion of a number of these, he is paid handsomely by the women and girls for his professional services with a quantity of bananas, yams, taro, sugar-cane, etc. The boys are taught to dance by the parents, and also learn much by watching their elders.

All Kiwai boys and girls may be said to be fond of flowers, which they put as ornaments into their hair, and into the grass bands round the upper arms. The children look very sweet when clean, and with a few bright red flowers stuck in the black hair over a dark face. They have no real love for flowers, and make no effort to cultivate them. If they were to grow flowers some other useful article of food would have to be left out of the garden. Flowers are good ornaments, nothing more.

CHAPTER III

YOUTHS & MAIDENS

KIWAI parents are very indulgent with their children and allow them to do pretty much as they like; the consequence is that the youths and maidens soon get out of hand and become troublesome. To counteract this evil tendency children from twelve to sixteen years of age were in olden times put through a ceremony named *wete*.

Some of the old men call this a *muguru* ceremony; others say that it does not come under that term. However that may be, it was an ordeal very much like an initiation ceremony, and served pretty much the same purpose. Mothers of children of the above-mentioned ages strongly urged their husbands to make gardens so that food might be provided on the occasion when the *wete* would be held. In accordance with the usual custom, plots of land were specially planted for this purpose. Gardens made at the end of the south-east season would be ready by the following south-east, when the ceremony would take place.

On the morning of the day fixed for the *wete* all young children who were not old enough to see the performance were sent out of the village for a day and a night, being provided with food and water for this period. They were instructed not to return to the village unless rain compelled them to do so; in that case they were commanded not to go near the men's club-house or dire punishment would be inflicted. At seven A.M., after breakfast, the initiates were taken into the men's house and placed inside an enclosure, which had been specially erected round the central post of the house (*bobo omabu*, Mawata), the walls of which were made of *tiro* mats or coco-nut leaves. The children, both youths and maidens, were confined within this structure till four P.M., being supplied with food and water during their incarceration. They were guarded by several of the old men of the village. Whilst the young folks were imprisoned they were subjected to various kinds of physical and mental tortures, deliberately inflicted with a view to make them submissive to their parents' authority. The first piece of torture was the throwing of a harmless snake amongst the company; then men with stone clubs would look over the fence and threaten to kill them; others with bows and arrows leaned over the wall and threatened to shoot them, placing the arrows on the bow-string as if they were really in earnest; others came along and poured water upon their bodies, whilst all the men in the house shouted and brawled as if quarrelling. The initiates wept and shrieked, but no mercy was shown to them. So great was their terror that before four o'clock the enclosure became like a cesspool.

On the island of Kiwai the children were not taken into the house as they were in the villages along the coast. The former dug a circular pit near the building where the men lived, and into this the initiates were placed, their heads being just below the surface of the ground. The same unpleasant experiences befell these as were experienced by those who were placed in the club-house.

At four P.M. the children were brought out of the house or pit and taken to the sea-beach to be washed. The boys were attended to by their male guardians, the mothers' brothers, whilst the girls were taken charge of by their aunts. After being bathed they were led to a good fire so that they might warm themselves, when they were permitted to sit on the ground and watch the women dance.

A large enclosed space, about forty yards long by five broad, had been built on the sea-beach, which served as a dressing-room for the women dancers, in which there was only one door for entrance and exit. This was the one time of the year when the women had an opportunity of making themselves really smart and coming out in their very best. Their heads were adorned with three or four head-dresses made of bird of paradise and cassowary feathers, with croton leaves of different colours mixed with them. Their faces were painted black, white and red. Their bodies were covered with banana leaves, which crossed on their backs and chests like sashes. The same kind of leaves were tied round the lower limbs from the ankle to the knees. When fully dressed they were unrecognizable.

Two women first emerged from the dressing-room and danced before the villagers and the initiates. The last-named were then informed that this was the *wete* dance; they were also exhorted not to reveal what they had experienced or seen that day to the younger children. The two dancers having finished their third performance, drew the coverings from their faces so that the initiates might see who they were. The women then retired.

After a short interval the whole company of women

BOYS GOING FISHING BY TORCHLIGHT.
The torches are dead and dry coconut leaves.
BOYS SHOOTING WITH SMALL BOWS AND GRASS ARROWS.
The Author has seen these arrows shot over 150 yards.

emerged from the green-room and danced until about five o'clock. When this was concluded they sat on the ground in two rows six feet apart. Two men then took up positions, one at each end of the passage between the two lines of women; both lighted torches at their respective ends, then rushed down the lane with the flaming torches held aloft, and on reaching the opposite end the torches were extinguished. The women then stood and received the food which had been stacked on the several stalls from the hands of the men-folks. This concluded the first act of the *wete*.

The second performance took place immediately after the evening meal was over, and was held in the men's clubhouse. Women and children were permitted to enter the building for the *wete* ceremony. Dancing, singing and drumming were kept up all night and lasted till daylight the following morning. Both men and women danced. The two sexes did not dance together, nor did they dance the same step. The women followed the men in a kind of procession round the long house, and all they did was simply to bob up and down with a few croton leaves in their hands, which were held in front of their chests. The men, like their wives and sisters, were dressed in their best. They wore long grass petticoats which reached down to the ankles, pearl shell ornaments on their breasts, and many had large headdresses filled with white feathers.

The Geno'o Kamara or the Rat Dance.—The poor initiates were again given a bad time. They were placed at one end of the house under the care of their guardians, and were permitted to view the dancing. Ashes were thrown upon them from time to time, and with small sticks the men occasionally struck them gently on their backs. The men with drums made a rumbling sound, and with their mouths imitated the horrid squealing of rats. The children were informed that rats were coming to fight them. The house was in semi-darkness, and add to this the noises of rats and drums and some idea may be formed of the terrified state of the youths and maidens, who were every moment expecting to be attacked by a company of rats. Before the performance ended in the early morning the children were informed that the noises they imagined made by rats were produced by their own people.

The object of the *wete* ceremony I will give in the words of the native named Uria, of Mawata. He said: " We made *wete* to frighten the boys and girls so that they would be more obedient to their fathers and mothers." Before the women danced in the afternoon each boy's face was painted red. A mark was put down the bridge of the nose, across the eyebrows and half-way down each cheek, as shown in Fig. 1 opposite. Fig. 2 was painted on the girls' breasts in red. This together with Figs. 3 and 4 were scarified on the chest, arms and legs when their brothers were undergoing the real initiation ceremonies. In after years these scars are pointed to with pride and shown as the decorations received when their brothers and cousins were initiated.

The *wete* is a thing of the past along the coast, but is carried out in the Fly river in places.

The next ceremony of importance for the youths and maidens is the *madia*.

Madia Dance.—Just as the bird of paradise is said to

Youths & Maidens

display its beautiful plumage in the presence of a number of female birds with the object of winning their affections, so the Kiwai young man in the *madia* dance or ceremony displays his strangely attired person, makes a show of himself and his dancing capabilities, that he may attract the fair sex and by his winsome qualities obtain one or more proposals of marriage. It is only the youth who has passed through all the initiation ceremonies, and is of a marriageable

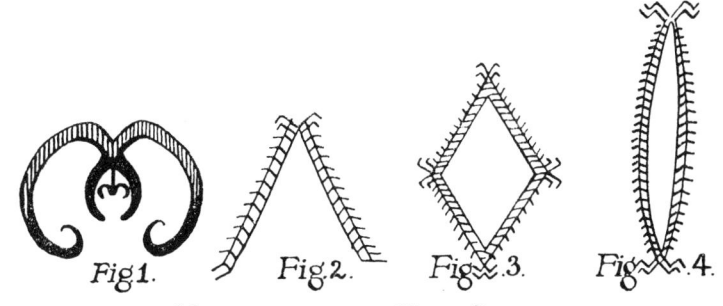

MARKS USED IN THE *WETE* CEREMONY

No. 1 is painted on the nose and face and is put on by the boy's guardians before the dance of the women in the afternoon.

No. 2 is painted upon the girl's breasts when a youth goes through the *gamabibi* and *mimia* initiation ceremonies.

No. 3 is placed on the girl's calf.

No. 4 represents a centipede and is cut into the back of the girl's thigh.

age, that dances in the *madia* with the object of procuring a wife. Some of the old men call this a *muguru*, but others do not class it under that head and call it simply a festive dance. There is none of the secrecy connected with this festival such as we find in the *muguru* ceremonies. All who desire to dance may do so. It is an occasion when both women and children are admitted into the men's club-house and take part in the performance.

The youth who is to go through the *madia* is a source of anxiety to his father and mother. They have to provide a large quantity of food, and prepare a small framework upon which this is placed, so that a good show can be made with a

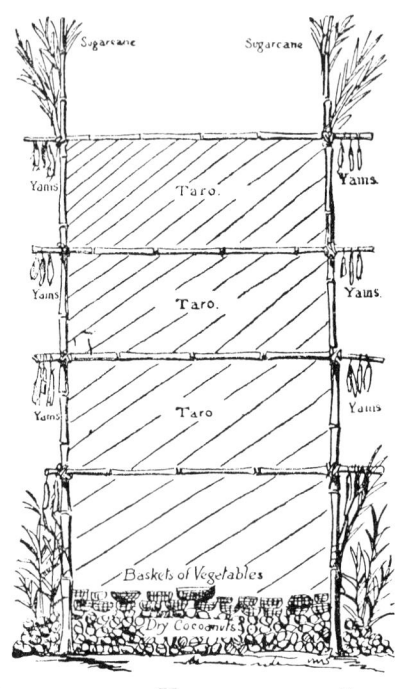

FRAMEWORK FOR VEGETABLES AND FRUIT
USED IN THE *MADIA* CEREMONY

view to impressing their neighbours with eligible daughters. The father obtains four long poles and makes a stall about six feet square, several tiers high—the height of the stall above ground is about ten feet. This is stacked with food from their own gardens and with contributions obtained from members of the father's and mother's clans.

Youths & Maidens

The Candidate for a Wife.—The father and mother of the youth who desires to take unto himself a wife spare no efforts to turn out their offspring in as attractive a manner as possible. After the garden produce has been collected they go out into the forest to procure charms—sweet-smelling plants, which are supposed to have some peculiar effect upon the fair maidens in the settlement, and which will draw them to their own child. The plants usually obtained are the *nibonibo, gauari, busumo* and *wabare*. The

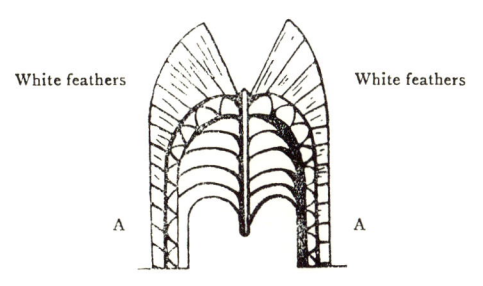

DIAGRAM OF HEAD-DRESS NAMED *DORI*

leaves of these plants are cut up by the parents and placed in a shell (*wedere*); coco-nut milk is then made and poured upon the perfumed leaves. This is laid aside until next day, when the ceremony commences. They make only enough medicine for their own child. The youth is decked out in the very finest garments that can be obtained.

It is an unwritten law that no man can take a wife until *madia* has been made for him. He must wear a *dori* head-dress, which when new looks really well. This is made of twine and wicker-work and is placed on the forehead and tied at the back of the head with two strings, which are fastened to the wicker-work, marked A. The young man's hair receives much attention. It hangs down on his shoulders in curls; the latter are not produced with hot curling-irons, or any such costly contrivances, but by taking a portion of the hair between the hands, adding a little mud mixed with oil, and rubbing the hair, mud and oil all together between the hands. The curls do not require daily attention and have a somewhat glossy appearance. I have known people who would object to the smell arising from a collection of a few such heads in a hot room at one and the same time. After being in curl for two or three days the mud is removed by the *tere iopu* (the end of an arrow) and the head covered with lime. This serves a double purpose—it is sanitary and, secondly, turns the hair brown or bleaches it: hair nicely curled and bleached adds much to the attractiveness of the love-sick youth.

The youth cannot under any circumstances put his own head-dress on or remove it when the *madia* is over. These operations must be carried out by the father and mother.

A nose-stick (*wodi muti*) eight inches long is placed in the septum of the nose, which is said to influence the fair sex not a little when making their choice of a husband.

All the men, the candidate included, wear long petticoats which reach down to their ankles. The garment of the youth is dyed in front, yellow, white and black. It is tried on by the mother, who cuts it the length required, and she teaches the boy the correct method of adjustment. It is hung out in the sun for a day. On the morning of the *madia* it is taken down from the place where it was hung and a number of perfumed leaves are fastened to the belt which

Youths & Maidens

is tied round the waist. He also wears a gauntlet on his left arm from which a stick of cassowary feathers projects beyond the elbow. Armlets are worn round the upper arms into which croton and other perfumed leaves are placed. One or more dog's-teeth necklaces and mother-of-pearl ornaments are placed round the neck and hung upon the breast.

Before the performance begins the father takes the shell containing the perfumed concoction and holds it in his hands, whilst the mother sprinkles her offspring from head to foot, using a little teased coco-nut fibre for the purpose.

Every dancer, or every two dancers, carries a round ornament of white feathers, named *gora*, in his or their hands. When two youths have only one *gora* it is carried between them, each youth holding it with one hand. The older men, those who are married, carry long ornaments decorated with white birds' feathers.

During the dancing, women carry young children on their shoulders. A mother never carries her own child. She hands her child to a sister and will carry the latter's child should she have one. When the children drop off to sleep they are handed over to their mothers, who place them in some secluded spot upon mats which they have provided for this purpose. Men also dance with small boys on their backs and shoulders.

The women dance in the same manner as in the *wete* ceremony, walking behind the men from one end of the house to the other. The *madia* dance is carried on all night and ends at daylight. The father removes the *dori* head-dress from the head of his son. In future years he may fasten his own head-dress for the *madia*. The majority of the people in the settlement sleep till about noon.

All the unmarried girls receive very strict instructions *re* their marriage proposals. They are commanded not to propose to any youth who is unfortunate enough not to possess a sister whom he can give in exchange for her. If a young woman marries into another family, the latter must provide a maiden in her place. This exchange of sisters is called *mori*. In this way the strength of the clans is kept up and consanguinity avoided. A girl may not marry a man of her own clan.

Should a maiden refuse to follow the advice tended and propose to a man without a sister, there would be very serious trouble. There would be no peace between the clans until a girl was provided in exchange. This difficulty was, and still is, got over by some other family in the young man's clan giving one of their girls to the clan from which he wishes to take a wife.

In olden times when an exchange of sisters took place and one of the girls rebelled against marrying a man she did not care for, she was forcibly dragged to her future husband's house and kept there. She might keep up her opposition for two or three months, but would eventually surrender. As a last resort her relatives would threaten to call in the sorcerer to put her to death. The old men say that this threat proved effectual in bringing the girl into a submissive state of mind. A girl placed in such a position, realizing that the whole community is, outwardly at least, against her, had a very bad time, and one is not surprised that she took the line of least resistance and yielded to the wishes of her parents and the clan.

Often marriages are arranged by parents when their children are quite young. This practice is still in existence. If when the girls grow up they do not wish to marry the men chosen for them, they will be compelled, by the force of public opinion and the methods already described, to give way and accept the arrangements made for them. I asked a man on one occasion, who had arranged an exchange of daughters with another man, what had led him to make the proposal. He replied as follows: " I saw that the girl I wanted for my son's wife was very smart in the garden, she always got firewood for her mother, fetched her water, helped her mother to look after the young members of the family, and was always willing to help any of her clan. My own daughter was like her, so I proposed the exchange, which was accepted." I then asked: " Suppose that your son had not wanted the girl, what would you have said?" He replied: " I should have told him that he had to marry her, and that I know what is good for him better than he does."

In the old head-hunting days, if a change of daughters had been satisfactorily settled, the girls would go to their mother-in-law's house, but the future husbands would not be permitted to occupy the same quarters unless both men had taken the head of an enemy in battle. It was absolutely necessary for a young man to be possessed of such a trophy in Mawata before he could take unto himself a wife.

Marriage was celebrated in olden times by an exchange of food between the two families. Food would be taken by the two girls from their own gardens and carried to their respective houses. The brothers and sisters of the two women would contribute a fair supply, including sleeping-mats (*tiro*), grass petticoats, wooden garden spades, and other useful articles. At the end of the first year another exchange of garden produce took place. On this occasion it was between the two fathers.

The girls were not expected to call upon their own mothers during the first year of married life. At the expiration of that period they would go to the old home with a broom and a basket of food. The ashes on the *momogo* or fireplace were swept away with the broom by both women. After the sweeping operation the broom was laid on the fireplace and left there. In case the parents were sick, the daughters might then go home and lend a helping hand.

The above regulation did not prevent mother and daughter holding conversations on the road to the gardens or in the village compound. The object of the prohibition was to prevent a young woman going home with any bit of trouble she might have with her husband, her mother-in-law or father-in-law, which might cause the two families to become estranged. The mothers would not visit their daughters except in case of illness.

Another interesting old custom was the case of an only son who might happen to have two or three sisters. An exchange would be demanded for each sister. The only son would therefore become possessed of three wives. He would be considered a very rich man, having three women to make gardens with him, and would always have a great supply of fish and other kinds of food.

What about the women and polygamy? The majority

did not object to being a second or third wife. The reason given was that it was easier for two or three women to look after a man than for one to do so. The women shared the work of gathering firewood, fetching water, cooking the food and attending to the gardens.

A Favourite Cicatrice cut on the Skin over the Biceps Muscle of the Arm.

This is done only by middle-aged men

CHAPTER IV

KIWAI WOMEN

THE Kiwai women, taken on the whole, are a hardworking and most industrious class of people. From morn till night, day in and day out, week in and week out, year in and year out, they live a life of drudgery. There is little of the joys or pleasures of life that falls to their lot. Two decades ago they were a sad and morose class, but during this period of time a wonderful change has taken place, and they now appear much more cheerful and happy than formerly. There were times, however, even in the old days, when they were able to cast dull care aside, as while making their garden, when they did not see their male kind for a month at a time, then they appear to have had some share in the delights of life, and in knowing that their husbands were cooking and fishing for them. During that period it must not be imagined that the women were idle; quite the contrary; they were doing what may be rightly called a month's hard labour. Yet it appears to have been a source of pleasure to them.

An Ordinary Day's Work.—At dawn of day—that is, about six A.M.—the woman is up and about. She has no bed to make and no anxiety about her husband's breakfast being ready in time for him to go to work or business, for the simple reason that she has no bed, and her husband has no work except his own garden or things connected with his own private affairs. In other words, he is not employed at so much a week or month. He has nothing except what he can get from his own land by cultivation. The woman first attends to her offspring, not by giving them an early bath, but getting them ready to make the journey with her into the garden, which may be two or more miles away, either by road or by canoe. If she has a young baby this is carried in a cradle, called *neteru*, under the arm with a piece of vine tied to both sides of the cradle and slung over the shoulder. Her lord and master precedes her as they walk to the garden; he carries a bow and several kinds of arrows. He is her natural protector, and one never knows what enemies in the shape of human beings, snakes, wild pigs, etc., may be met on the road. This is not the only idea of his carrying the weapons; he carries them in case he may be able to obtain a little animal food by shooting either bird or beast.

The woman's work in the garden varies according to the season and time of the year. When new gardens are being made her task is very heavy. Upon her shoulders rests the burden of digging up the ground, and in olden times this was done with a *wederemoa*, a shell fastened into a stick, which was used as any ordinary adze for digging the ground. She takes the bulk of the planting, weeding and trench-digging. She has also to see to the food supply of herself and family, and attend to the cooking of this. Her time is occupied in the garden until about three P.M., or maybe four P.M., when she wends her way home with the baby, a bundle of firewood, and often a basket of yams, taro, or a bundle of sago or a bunch of bananas on her shoulder. Her husband walks on in front, ever alert to catch the sound or sight of anything that will add to the food supply. There is nothing incongruous in the woman carrying this load, whilst the man walks behind empty-handed. She would resent her husband's offer to carry her load, and would look upon such an offer from him as being an unwarrantable interference with her rights. She would no more tolerate such a thing than a white woman would tolerate her husband taking over the management of the kitchen or laundry.

If the journey to the garden has to be made by canoe, the baby, which always comes first as in every other home, is placed on the little platform amidships or inside the canoe, whilst the mother takes her paddle and assists her husband to propel the small craft along the coast or along the creek. If the husband has two or more wives he may be seen sitting in the middle of the canoe without a paddle, but if necessity should arise and his help is required he has a paddle at hand to render assistance. I once saw the chief of Suwame, a village a little beyond the outskirts of what we might call civilization, being taken to the gardens in his canoe with seven wives. He was seated in the middle beating time to the rhythm of the strokes of the paddles. Such a one is considered a man of wealth, having so many wives, all of whom are expert gardeners. The women are skilled paddlers, and whilst they might not have the endurance of the men in paddling long distances, or in rough seas, there is a style or finish about their paddling not seen in that of the men-folks.

The chief meal of the day is in the evening. The woman has brought the food with her from the garden, and immediately on arriving at home commences the cooking. She has

Kiwai Women

no stove, fire-grate, saucepans, kettles or boilers, etc. She is spared the worry and trouble of such cumbersome articles. She manages quite well without them. She is able to boil a little meat in a large shell named *wedere*, and other foods may be roasted in the fire or on the fire, or in front of the fire.

The menu or bill of fare varies. Often it consists of only one course, which may be roasted sago, roasted bananas, or yams, or taro, or sweet potatoes, just these and nothing more. On the Fly river sago is the staple food, and it is interesting to see what a variety of dishes the women can make with sago and other things combined, all without the assistance of cookery books.

Sago and Coco-Nut.—Coco-nut is nearly always eaten with sago; even when the latter is simply roasted, coco-nut direct from the shell is generally eaten with the sago. A very palatable dish is made with sago and scraped coco-nut. The latter is prepared by scraping the white portion of the nut from the shell with a nipa shell. It is then very like grated coco-nut. This is mixed with the sago and laid in a leaflet of the nipa palm, and sometimes in a leaflet of the coco-nut leaf, stitched up with small pieces of fibre about the size and thickness of pins, and roasted by laying the rolls of sago upon sticks a few inches from the ground and placing fire underneath. When this mixture is nicely prepared and sufficiently cooked it would satisfy the most fastidious taste, provided that such a one does not wear false teeth, as the compound is somewhat gluey or sticky and causes unpleasant consequences. The natives having not yet attained to that state of civilization when false teeth are necessary, they do not suffer as a European would when eating such a delicious meal.

There is hardly anything that sago may not be cooked with in the same manner as the above mixture. Fish, cooked whole or cut up and mixed with sago; turtle, dugong, crabs, prawns, fruits and leaves of different kinds are all mixed with sago and cooked inside nipa-palm leaves. I have tested all the above mixtures, and several others in addition, and can say that they are very tasty dishes. Another favourite dish is made by cutting up yams, sweet potatoes and bananas into small pieces, covering them with coco-nut milk and cooking in an earthen oven named *moboro*. The term coco-nut milk does not mean the water which runs from a coco-nut when it is split open. Real coco-nut milk is made by scraping the coco-nut with a shell, or grating it, placing the grated nut in a dish, covering with water, then kneading the coco-nut and water together, and afterwards straining this by squeezing the mixture in a piece of cloth. The natives use the cloth from the coco-nut tree as a strainer. The result is a very rich milk which is somewhat sickly when strong, but if watered down is very palatable to the taste.

Meats, fish, crabs, crayfish are generally roasted by placing the joint on the top of the fire, or by laying it across two pieces of wood raised a few inches from the ground and placing fire under the food which is to be cooked. Another toothsome morsel is the flesh of the carpet-snake roasted with sago, the smell of which is enough to tempt a delicate appetite. The flesh of the carpet-snake is very tasty. I have eaten a small portion, and had I not known what it was beforehand, should without hesitation have said that it was ox tail. I

1. Scraping a Coconut.
2. Auti Women cooking the evening meal. The tongs in the woman's hands are for removing the food from the fire.
3. Bugi women on their way to their gardens for food.

have also tasted crocodile; the flesh was rather coarse and tough, but as that was part of an old male one could not expect him to be very tender. The natives are never averse to eating crocodile meat. There are two dishes which I have so far not ventured to touch—namely, roasted dog and cat. The first time I visited Auti I had a nice leg of a roasted dog given to me as a present. In thanking the givers I promised to take it aboard my vessel, which promise I faithfully kept. I did not, however, indulge in the luxury provided by my kind and hospitable friends.

The evening meal is finished about sundown. The women have then to attend to the babies, and afterwards may spend the rest of the day, or rather night, in conversation, or, if there is a dance, they may watch or take part in it as they desire. So ends the day's work.

There are many other kinds of work which the women have to do in addition to their work in the garden. They often get home about noon, when garden work permits. The afternoons will be spent in making mats, dresses, or petticoats, baskets, string bags, wicker-work fish traps and many other kinds of articles.

Mat-Making.—The *tiro* or sleeping-mat is made from the leaves of the pandanus-tree. These leaves are about four feet long and about an inch and a quarter broad when first cut. They are laid out to dry for a time in the sun, and at night they are taken into the house and placed upon the *dodo* or shelf. Next day they are rolled up into a kind of ball and again placed in the sun. After some three days' drying the leaves are unrolled and sewn together leaf by leaf. An *iro* or needle is used for the purpose of sewing. The needles are all home-made, being fashioned from the small thin bones in the wing of the flying-fox. They are two or two and a half inches long, with an eye bored through the bone at one end, which is blunt, whilst the thin end is fairly sharp. As they do not possess sewing cotton, a strong native-made vegetable thread is used in its place. The needle is used in the ordinary way, but the stitches are somewhat wide apart. The women are quite skilful in sewing these mats and take no little pride in their work. Other kinds of mats are made from grasses which are pleated.

The *eere* or petticoat is made from shredded young leaves of the sago palm and from fibre made from the body of the banana plant, which is much softer than the first-named. There are generally three kinds of material used in each petticoat, often more. It looks a simple kind of garment, but there is much skill required in the making.

To begin with, a piece of fibre from the inner part of the bark of the *warakara* tree is obtained. This is easily procured. The bark is stripped off the tree in long pieces. The woman, sitting on the floor, holds the bark with her toes and taking a shell cuts it across and she is then able to pull the inner bark off to the length of the outer bark. She takes a piece of the inner fibre about four or five feet long, which she splits into four pieces longitudinally. These are then pleated and made into a strong waistband with a loop at one end. The next step is to take about a dozen different pieces of fibre and put one end of these through the strands of the girdle, and by interweaving the strands and bending over the ends of the fibres the latter are securely fastened. Close to the looped end of the girdle some four inches of fibre are spliced along the waistband; the next part of the waistband is not covered with grass or fibre. This goes across the right hip. Some eight or nine inches of the band are spliced in the manner related above, which fits the middle of the back. The one end comes round by the left hip and passes through the loop in the waistband. The fibres hanging down the back are passed between the legs and also through the loop, when they are firmly secured. The fibres hanging down the front are then tucked round the girdle in front. The native name for the waistband is *eere iawa*, the petticoat teeth. The part which rests upon the lumbar region is made very strong by extra splicing and is about four or five inches broad, something in the shape of a collar, which is often decorated with fibres dyed in different colours.

Sago-Making.—There are no less than eleven different kinds of sago-trees on the island of Kiwai in the Fly river. When sago is first made it is white. If a good supply of water is used in the making it is said to remain white, but if only a moderate amount of water be used the sago turns blue, whilst if only a small quantity of water be used it turns red. The eleven varieties of sago may be divided into two classes, those with thorns and those without thorns.

The propagation of the sago palm is from either seeds or suckers. They flourish in low, swampy land and attain a height ranging from twenty to thirty feet. The trunk is thick-set and some fifteen to twenty inches in diameter. They come to maturity in fifteen years after they are planted. The trees used for sago-making are not allowed to flower. As soon as they mature the centre bud is cut out and all further growth prevented; the other leaves are left standing. The centre bud which is cut away is considered a delicacy and is cooked and eaten.

The decapitated palms are left standing for a considerable length of time, from one year to as many as five years, before being cut down and made into sago. Should a tree be allowed to flower or seed it is useless. After the seeds are ripe the tree begins to die. A grub, named *koni*, which is prized by the natives and considered a luxury, is found in trees which have run to seed.

When the sago-tree is considered to be ready and dry enough it is cut down by the owner. The bark is then nicked the whole length of the tree. On one side of the tree the bark is removed from the trunk and pressed down until it lies flat on the ground. On the other side of the tree the bark is removed only a few inches from the middle of the tree trunk and is left standing. The part of the bark which is laid upon the ground is covered with a mat, upon which the pithy substance of the tree falls when it is dug from the trunk with a wood adze. As soon as the bark has been placed in position the man retires and hands over all further operations to his wife, whose duty it is to make the sago. Before beginning she has considerable preparations to make. She has to procure an *oto* or adze, for the purpose of chopping up the trunk of the tree, to fix up a kneading-trough and a receptacle for the sago. To make the kneading-trough some six feet of the thick end of the midrib of the sago leaf is cut off, one end of which is about eighteen inches broad, the other tapering to about three or four inches. This is called the *wowo* or kneading-trough. It is supported at the thick end upon a piece of wood or post three feet above the surface of the ground; the other—thin—end rests upon the *baru* or receptacle for the sago.

The *baru* or sago receptacle is made from the bark of the *te* tree. Midway in the *wowo* or kneading-trough is a strainer, a piece of *sugu* or cloth from the coco-nut tree, which is fastened in by two wooden pegs.

When the woman has erected her kneading-trough she stands upon the tree trunk and with adze in her hands chops it into fine pieces like thin shavings. These fall upon the mat and are thus prevented from being contaminated by dirt. The shavings are then collected and placed into the *wowo* or kneading-trough. Water is then poured upon this and the pulp is pressed between the palms of the hands and the water runs down towards the strainer with the particles of sago held in suspension. The strainer prevents the pulp from getting into the sago receptacle.

There is a great art in using the wood adze for chopping the sago. I have tried several times but was unable to make a decent show of cutting out the sago pith. The adze is aimed to fall on the side of the foot.

The amount of sago procured from one tree varies much. Five bundles weighing about thirty pounds each are made from an ordinary-sized tree, but as many as ten bundles of the same weight may be made from a large one.

The method of cutting out the central bud mentioned above and allowing the tree to dry for years is not practised by the bushmen in the western division, who use the trees as soon as they are mature. The natives say that the object in allowing the tree to stand for years is that it improves the quality of the sago, and that the sap has time to dry or fall back into the earth, and, secondly, that the quantity of sago is increased. I endeavoured to find out the reasons why they had come to these conclusions, but was unable to do so. Such, however, is their theory.

Childbirth.—Children on Kiwai Island are generally born in the apartment or quarters inhabited by the parents, named *motee*. This is about the size of a stable, or maybe twelve feet by twelve feet. It is fenced in by placing *tiro* mats on three sides of the room, the fourth side being the wall of the house. The woman is attended by her own mother or by some of the women of her own clan.

In the village of Mawata, which is on the coast, the children are all born under the house. In the village of Kunini, some twelve miles from Daru, which is also a coastal village, though the people came originally from the bush, the women are often confined in the woods or in a special house erected some distance away from the village for the purpose. Here they may be attended by the mother or female relatives, or they may be left entirely to their own resourses to do the best they can. Some months ago the wife of one of my work-boys went home for her confinement and was sent into such a house as described above. Her mother was too old and infirm to go with her, so she had to carry on all alone.

Home Life.—There is no such thing as home life as understood by Europeans in the large houses on Kiwai Island. Most of these houses have disappeared in the coastal villages. Formerly on the coast and now on the Fly where the large houses are built there are some twenty or thirty families living in one house. This is divided up into

Kiwai Women

compartments. There is a wide passage running the whole length of the house some twelve or more feet broad. The two sides are divided into booths or rooms just like a stable. One family inhabits each *motee* or apartment. There is a fireplace in each room and a *dodo* or kind of roughly made framework which is used for storing firewood, food and other treasures. There is no furniture of any kind whatever. The *tiro* mats are laid upon the floor, which consists of the bark of a tree named *te*; the flooring bark is called *teere*. These are the beds. Some have bamboo pillows; others have rudely carved pieces of wood which serve the purpose of pillows; others have none, but use the hand or arm to rest the head upon.

A fire is kept burning on the *momogo* or fireplace, which is seldom allowed to die out. It is really wonderful how these folks manage to make so little smoke when there are some twenty or thirty fires smouldering in a house at one time. In olden times there were no lamps of any kind and the only light they had was fire. When a man walks about in the dark he generally carries a fire-stick, keeping the lighted end against the wind so that his stick burns quite freely. There are not many lamps in the river villages, though there are a fair number in the coastal ones, but none of these ever has more than a few days' supply of kerosene on hand, except occasionally when a man indulges in the luxury of purchasing a four-gallon tin.

Dyes.—There are only four distinct colours as far as I can make out. White fibres are produced by bleaching the vegetable matter in the sun.

Red dye may be made in three different ways. The first

is from a native fruit named *buma iopu*, the skin of which is very red. This skin is taken off the fruit and is rubbed upon the fibres that require to be coloured. The second is made from the skin of the fruit called *iriri iopu* and is used as above. The third method is by scraping the bark of the *gagoro* tree (mangrove) and placing the scrapings in a *wowo*, upon which water is poured. It is not only used for dying fibres, but also for painting canoes.

Yellow dye is made by pulverizing or scraping the root of the *agoago* plant, pouring water upon the root in a kind of dish.

Black colour is obtained by burying the fibres in mud for two or three days.

Fibres.—The Kiwai women make no less than sixteen different kinds of fibres. The softest, as far as I am able to judge, is made from the trunk of the banana plant. A piece is simply stripped off and the pith removed by means of a shell; it is then hung up and dried. The strongest fibre is perhaps that made from the skin of the coco-nut. To make the fibre into twine all that is required is to roll it under the palm of the hand upon the thigh. They make most, if not all, of the twine used by their husbands when rigging canoes and fixing the outriggers.

The women render most valuable assistance when houses are being built or re-roofed. They are really splendid thatch-makers and do not need to knock off every hour or so for a smoke.

Character.—Many of the women are really fine characters. If they make a promise they will keep it. I frequently lend sago to them in the north-west season—that is, to the women

ECONOMY IN DRESS.
A native of Tirio, Fly River.

on the coast—to be repaid with taro when the produce is ready for harvesting, and I have never known one of them to fail in repaying the debt, and I do not have to remind them of it. Generally speaking, they are kind, sympathetic, generous, obliging and trustworthy. They are ever ready to help one in trouble.

The lives of the women cannot be considered happy ones. The greatest obstacle to their peace of mind is the haunting fear of the evil spirits which they believe are everywhere around them, and their dread of the sorcerer. They are easily duped by the men-folk, who are constantly devising imaginary ghosts of a malignant character in order to produce a scare. To see the women in tears is a source of much enjoyment to the male members of the community.

This state of affairs is rapidly passing away and the women will at an early date have more say than at present in the civic life of the community.

The women have, as a general rule, no real appreciation of the beauties of nature. Most of them are fond of flowers, but only for personal adornment.

There are two kinds of amusement in which the women shine and derive a lot of pleasure—namely, dancing and the making of cat's-cradles, which will be dealt with in another chapter.

> "As unto the bow the cord is,
> So unto the man is woman,
> Though she bends him, she obeys him,
> Though she draws him, yet she follows."
> *Longfellow*

CHAPTER V

WIDOWS

ON the death of a husband the wife, or wives, as the case may be, sits by the corpse until it is removed from the house for burial. Like women all the world over, the Kiwai woman goes into mourning, no matter whether she revered and respected her husband's memory or not. She must exhibit some symbol of sorrow and manifestation of grief. Custom demands that she shall do this, and were a woman not to show some outward signs of lament she would be ostracized by society. After the body has been removed from the dwelling-place the woman sits in her own *motee* or apartment where she lives. The married women of the village proceed into the bush and begin to make fibres for the mourning costume. Two armlets of pleated grass, or fibre, are put on each arm, one on the wrist and another above the elbow. Two leglets are also placed on each leg, one on the ankle and the other below the knee. It takes about four days to make these. The head-dress is then made. It may be a week or a month before all is completed. The number of mourning garments, and the nature of these, varies in different parts of the Fly river.

I have seen widows decked out in head-dresses of the very best fibre, which has been rolled into twine, and a kind of short cloak, made from the same material, hanging from their shoulders; necklaces of dog's teeth wound round the

Widows

neck, pig's tusks and mother-of-pearl ornaments resting on their breasts.

In some villages the head-dresses are made of grass only, with long streamers of the same material hanging down the back, the sides of the face and in front of the face, leaving the eyes, nose and part of the cheeks visible.

I have, some little time ago, purchased the latest 1923 fashion at Samari, Kiwai Island, Fly river, which consists of no less than eight pieces. Five of these are a kind of collar which goes over the head and rests on the neck, with fringes hanging on the breast and between the shoulder blades. Two pieces, named *bara sogere*, are for covering the sides of the body. One is put under the arm on the right side and, with strings crossing the breast and back, is fastened on the top of the shoulder on the left side. Another is put under the left arm and fastened above the right shoulder. The last piece belongs to the head with its flowing streamers. When a widow wishes to wear very deep mourning she increases the number of garments worn on the sides of her body. Farther up the river different fashions or styles of mourning attire are worn.

Some women, however, do not wear mourning garments at all, but show their grief and conform to custom by simply besmearing their bodies from head to foot with charcoal and coco-nut oil, or by plastering them with white clay. Women so attired may not bathe. They can wash only their hands and feet. When the charcoal and clay begin to wear off another supply is immediately put on.

Some time ago a friend of mine, an Englishman, who has charge of a large plantation on the Fly river, was purchasing a quantity of sago from a number of natives who had come from a village some considerable distance up the river. One of these visitors was a widow in mourning costume. My friend, who is much interested in fibres from a commercial point of view, was anxious to find out what kind of materials her mourning garments were made from. He walked round to the place where the woman was standing several times, but was unable to accomplish his object. The widow, knowing something of the craftiness of men, had become somewhat suspicious of his movements, watched him carefully and kept out of his way. He asked her several times to allow him to inspect the head-dress, but without success. She did not understand a single word of his language, nor did he of hers. He tried gesture language but it was no use. She was not to be caught by chaff of that kind.

After a time he hit upon another plan. He went into his store building and soon emerged from another door with a pair of scissors in his hand. Unseen by the widow, who was engaged in conversation with her friends, he managed to get behind her and snipped off a piece of the fibre from her head covering, which was hanging down her back. As soon as the poor soul realized what had happened she uttered a piercing shriek and rushed off to her canoe in the river, howling as she went. The rest of her friends, terror-stricken, and not knowing what had happened, fled in her wake, howling and screaming as they frantically rushed towards their canoes. All embarked with haste, seized their paddles and paddled for dear life. This was more than my friend had bargained for. He called after them, but his call was the voice of one crying in the wilderness. He was considerably

Widows

upset by what he had done and the manner of the visitors' departure, fearing that the incident would get the plantation a bad name. He immediately sent a native who was in his employ to the nearest village, where he considered it most likely they would call in at and probably stay the night, to endeavour to get them to return. The native departed and on reaching the village found the people ashore and much excited. After three days he succeeded in allaying their fears and persuaded them to make the journey back with him. On their arrival, by means of the said native acting as interpreter, the plantation manager further calmed their troubled hearts. He, however, was most horrified to learn the significance of his action with the scissors. The long-established custom amongst those people is for the man who removes the mourning head-dress from the head of a widow to take her for his wife. The poor woman had vainly imagined that the white man, charmed by her beauty, desired to take possession of her and make her his wife. She was much relieved when informed that such an idea had never entered his head. The natives who were with her were then paid for their produce and departed, well pleased with themselves and all concerned.

In olden times the widow had to remain in her house all the time she wore her weeds. She left the house only when actually compelled to do so. She did no work of any kind, just sat and moped in the house. All her food was supplied and cooked by the women of her clan. During recent years widows have obtained much greater freedom.

There is no law or custom regulating the length of time a widow is to wear her mourning costume. The time may be long or short. It depends mostly upon the character and attainments of the woman herself, upon her past experience of the married state, and upon the size and age of her family, if any.

If the widow is a woman of sterling character, with comely manners, agreeable in disposition, pleasing to the eye, a good gardener, a good cook, a good fisherwoman, a good mother, and has been a model wife to her late spouse, she will not wear her mourning dress for many months; if she does, it will probably be her own fault.

Or again, if the widow's married life has been a happy one, she herself may desire the companionship of a husband, after a reasonable time of mourning has passed. Mr Serjeant Buzfuz said of Mrs Bardell that her "opinions of the opposite sex were derived from a long contemplation of the inestimable qualities of her lost husband. She had no fear, she had no distrust, she had no suspicion, all was confidence and reliance. Mr Bardell was a man of honour, Mr Bardell was a man of his word, Mr Bardell was not a deceiver." Now when a widow on the Fly river has had a similar married experience to that of Mrs Bardell she is no more averse to marrying again than was that distinguished lady. This being the case, and in accord with human nature at large, the lone widow does not mind proposing to some unmarried young man, or to a widower, or to a man with one or more wives, nor does she object to receiving proposals of marriage from any of these different classes of the opposite sex.

How then does the widow or her admirer propose? I think it can be safely said that a great majority of such proposals, on both sides, are made by wireless communications. The Morse code method of signalling is too antiquated and intricate. A much simpler method is used, one that can be repeated with ease if necessary and is without difficulty understood. An upward movement of the eyebrows, a wink of the eye, some movement of the eye itself, a slight cough when passing on the road, or the smell of perfume which may be blown upon the fair widow as she wends her way home from her garden. A man will decorate himself with sweet-smelling flowers or blossoms, and stand or loiter on the windward side of the woman he wishes to attract, so that the wind will carry the perfume to the dear heart as she passes the place where he is. If she turns her head in the direction from whence the perfume comes, he is a happy man; if she does not, he is stricken with sorrow.

All such messages are answered in the same way, a flash of the eye, a look, an answering cough, a quick forward motion of the head, and the matter is settled as far as they are concerned. There is no beating about the bush. No sending the boy up to town, out of the way, as Mr Pickwick did.

Proposals may be, and are, made by a third party. It often happens that the marriages of widows are not arranged by themselves, but by relatives or friends. This is not an unusual proceeding in more civilized parts of the world. The relatives or friends may arrange these marriages without any knowledge of the parties concerned, or the widow may just mention, to some kind soul, that she likes so-and-so, and will have no objection to sharing his joys and sorrows. Such a message would be delivered with dispatch, and an affirmative or negative reply sent back without much delay. If a widow proposes and a favourable reply is received, a dainty morsel of food is immediately sent along to the fortunate man. The omens are then propitious.

Should the widow's experience of the married state have been unfortunate, and not as satisfactory as that of Mrs Bardell, she may not desire to barter away her freedom a second time. She will neither make advances nor receive them. Under such circumstances she may continue to wear her mourning costume for two or even three years. When the costume is finally removed, she may even then refuse to marry again, though great pressure may be brought to bear upon her both by her relatives and the whole of the native community. It requires very great strength of character to stand against such a combination of forces. I have known many women marry men they did not care for because they were daily harassed by their relatives. They took the line of least resistance and married for the sake of peace.

The Removal of the Mourning Costume.—On the island of Kiwai the mourning garments are not removed by the person who is to take the widow to wife, as in the incident of the plantation manager already related, but by the women members of her own *gu* or clan.

I have stated above that the length of time the weeds are worn may depend upon the size and age of her family, if any. Now when the husband passes that bourne from which no traveller ever returns, all the children are taken away from the mother by the members of her own clan. Whilst wearing the weeds she cannot have any dealings with her

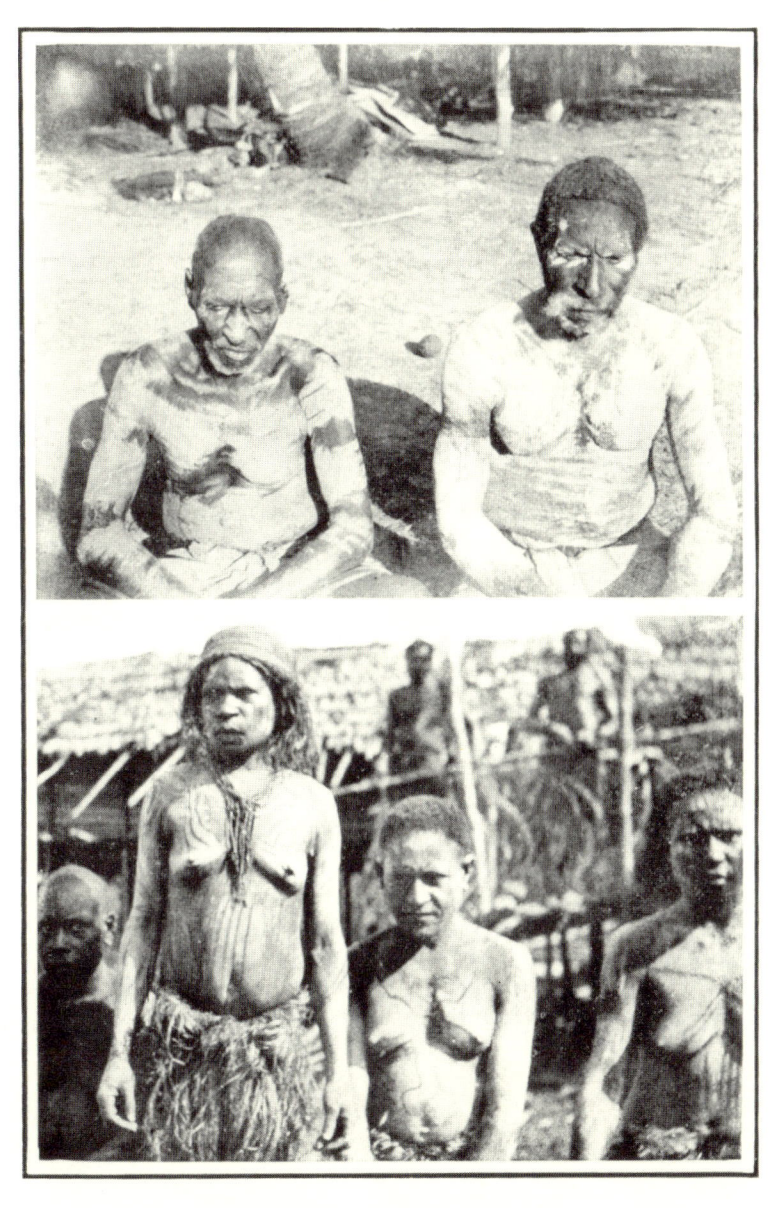

WIDOWERS OF DAWARE, FLY RIVER.
Their bodies are painted with white earth.
SUWAMI WIDOWS IN MOURNING COSTUME.
Consisting of mud and grass.

own bairns. If she has a very young child at the breast she will urge her people to speed up the feast for her dead husband, and when the festival is over she casts off her costume and takes charge of her baby once more. It is very seldom that she recovers possession of the whole of her family, if there should happen to be several children.

The mourning dress may also be removed after another marriage has been arranged, or it may be removed when the period of mourning is considered to be satisfactorily observed. In either of these cases great preparations are made for a feast, which is followed by a great dance. Some of the clan are sent into the bush gardens for bananas, yams, taro, sweet potatoes, sago, sugar-cane and other native vegetables. Others, again, go out seeking crabs; others go fishing, when turtle and dugong may be procured; others go hunting for pig, wallaby or cassowary. When all these edibles are brought into the village they are piled or hung upon a stand erected for the purpose. The members of the widow's family then proceed with all solemnity to the grave of the late husband; only the males take part in this ceremony and not the females. The small wooden house or platform which had been erected over the grave of the deceased is taken down and the wood heaped up and burnt. Before the fire is lighted the dead man's bows, arrows and all other personal property are piled upon the timbers and destroyed.

During the time these rites are being observed the female members of the family are assembled in the house where the widow lives. They first cut off the armlets and leglets; then the other eight or more garments, together with the head-dress, are removed. When these have all been taken off they are burnt in the fire inside the house. The widow is then taken to the nearest bathing-place and is permitted to bathe. In some villages she is actually bathed by the women who have accompanied her. The attendants place their hands upon the neck and back of the woman and duck her head into the water for some considerable length of time. When the ablutions have been completed the widow is thought to have paid the respect to the memory of the dead which society demands. She is now at liberty to forget the dead, if she has not already done so. She is now free from the restraining hand of custom and may take another helpmate.

There are times, however, when a widow does not wear her weeds more than six months, or even a shorter period. I know a widow who had proposals of marriage by several suitors before her busband had been in the grave a month, one of whom was considered satisfactory and accepted. Another case which came under my notice was a widow, whose husband had not been dead three months, who imagined herself to be passionately in love with a man who had two wives, both of whom were living. Whilst walking from her garden she met the man on the road and poured out her soul to him. Late the same afternoon she took her sleeping-mat and her few worldly belongings to his house and made her abode there. The other two women, who were by no means too friendly with each other, now joined forces, and though they did not actually resort to violence, came very near doing so. After the quarrel, which lasted over an hour, the two wives picked up their beds and departed, leaving the new arrival in full possession, and spent the next few days with their respective friends. Within a week they were both back again, but the husband had not a happy time. The feast which released the third wife from her weeds took place only two days before she joined the new household. The amusing part of this story is that the man was kept out of the quarrel when number three came on the scene. He did not say a word.

There is often great trouble over young widows. They are, generally speaking, the hewers of wood and the drawers of water for their mothers-in-law. The latter will hold on to the daughters-in-law as long as possible, and will do all in their power to delay or prevent their remarriage. Keeping the young widows single means not only service but an addition to the food supply, as they are good gardeners. In such cases great tact is required to placate the mothers-in-law, and an inducement in the shape of a handsome present must be given if the marriages are to be peaceably arranged.

It is a custom in some villages that when a widow does not get an offer of marriage after casting off her weeds, or refuses an offer, she becomes the wife of her late husband's brother. Several such women have appealed to me for advice and help when their brothers-in-law have desired to take them to wife. In all such cases the women's wishes have been realized.

CHAPTER VI

KIWAI MEN

A KIWAI man has a very dark skin, black frizzy hair, a long narrow head, an arched Semitic nose, is somewhat flat-chested, and stands, on an average, about five feet six to five feet eight inches in height. He is somewhat sullen and austere in appearance and does not make a good impression on a first acquaintance. He is very overbearing in his treatment of those he considers much below himself in the physical, social and intellectual world, such as the bushmen or inland people, whom he despises and derides. He is choke-full of an inordinate self-esteem and empty pride. He appreciates a joke, if it be at another's expense. He is cunning—a necessity of his environment—deceitful, suspicious, very forgetful of a kindness or help given in time of trouble or difficulty, is wanting in sympathy, except with himself, family and clan; he is very revengeful, does not forget an injury until he has squared the account; he is selfish and disobliging, and acts upon the principle: "If you do anything for nothing, do it for yourself." He is not lazy. I do not mean by that sentence that he rushes round with cyclonic energy to tackle any job he may have on hand, or that he is a hustler. There are Kiwai men who cannot be said to love work, just as there are white men who do not love it. He is not by nature a hustler, but he can and does get a hustle on. See him when he is hunting a pig and hot

Kiwai Men

on the scent, or when he is turtle or dugong fishing, or when he is dancing or engaged in some congenial pursuit. He is a keen trader, but is not conscientious in his dealings. He does not consider it a heinous crime to break a promise or go back upon a bargain; he will appropriate the private property of a white man, provided he can get away with it unobserved. I know a white man who was once building a house and had to tie his hammer and saw to his body with a piece of string lest they should be stolen. The first time he omitted to make fast the saw it vanished, and he did not see it again for years. It was returned many years later, and when the thief was asked how he managed to take it he informed the European that when he laid it on the ground he, the thief, picked it up with his toes and managed to place it behind his back, then retired out of sight walking backwards in an easy manner.

I have seen a trader on Kiwai Island buy coco-nuts twice over. He would buy a number from several natives and throw them in a heap behind him. Two men walked round, picked up about twenty each, and quietly presented them to the white man, who paid a second time. This is often done.

Another example of dishonest trading was brought to my notice only a short time ago, where a native canoe-maker had sold a canoe to two different men. The first buyer paid half the price demanded when the canoe was started. When it was finished buyer number two came along and purchased it outright. When the former heard of the sale he rushed off to the maker and asked for an explanation. This was duly given, but considered unsatisfactory. Buyer number one demanded back his arm shells and other articles of trade. These, however, had vanished and so could not be returned. After some protracted negotiations an agreement was fixed up whereby a new and larger canoe was to be provided to replace the one which had been previously purchased. As this bargain was made in the presence of the headmen of the village it will most probably be kept.

He is a keen observer of men and nature, but possesses no powers of deduction of things outside his daily life. He is very superstitious and imaginative, especially with regard to the spirit world. His mental powers are not highly developed. He is, however, clever in many ways. He is smart at improvising. I was once benighted in the bush and in the space of half-an-hour a few boys set up a small humpy and provided a decent shelter which would keep out the rain; and the only thing they had was a knife. Here is an illustration of their resourcefulness. I took a man on board my boat as pilot. When out at sea he sighted a canoe from his own village and signalled by waving a piece of print for it to come towards us. He wanted to send a message back home to his brother. The tide was too strong for the canoe to do so, though she was under sail, and the water was too shallow to permit the boat going to the canoe. As soon as the pilot discovered that the canoe could not get within hailing distance he cut the stem off a bunch of bananas and with the point of a six-inch knife scratched a message upon it. Had he thrown this into the sea it would have sunk; to prevent its doing so he took the skin off two old coco-nuts and tied the banana stem to the skins and threw them into the sea. He again signalled the crew of the

Kiwai Men

canoe, pointing to what had been thrown overboard. The canoe went about and the tide carried the message alongside and it was easily picked up.

There is something lacking in the mentality of all the Kiwai men and women. They have no appreciation of the beautiful. The pleasing combination of colours in nature makes no appeal to their souls. A gorgeous sunset leaves them cold and unmoved. Trees laden with blossom, a bed of flowers or a picturesque landscape, have no interest for them. Utility is the only thing that appeals to them. Nature is only interesting when it supplies them with something to eat, or with some object which will be of service when hunting, fishing or dancing. They love flowers and ornamental trees in a way, but it is only because they are useful for adorning the body and making a dancer or lover look smart. A man will often decorate himself with flowers and sweet-scented leaves to catch the eye of some fair maiden or lone widow whom he may desire to know more intimately.

Many years ago I travelled up the Binature river in a whale boat, pulled by ten good oars (double banked). When we had travelled about eight miles we came in view of the most gorgeous piece of natural scenery that I have ever set eyes upon. Two huge trees, one from each bank of the river, owing to the water washing away the soil from the roots, had fallen, one against the other, in the middle of the river. One was wedged in a fork of the other, so that they were holding each other up. The two trees combined formed a very beautiful arch from bank to bank. The trunks of both trees and the whole of their branches were covered with the

De Albertis creeper. The arch was one mass of fiery red, some thirty feet high in the middle, in which were patches of dark green leaves, whilst under the arch flowed the bluish green waters of the river, making a picture which I have not words to describe. As soon as I saw this I stood up in the stern sheets and pointing ahead said : " Look there ! " The crew instantly stopped rowing and turned round to look. One of them asked : " What are you looking at ? " I replied : " The red flowers on those trees." The boys smiled, and the former spokesman politely said : " I thought you had seen a crocodile or a cassowary on the bank of the river." My shooting-boy, who was perched in the bow of the boat watching both banks of the river in the hope of finding something for the pot, rose when I first spoke and held his gun ready to fire, but when he discovered that the cause of my remarks was " nothing but a few flowers," sat down again, disgusted and disappointed.

I have stated that the natives are ungrateful, and so they are, but still I think that they feel much more than they appear to do, as the following illustration will show.

Many years ago an Assistant Resident Magistrate sent a woman and her husband, in charge of a sergeant of police, to my house for medical attention. The lower end of the humerus of her right arm was fractured. This had been done by her husband striking her with a heavy piece of wood. The bone was duly set, the arm put in splints, bandaged and placed in a sling. They then returned to the care of the Magistrate. I gave the sergeant a note for the officer asking that she should be sent to me next morning at eight o'clock for inspection. Promptly the same three

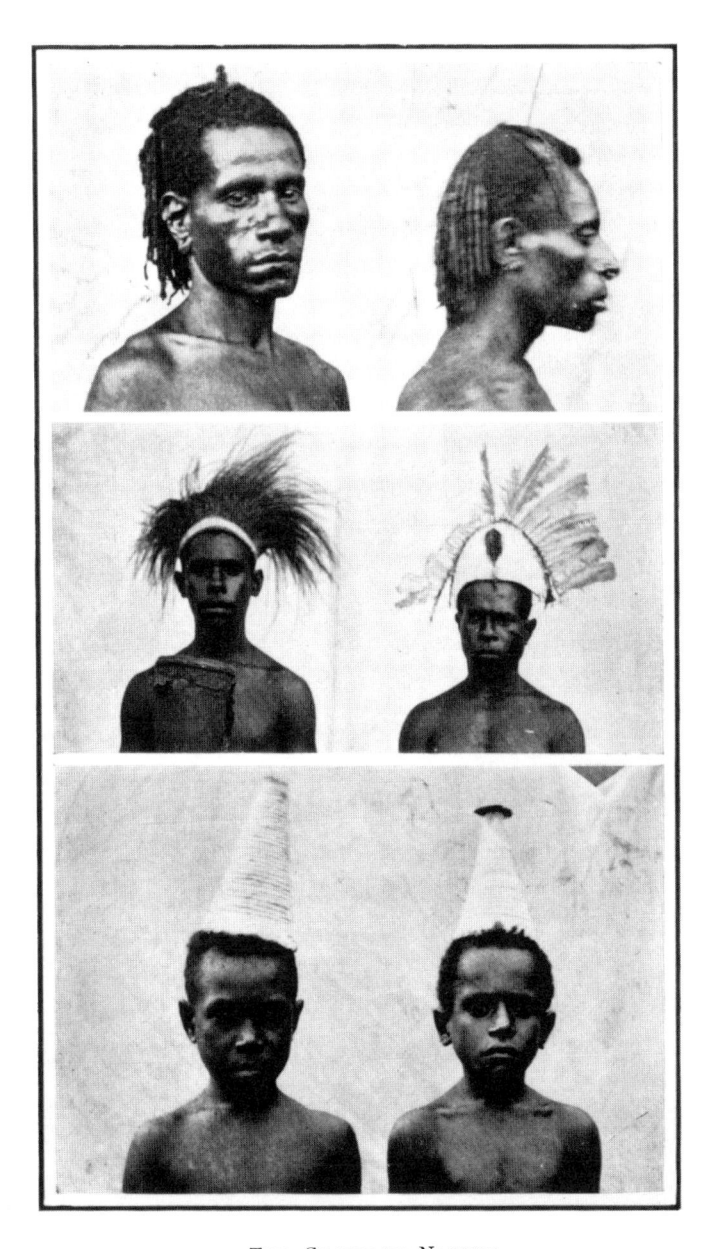

1. TWO GOARIBARI NATIVES.
2. NATIVE DANCERS.
3. CAPS WORN BY GAIMA NATIVES ON THE NORTH BANK OF THE FLY RIVER.

Kiwai Men

persons made their appearance next day. I was not a little surprised to see the woman carrying the splints and cotton-wool in one hand and the bandages placed round her neck and hanging down her back as streamers. Not understanding her language, as she was a bush woman, I could not speak to her except through a very indifferent interpreter. I did, however, learn that she had removed the dressings because she did not wish to have her arm tied up. I again rendered the necessary service and sent them back, telling the sergeant to bring her next day. She was understood to promise not to remove the splints a second time.

At eight A.M. the patient arrived, bandages round her neck and splints as before. I dropped a note to the Magistrate, who quickly appeared on the scene. He spoke to her in choice English, and though she did not understand a word he said, the admonition was effective. The splints were not removed again by her. After some six weeks she left Daru with her arm quite well, but with no word of thanks from either the woman or her husband.

Five years after, I was coming down the Binature river in a whale-boat and was hailed by a man standing on the bank of the stream, who motioned with his arm for us to come to him. I approached very cautiously, as there had been some fighting amongst the bushmen a few days before, not wishing to run into a trap, and when nearing the bank a woman appeared. The two rushed into the water, seized the gunwale of the boat, and hauled it into the soft mud. They both laughed and gesticulated and were highly amused at our wariness. The man shouted, his wife shouted, and then they shouted together; an answering voice came from the thick bush and presently a native emerged carrying the largest bunch of bananas I have seen. There were over four hundred on one stem. I did not count them but my boy did. I offered payment in accordance with the usual custom, and to my great astonishment this was refused. The man pointed to the woman's arm, but I did not understand the expressive action. One of my crew at length informed me that she was the woman whose arm had been broken. They showed their gratitude after five years and would not accept a return present.

House-Builders.—The Kiwai men are very clever house-builders. In the old days they had no tools except stone axes and adzes, yet they could build a house three or four hundred feet long and forty feet broad without a saw, hammer, nail or any other tool of iron. To-day they will build such a house with only sixteen-inch knives and tomahawks. All the timbers required would be cut with these implements and used without any dressing. I have seen huge posts thirty-five feet long (five feet being sunk into the ground and thirty feet above the surface) put into position by means of long thick rattan canes, used as ropes.

I will now briefly describe the building of a *darimo* or men's club-house of olden times. All Kiwai houses are built upon piles sunk into the ground. Before building operations are commenced all the posts, and a great part of the timber to be used, are assembled on the ground. The posts upon which the building rests are about five feet above the surface. Previous to the first post being put in position a pig hunt takes place. When the pig has been caught and killed all the skin is taken from its head and back, including the tail.

Kiwai Men

This is dried on the *dodo*, a kind of shelf, in the old club-house. No woman or child is permitted to partake of the meat or even to look at the pig. The men alone eat the flesh. The use of the skin will be related later on.

The ground for the new house will be measured by two or three of the old men and the position of the middle post decided. The holes for all the piles will be dug, and when these are finished the pile for the middle hole is brought and laid alongside, after which there is a ceremony of great importance performed.

In the middle of the end of this particular post, the part which will be buried in the ground, a hole is bored. Into this hole is placed a piece of skin taken from the head of a snake, named *dirioro*, a portion of the pig's skin, two dried eyes of an enemy killed in battle, a small piece of the mouth and parts of the mutilated bodies of both sexes, also slain in war. In the Fly river the end of the post was then wrapped up in the leaves from the *puruopuruo* tree. Among the coastal tribes the practice was to cover the end of the post with the skin of a snake. *Karea* is then made. The post is sprinkled with *gamada*; the ceremony is invariably performed by an elder of the Doriomo clan, when the following invocation will be spoken: " When we go to fight, let your spirits go before us and first overpower the spirits of our enemies. Give us good fortune when we go fighting, fishing, hunting and buying canoes. May all the people be kept free from sickness." The post will be erected, great care being taken to see that it is perfectly straight in the ground. The rest of the piles are afterwards put into the ground and in the evening much *gamada* will be drunk.

Kiwai Men

A raid upon some enemy is the next item on the programme. The ceremony related in the chapter on "Headhunters on the Warpath" takes place, followed by a raid. When the heads are brought home they are hung upon the posts and the *pipi* war dance is performed, which lasts a week.

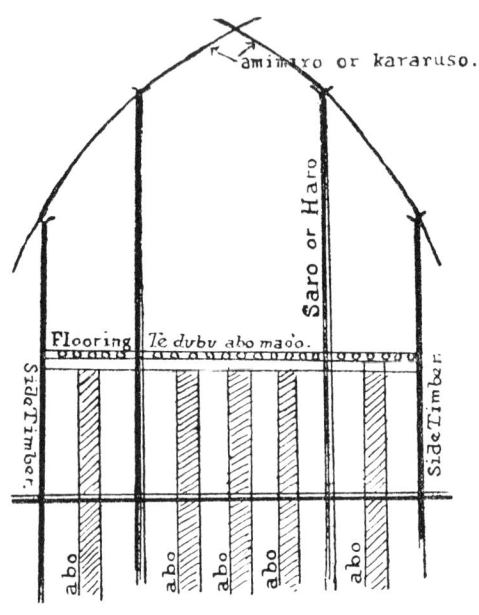

ELEVATION OF THE FRAMEWORK OF A HUT IN COURSE OF ERECTION

Building operations are then resumed. The posts under the house are called *abo*. In the plan it will be seen that those on the outsides of the house are three feet six inches above the floor. These determine the height of the walls. All the posts used in the building are cut with the top like a two-pronged fork, so that the plates can be laid inside the fork and firmly lashed with rattan cane, thus giving greater stability to the building. Two other lines of posts, named

Kiwai Men

saro on the river and *haro* on the coast, are then erected. These are fifteen feet above the floor of the building and determine the height of the roof.

The Floor of the House.—Bottom plates are laid upon the piles, which form the foundation of the floor (these are called *abo maoo*), sometimes lengthwise, but more often right across the house. They rest in the forks of the timbers. Upon the plates rafters (*tedubu*) are placed, and upon those the flooring-boards. The latter consist of the bark of the *te* tree and are called *teere*, and are about one and a half inches thick. When the *te* tree is felled the bark is split down the middle the whole length of the tree and can be taken off in two halves, which may be from ten to fifteen inches broad and twenty feet long. The outer bark is placed uppermost, and when new makes a good substantial floor, but must be trodden on carefully by strangers as the ends are not fastened down. When old it is not very safe. I have several times put my foot through the floor and had nasty jars.

The Superstructure.—Top plates are set upon the studs forming the sides of the house and also upon the *saro*. These are laid lengthwise from one end of the building to the other and are securely fastened with strong lashings.

Rafters to form the roof of the house, named *amimirio* or *kararuso*, are fixed to both lines of top plates, overhanging the outer studs about eighteen inches and meeting together in the middle of the house, forming the arch of the roof. Two thin ridge-poles are fastened to the rafters where they meet in the middle, one on the inside and one on the outside of the house. The framework is now ready for the thatch to be put upon the sides and roof.

Kiwai Men

The thatch is made from the nipa-palm leaf. The longest leaves possible are obtained and the leaflets, which measure about two feet six inches long, are stripped from the midrib by hand. Sticks are produced six or eight feet in length, one and a half inches broad and an inch thick. The leaflets are then bent over the sticks, one at a time, and fastened with two pins. The pins are obtained from the midrib of the leaflets before they are placed across the sticks. The pins are not put into the sticks, but simply through the double leaflets. When the *were* or thatch is completed, the sides of the house are first covered in and afterwards the roof is put on. The long sticks of thatch are tied to the framework by three kinds of vines: *aaro* or rattan cane is the best. The cane is split into three of four pieces and the pith scraped off with shells or knives before being used; when dry it is very strong and durable.

Explanation of the Plan of Darimo or Men's Club-House.—(1) The two circles with dots inside represent two human eyes of enemies let into the flooring-boards and covered by two red beans.

PLAN OF *DARIMO*, OR MEN'S CLUB-HOUSE

Kiwai Men

(2) The mark in the centre shows position of the central *saro*, near which the most important ceremonies are conducted. See Mimia and Gamabibi ceremonies.

(3) It will be noticed that there are thirty-two compartments in the *darimo*, and that every compartment contains a fireplace or *momogo* marked m, with two extra ones, one at each end, in the middle of the hall floor.

There are two men to every fireplace and therefore two men to each *motee* or compartment. Generally speaking, one man sleeps on each side of the fire. The fireplaces at the two ends are bigger than the rest.

(4) There are four doors, one at each end and one on each side; the former are called *gabo* and the latter *ipisurumoro* or *pipihurumo*.

From the ground plan it will be seen that the house is divided into a number of compartments. Two men have the use of one room only. They must build and complete that particular apartment of the house they will live in when not at home with their wives and families. It will also be seen that each room has a fireplace or *momogo*. This is the last piece of work to be done after the rest of the house is completed, and is done entirely by the women. The wives of the two men who are to occupy a room make the fireplace. The *tedubu* or joists of the floor are cut out for a space of about three square feet and stronger timbers, chiefly mangrove, are laid in their places. Upon these several layers of nipa and coco-nut palm leaves are placed, which are covered with clay three or four inches deep. Hot wood ashes are spread over the clay to make it firmer. In the course of twenty-four hours it is dry and a fire may be lighted upon it.

The plan shows that at each end of the house the rooms are somewhat larger than the others, and that there is a fireplace in the middle of the hall floor. These are convenient places for gossiping.

At one end of the central hall will be seen two circles, in which are two dots. Two small holes are made in the flooring-boards with fire. In each hole is placed a dried eye of an enemy put to death in battle. The dot marks represent the two eyes. These are covered over with a bean named *ibure*, which is a scarlet-red. The beans are fastened in the holes by means of the latex from a tree named *daha*. A branch is broken off a tree and the bark stripped from it; this is held over the bean and the latex runs from the branch and cements the bean to the flooring-board. It is then left to dry. Spirits of slain enemies are supposed to inhabit the two eyes, and when the builders of the house go forth to war the spirits have the power of capturing those of the enemy, thus making them weak and impotent, and giving the attacking party an easy victory. The eyes are called *ee rubi damari*: the eyes of the people who have been slain.

The Central Saro or Post.—This is the most important part of the whole house, and is marked by a small circle on one side of the ground plan. In the coastal villages this *saro* had to be placed on that side of the building which was nearest to the island of Kiwai. Around this post most of the initiation ceremonies take place. Around it the elders meet in council and discuss all matters affecting the community, their agriculture, hunting, fighting and fishing pursuits. It is considered *tarena*, something to be afraid of, hence sacred. Human figures, representing men and

Kiwai Men

women, were carved on most of the *haro*. The carvings of some of the faces, which were done in hardwood, were, or appeared to me at all events to be, well done. I think these carvings were done for ornamentation only and that they have no inner meaning. It owes its sacred character to another cause than the carvings on the posts. This is hidden away in the form of a package which is tied on the inner side of the top plate and not on the side facing the central hall. This package contains the skin of the pig which was killed before the building operations commenced, two dried human eyes, a part of the upper lip of an enemy, and similar parts of the human body as were put inside the first *abo* or post. These are tied in *aaro* leaves and form the package already mentioned.

One head-hunting expedition has been already mentioned. A second takes place when the framework of the house is completed, and a third when the house is finished. After these raids the usual head dance, *pipi*, is held. No near neighbours or distant friends would ever dream of visiting a village where a new club-house has been built until they had definite information that heads had been taken to celebrate its completion.

When the third raid has been made the house is opened and a great *karea*, good-luck ceremony, is made. The central *saro* is sprinkled with *gamada*, a drink made from a plant named *Piper methysticum*, and the spirits are called upon for help in the same way as when the first post was erected. A great feast takes place and much *gamada* is drunk.

In olden times it was the custom for all warriors going

out to fight to spend the last night in the club-house. Some of the men would remain awake all night to watch the *bisare*, or charm, resting above the central *haro*, and also the men who were to do the fighting. The charm, containing the pigskin, which was to make the men fierce in battle, and the human remains, which contained the spirits of the dead enemies and which were supposed to go ahead of the fighting men and capture the spirits of the prospective victims, renders their eyes as those of the dead, so that the raiders would have little or no trouble.

The watchmen fixed their attention first upon the *bisare* and secondly upon the men. If the spirits in the *bisare* moved, and the covering of the package made a crackling noise, all would go well with the expedition. If no movement whatever was noted, the bushmen would not be at home and the projected fight would be abandoned. Should the roof move or shake, the omen was excellent and good fortune would favour the undertaking. The name of the spirits in the package is *kokokoko*.

Should the watchmen observe a faint white light above the body of one of the sleeping warriors, they inform the person concerned of the fact as soon as he wakens, and advise him not to march with the fighting forces, the appearance of such a light being a sure indication that the man would be slain.

When a widower went on the warpath and was successful in decapitating an enemy, he took off the *sogere* or mantle and, with the assistance of a friend, tied it to the *udurumo* or headless body of the victim; the grass armlets and leglets were cut off his arms and legs with an ipa shell, then tied on

Kiwai Men

the arms and legs of the dead body. A belt made of leaves was also taken off and tied round the waist of the slain, which was then left. On the widower arriving in the village his mother and sisters would take off their mourning costumes and burn them in a fire underneath the head. The widower's mourning was then ended.

Gesture Language.—The natives are able to communicate information to each other by signals which are readily understood by all. Affirmation or yes is signified by raising the eyebrows or by tilting the head upwards; no, by shaking the head from side to side. To indicate a young child the closed fists are placed one on each breast and the index finger put into the mouth, showing the child is still at the breast. If it is desired to say that a child is dead, the above gestures are made and the arms brought stiffly to the sides of the body. Death of a man is signalled by touching the end of the chin with the right hand, indicating a beard, then bringing both arms to the sides of the body. If a woman is dead, the closed fists are placed on the breast and the arms stretched on the sides of the body.

To signal that a canoe has reached the reef out at sea, all the paddles are held aloft in a vertical manner. At night the signal is made by fire. When a canoe is returning at night and wishes to announce the number of turtle or dugong caught, two lighted sticks are struck together at intervals, making sparks fall into the sea signifying the number caught. A fire lighted in a village or the blowing of the conch-shell will recall every canoe out fishing. This means that guests have arrived or enemies have been sighted.

CHAPTER VII

GARDENING

ALL the Kiwai natives are proficient in the art or practice of cultivating the land. It is their only means of sustenance. Every adult realizes that unless the soil be tilled there will be no food to eat. Generally speaking, they grow only enough for their own needs. At harvest-time they often have more than they can eat whilst it is good. The surplus in such cases is bartered or sold. The above remarks refer to garden produce only, and not to coco-nuts and sago, which may be bought practically all the year round. Comprehending, as the natives do, that gardening is essential for their very existence, it naturally follows that their minds, thoughts and time are all concentrated towards one end—making it a great success.

Making a Yam Garden.—Yams are very thick tubers. They are said to contain more nitrogenous matter, but less starch, than the potato. They sometimes strike down two or three feet into the soil. I have weighed a medium-sized one grown in my own garden at Daru which turned the scale at five and a half pounds. They may be boiled, roasted, or grated into a powder and cooked in fat or butter as a kind of fritter. There are forty-four different kinds of yams in the Fly river district and possibly more. I have the names of the above number.

Gardening

When making a yam garden a suitable site is selected. If the land has not been used as a garden before, a small ceremony takes place in which *gamada* is sprinkled upon the trees and the spirits inhabiting them are requested to take their departure and make their abode elsewhere. If the ground has been used for a garden in years gone by, the spirits of their ancestors are called upon to assist in the making of the fence, and to produce an abundant harvest. The burning off then takes place.

The making of the fence is a great task, and also a great necessity on account of wild pigs, wallabies and cassowaries. It may be made by one clan, or by two or by three, and takes two or three months to make, according to the size. Some of them are a good half-mile long, and as straight and square as if a theodolite had been used to mark the lines. Men, women and children all assist in the fencing of the ground. The material used may be near at hand or may have to be carried some distance. It consists of small timbers, saplings and often bamboos. Two rows of straight sticks, six feet long, about four inches in diameter, and about six inches apart, are driven into the ground in an upright position. Between these other timbers are placed in a horizontal position and all are lashed together by rattan cane and other vines. The women and children help to carry the materials, but the men do all the building.

Charms.—No yams are ever planted without charms, which are supposed to make the garden more productive. The following are used for yams—leaves of several plants; *nibonibo*, which smells like mint; *hiware*, aromatic leaves; scraped coco-nut; dugong skin roasted in the fire and grated; a grass named *esame*, which is perfumed, and another plant named *sanea*. All these are cut up and mixed together in a *wedere* or large shell. Banana leaves are placed all round the shell, and the person who has compounded the charm places a portion of the mixture into each leaf lying around the shell. The medicine is wrapped up in the leaf and placed in a basket, along with four yam tops, not more, ready for planting. One man mixes for each clan, and each member gets a fair portion of the compound. It is then left until the following day.

After sunset the bull-roarers are brought into play. These are thin egg-shaped slats of wood from nine to fifteen inches long and three or four inches broad; a hole is bored through at one end and a piece of string inserted, then tied. Women and children are not permitted to see them. These are whirled by hand round the heads of the men using them and make a most weird noise, which terrifies the women and children. The swinging of these is carried on all night long, and is very annoying to a European who happens to be in a village when these operations are in progress; this at least is my own experience; others may, of course, find such noises to be entertaining, but I have never done so. There is no dancing.

At four A.M. next day all the women are up making a *moboro* or earthen oven and preparing for a feast when the first four yams have been planted. At six A.M., when the sun appears on the horizon, the men, with head-dresses of the bird of paradise and cassowary feathers, bows and arrows, with *adigo* or gauntlet on the left arm, take their departure for the new garden, carrying the basket with the medicine and four yam tops. On their arrival every man takes an *ea*, or wooden

Gardening

garden spade, and digs four holes in the ground on his own particular patch. These are about eighteen inches broad and about twelve inches deep. The yam tops are then taken out of the basket one at a time and placed alongside the four holes. The medicine packet is then removed from the basket and opened up. Each man takes one yam top in one hand and a portion of the charm in the other. The plant is held over the hole and rubbed with the concoction. What medicine does not adhere to the plant falls into the hole, so that nothing is lost. The yams are all treated in the same way, planted, and the soil heaped upon them and the holes filled up.

Any medicine that has not been used is carefully wrapped up again in the same banana leaf and put back into the basket. A *woto* or planting-stick, five feet long, is put into the ground in a slanting position in the middle of the square of yam holes. A bunch of grass (*esume*) and a few croton leaves are tied to the top of the stick. A small quantity of the medicine is buried in the ground near the *woto*. Coconut skins and the shells of these, which must have been used the previous day, are put on the ground at the base of the stick.

When every man has finished planting the four yams and made the charms fast to the *woto*, the bull-roarer is placed on the ground on the left-hand side of the *woto*, then all stand erect alongside the garden fence, with bow and arrow in hand, and earnestly implore the assistance of the spirits of all their neighbours from north, south, east and west, concluding the appeal with the mention of their ancestors, who are requested to come and produce a good crop of yams. During this invocation an arrow is placed to every bow-string and held aloft as if the arrow is about to be shot away. The arms are then laid upon the ground, and the bull-roarers lying near the upright stick are picked up and whirled and whirled, with deafening noise, until the men are tired out. Each man calls upon the *maigidubu*, a huge mythical snake, to come and guard the garden fence, so that nothing may enter which is likely to spoil the yam harvest. The bull-roarers are all wrapped up in mats or bark again, and the men return to their homes. The banana leaf containing the medicine is carried back to the village and thrown into the sea.

The women have in the meantime been cooking in readiness for the return of their husbands and sons. On their arrival the oven is opened and the food divided into five different portions, one for each clan. This is again subdivided among the different families of the clans. The rest of the day is spent in feasting and drinking *gamada*. There is no bull-roarer performance nor any dancing. The noise made by the bull-roarers is called *ububu overa*, which the natives can imitate in a wonderful manner.

Early next day all the men and women go to the gardens; the latter dig the holes and the former plant yams in them, using a similar kind of medicine as on the previous day on every plant. Before the yam seeds are put into the ground all are rubbed with medicine, and *manababa* spat upon every seedling. When the last hole is reached there is some slight variation in the performance. Before spitting on the yam root, the gardener spits the *manababa* on his own hands, rubs them together, jumps with both feet into the hole dug for the seed, places his hands flat on the ground, jumps

How the Bow of a Canoe is Built up to make a Double Outrigger Sailing Craft.
A Double Outrigger Canoe with Platform.
The boy has a dugong spear in his hand.

Gardening

back again without turning round, spits another dose of *manababa* on his yam seed, and then plants it in the ordinary way. This little ceremony for the last yam I have seen performed. The object is to keep sickness away from the community.

When this is finished the women return home, and as soon as they are gone out of sight the invocations of the day before are repeated, and the bull-roarers' piercing shrieks celebrate the fact that the yams are planted. These plants are all climbers, and as soon as the shoots come above the surface sticks are placed in the ground for the plants to climb. Before the sticks are put in, the *manababa* root is chewed and spat upon the end that is put in the earth. Such is the ritual of the coastal Kiwai people.

In the Fly river the ritual differs much from the above, and on the island of Kiwai almost every village has some little ritual of its own.

At Iasa the following method is employed. The charm is made of *wapase, nibonibo*, a wood named *kurumi*, a *kamuka* egg (*kamuka* is a wild fowl), a red earth named *were*, and water which is obtained from some creek where a certain fish (*geewa*) is found. This fish hides itself in the mud, and the water is scooped up in a coco-nut shell just above the place where it has been seen to enter the mud. The water is carried to the garden. The leaves of the plants mentioned above, together with the wood, are all cut up into small pieces with an ipa shell. The fowl egg is broken and mixed with the red earth in another coco-nut shell. *Manababa* is chewed and spat into the shell, after which the yam to be planted is rubbed with the mixture of earth, egg and *manababa*. A hole is dug, into which the plant will be placed, and a small portion of water is poured in. An old woman and her husband plant the first yam. This is laid on the ground near the hole, and the old couple stand, cross the left and right foot—that is, the man puts his right foot over the left of his wife—then both stoop down, each with the right and left hand respectively, take the yam and together place it in the ground. All the men from the village stand round watching the operation, and when it is over the bull-roarers are swung for some time. It is unusual for a woman to see the bull-roarer, but in this case an exception is made because of the woman's age. When the first shoots come up, sticks for them to climb up are placed in the ground. *Manababa* is not used as in the case of the coastal folks. Instead of that, certain parts of the flying-fox, which have been previously dried, are put into a hole which is made at one end of the sticks. The flying-foxes in the Fly are very prolific; hundreds may be seen hanging to a single tree at certain times of the year. The idea in the native mind is that by using this charm their yam gardens will be as prolific as the flying-foxes. At Sumai and Auti when yams are planted the people call upon two spirits, Nabodi and Sabodi, to come and make their gardens grow. The bodies of all the men are covered with charcoal at the planting season.

At some places on Kiwai one of the men goes daily to swing the bull-roarer near the yam fence. On the coast this is done only once after the planting, the object being to ensure a good crop and to ward off misfortune from the garden.

Yam Harvest.—This is arranged by the head men of the

Gardening

club-house. *Karea* is made in the club and the *maigidubu* is addressed and told to clear out of the garden which he has guarded for many months, and that at an early date another fence will be made, when he will be again called upon. Next

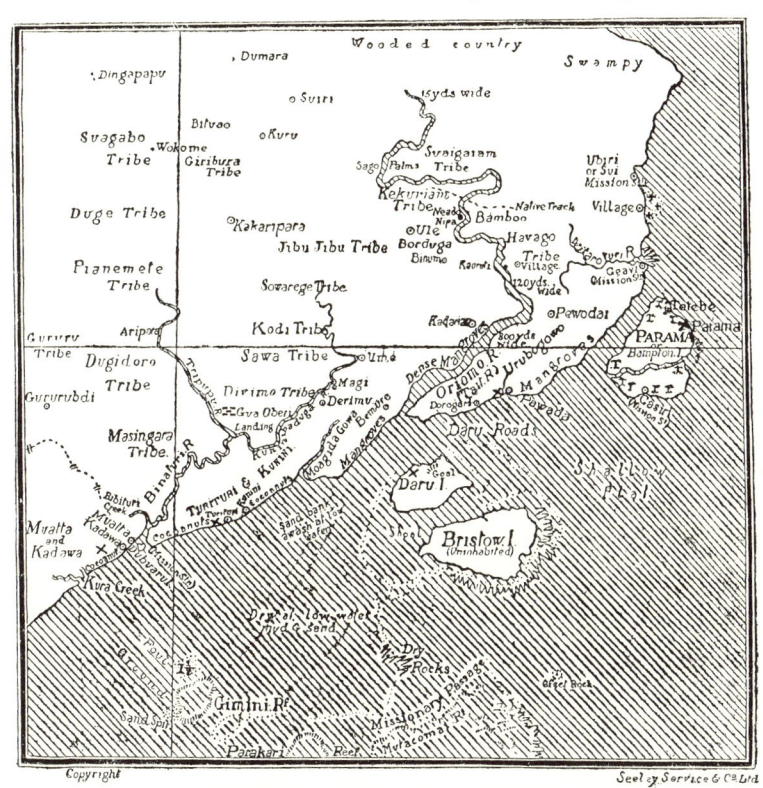

SKETCH MAP OF DARU DISTRICT

morning the announcement is made in the village by two men appointed for this purpose. Men and their wives march to the bush in single file; every man and woman in the village enter the gardens, and find the first yam that was planted the previous season. This is dug up by the whole community on their several patches at one and the same time. A planting-stick is used for clearing the soil away, and one yam for each child of the family, one each for father and mother, are laid on the side of the hole. The person who made the medicine for the clan at planting-time now receives one yam from all who partook of and used his medicine.

The man and his wife divide the yams presented to them, and afterwards hand them back to the givers. Young coco-nuts are collected, and the women go away to fish and prepare for a feast. Whilst they are away the husbands fill up the baskets, which must be absolutely new, with yams, and carry them back to the village. The eldest son of each family now makes an earthen oven, assisted by his wife, in which the yams are cooked. The men eat their food in the club-house, make another *karea* for the *maigidubu*, and spend the night drinking *gamada*.

In the Fly river the first yam is taken out of the ground by the old couple who formerly planted it. They are not permitted to dig the soil away with their hands or a stick. Four or five feet of the bush or scrub hen are tied together with a piece of string, and with these the soil on the top of the tuber is scraped away. The woman does not sit on the ground to do this but bends double with feet apart. As soon as the yam is seen the husband takes the *woto*, passes it between his wife's feet, then very gently loosens the root; when sufficiently loose, the woman picks it up with both hands and presses it against her abdomen; she then lays it down again on the ground; she goes in this manner to all the first yams planted by her own family. During this initial

Gardening

ceremony the man and woman must have their backs turned to the south-west and faces to the north-east. As soon as the yam is laid on the ground by the woman the husband steps in front of her, and away they march to the next patch, where digging continues.

On the Fly the bull-roarer is swung for one whole day after the yams are taken up. This is not the practice along the coast.

Taro.—This is one of the many tropical plants of the arum family. These are closely allied to the ornamental plants caladiums. The root is a little acrid, but when roasted or boiled is very palatable. Some, however, have a very peculiar taste, especially those grown on very swampy ground. There are forty-six different kinds cultivated in the coastal district. The young taro leaves are used as vegetables; when cut up, mixed with coco-nut milk, and cooked in a banana leaf in an earthen oven, it makes an agreeable addition to the menu. The coco-nut milk is prepared by scraping or grating the flesh of the nut, pouring water upon this and straining through a piece of cloth. This is very rich and rather sickly to the taste.

The medicine for producing a good crop of taro differs from that used for yams. It consists of young shoots from the nipa or sago tree palms, the grated bark of a tree named *sanea-ere*, and scraped coco-nut. These are all cut up and mixed together. The above prescription is by no means used by the whole community. Every person has his own special charm, and does not divulge his secret to those living in the same village.

When the fence for the taro garden is being built, a portion of it is not completed, but left open for a few days. The reason for this is that the *maigidubu* and the *ororaorora* (earth spirits) may enter to guard the ground and crops. A big feast is made, named *arapoo*, to celebrate the finishing of the fence.

Karea is made, one for each clan, after the fence, as stated above, is completed, and the night is spent drinking *gamada*. Next morning two men go alone to the garden. Every man who has helped to build the fence has a certain amount of ground inside the fence. The women have previously cleared a small piece of land and dug up the soil, just enough for the planting of one taro. On this cleared spot a planting-stick and one taro top, ready for being put into the ground, are laid. These await the arrival of the two men who are to do the initial planting. They leave home at sunrise the following morning and plant every taro laid on the ground, using the stick, which has been left for the purpose, for making the hole in the ground. They plant for each clan and for every family in the different clans. This generally occupies the two men a whole day, and on their return to the village they report the completion of their task. Next day four other men go into the bush to complete the building of the fence, and shut up the part which had been left open. *Karea* is again made and *gamada* drunk by the elders of the settlement.

Early next morning the women and children go and collect a quantity of food for their immediate requirements, after which they return home, and representatives of each clan go into the garden and plant a certain number of taro. Each man chews a piece of *manababa* root, then spits upon

Gardening

the planting-stick; he afterwards makes a hole six or eight inches deep in the ground, pours a little water into the hole, then a small quantity of the medicine, and finally places the taro top in the ground. The first one planted is on the elder brother's land; then follows one for each member of the family, and the last one to be planted is for the man himself. During the time these operations are in progress the men who are not engaged planting, also the women and children, may not walk about in the vicinity of the garden, lest the earth should be shaken.

The natives say that the object of this regulation is that the spirits which inhabit the forest, and those of their ancestors, who have been called upon to make the garden productive, should not be disturbed or displeased by the shaking of the ground. When this task is finished the men return home, make *karea* again and spend the night drinking *gamada*. It is now permissible for the whole village, men and women, to go to work and complete the planting of their own particular part of the garden. Children are not allowed inside the garden fence whilst the crop is growing for fear that a leaf of a plant should be damaged or broken. Should a man break a leaf of a taro or banana plant he would have an attack of fever. In order, however, that this may not happen, he would inform a friend, who would take a mouthful of fresh water from an *oboia* (a coco-nut shell from which the flesh has been scraped and which is used for carrying water) and spit upon the offender's back, at the same time asking the goblin to come from his body. The man would then escape the penalty of the misdeed.

When the first-fruits of the taro garden are taken up they

are removed from the ground in the same order in which they were originally planted, by the heads of the clans, and laid upon the ground near the hole from which they have been pulled up. The men then return to the village and inform the women and children that they may go to the garden and bring in the taro. The youngsters carry the baskets for the food which is collected and carry it back to the village. The women cook the taro in an earthen oven, and the children with ipa shells scrape the flesh from a large number of coco-nuts. When the taro is cooked it is mashed with a stick or masher and then mixed with the scraped coco-nut. This mixture is called *mabusi*. A few croton leaves are taken and one end of the *mabusi* is made into the shape of a man's face, the septum of the nose is punctured, and a nose-stick put through the hole; the remainder is shaped like the body of a dugong minus the tail and flippers. The whole mass is put into a *baru* or thick end of a *te* tree leaf. Shells are put all round the *baru* and then *karea* is made, after which portions are placed in every shell for the different clans, amidst great rejoicing. I have seen this ceremony performed at Masingara, which was carried out with great solemnity.

A very curious custom exists in Mawata for increasing the supply of taro when it is imagined that a crop has been somewhat smaller than usual. For the following season new and powerful charms are stealthily stolen from the bushmen. A man will call upon his friends inland and take with him a basket. He will sit down in the village near the earth oven, and with the claws from the leg of a wild fowl pick up all the rubbish from the oven fire, consisting of bits of stone,

Gardening

charcoal, half-burnt wood, etc., and put these into the basket. He goes from earth oven to earth oven, taking as much as he can from each, and exercising great care lest he should be discovered. Were he to be found out there would be very hard talking, and the offender would be asked if he wished the people from whom he was stealing to be short of food during the next year.

All these stolen things are mixed with scraped coco-nut, cut up young nipa-palm leaves and coco-nut milk. Taro is cooked by the man's wife and mixed with the stolen rubbish. Portions are cut up and given to every clan in the village, and this is again divided into many parts, one for each family in the clan. The head of each family places his portion alongside one special taro in the garden. It is not broken up but is planted whole.

The point of this ritual is that the medicine must be obtained by theft, or it would not be considered efficacious or produce the desired results.

When bananas (I have the names of fifty-six different kinds grown in the Fly), sweet potatoes, sago, sugar-cane, etc., are planted a different ritual is practised; different medicines and charms are used for each.

Whatever is being planted, the planter's face must be turned toward the east. Yams must be planted sitting, with the legs outstretched, one on either side of the cavity into which the seedling is to be placed.

The Seasons.—The Kiwai natives divide the year into two seasons, the north-west, Suruma, or rainy season, and the south-east, Uro, or the dry, windy season. In the Fly river there are five moons in the former and eight moons in the latter. Amongst the coastal people there are only twelve months in the year. At Tureture there is a man named Oroga who is in possession of twelve sticks about as thick as a lead pencil, all of different lengths and sharpened at one end. Several of them have a small bit of carving at the thick end. Every new moon one of these sticks is turned over and so the reckoning is made. As these do not make a complete year they have some arrangement for rectifying the difference every *keke* month. I saw these sticks some time ago, but had to give a promise that I would not attempt to buy them before I was permitted to see them. They are said to be a very great age, and I have not been able to trace another lot in the whole of the district.

Each month of the year is distinguished by some particular phenomenon. The Fly river months are as follows:

Dogai: strong winds, much rain and thunder.

Karogo: calms, with wind and rain.

Keremotoworo: north-west winds till midday, then south-east winds for the rest of the day.

Keke: strong winds and much rain; first-fruits are gathered.

Utiamo: so named from particular stars in the heavens.

Segerai.

Uro naturaime: very strong south-east winds.

Baidamo: sharks come up from the sea near the land and travel up the river. A star appears in the heavens which is like a shark, and two other stars seem to be its eyes. The word *baidamo* means shark.

Abu: the sharks turn seaward and leave the river. The word *abu* means to cross over. The sharks cross over the land to the sea.

Gardening

Durupi sagana : this is the month of very high tides (about September).

Dibiri dubu : no wind, sea very calm. Turtle go ashore to lay eggs.

Tagai : turtle-time. Dugong come over the reefs near the coast when the moon comes up.

Bunie Suruma : light winds, the beginning of the north-west.

The natives on the coast start their year, counting from *Keke*, about May; their months are : *Keke, Utiamo, Segerai, Koziguba, Wapi, Opukoruo, Abu, Tagai, Naramaduba, Niradubu, Karaguti, Goibari.*

CHAPTER VIII

CANOES & CANOE-MAKERS

A NATIVE may cut down a tree on his own land and make it into a canoe if he so desires. If he has no suitable timber on his own land he may purchase a standing tree from some neighbour, provided the latter is willing to sell. In olden times the price was one arm shell. If a person were to cut down a tree without permission, or without first paying, there would be serious trouble. A buyer having completed the purchase cannot sell the standing tree without permission of the original owner.

No man may cut down a tree for a canoe whose wife is in a certain condition, or who is suffering from a certain ailment. Almost any native in the district can make a small canoe. A short time ago I saw two which had been made by boys not more than twelve years of age, both of which were remarkably well done, and showed considerable ability in both design and craftsmanship. The largest canoes are made by experts, or under the guidance of experts, assisted by their relatives and friends. The period required for making one of the large craft depends upon the skill of the men, the number engaged upon the work, the quality of the tools, and the amount of time they are able to devote to the work. They are not in a position to give the whole of their time to the task, owing to the fact that they must attend to their gardens or they will go hungry. Time is put in as opportunity permits. To complete one may take from six to twelve months, after which finishing touches are given to it.

Making a War Canoe.—The first thing to be done is to select a tree suitable for the purpose required; the second, to determine the direction in which it will fall. This is easily determined by the bend of the tree, the prevailing wind, or by a combination of the two. The place where the tree is to drop is then cleared of all its timber and undergrowth. Logs of wood are laid upon the cleared ground after the manner of sleepers on a railway line, but are laid only upon the surface of the ground. This is to break the fall of the tree and prevent its splitting. A platform eight or ten feet high is built all round the base of the tree and upon this the men stand when felling it. Operations will then be suspended for two or three days.

In the meantime great preparations are made for the feast which is to follow the ceremony of bringing the giant to the ground. Large quantities of sago will be made, two or three days spent in catching crabs and fish, collecting bananas, coco-nuts and other native products from the gardens. Invitations will be sent out to friends in all neighbouring villages requesting the pleasure of their attendance at the forthcoming banquet and informing them on what day it will be held. A day or so before the appointed time the river will be alive with canoes of all description, some propelled by paddles, others under mat or canvas sails, all making their way to the festive spot; all full of interesting specimens of humanity.

In the early morning of the appointed day, just after sunrise, an old woman and an old man, unaccompanied by any other person or persons, proceed into the forest carrying a tomahawk with them, to the place where the tree stands which is destined to be cut down. The woman breaks a leaf from a tree named *dudoro*, wets it with fluid, and rubs the sides of the tree with it. This leaf is not thrown away but kept for another and similar purpose. The old man then takes the tomahawk and marks the tree with the blade in the same place which the old woman rubbed with the leaf. The object of this ceremony is to prevent the tree splitting when it falls to the ground. After the little ceremony is finished they both return to the village, or the camp, and inform the inhabitants that their task has been successfully accomplished. A procession is then formed and marches behind the old couple to the immediate vicinity of the tree, where a big *karea* is held. The *ororaorora* (fairies, goblins) are first dealt with and addressed as follows : " *Ororaorora*, you come out of that tree. We want you to leave it and go to live in another one. We want to cut it down and make it into a canoe." *Gamada* is then thrown into the air to propitiate the spirits residing within it. Another *karea* is made for the tree itself with a few choice words : " You now stand up a tree ; we are going to cut you down ; you will presently walk about on the top of the water ; by and by we shall decorate you [paint you]."

The ancestral spirits are then invoked to keep sickness away, to prevent any accident to the men who are going to cut down the tree and make the canoe ; that the men may not be lazy and that they may have strength for the work that lies before them. At the conclusion of this ceremony the operation of cutting down the tree commences. It is cut all round but not right through. As soon as the owner or any of the old men think enough has been cut away, operations are suspended, and the log is left for the wind to blow upon it and ultimately bring it to the ground. By not cutting through the natives say that it prevents shakes in the timber (namely, splits in the log). The tree sways, cracks, and finally falls upon the sleepers which had been previously laid to receive it. As it is falling the owner shouts the name of the man for whom he is about to make the canoe. That is to say, if one named Kobo is to make a canoe for Soko, he would call out at the top of his voice " Soko ! " whilst the tree is actually falling, or as soon as it is on the ground. A loud and long-continued shout, expressive of pleasure and joy, arises from every throat of the assembled crowd. The desired length is then measured off when the tree lies on the ground.

The old couple who first marked the tree now appear on the scene. The leaf which the woman used to make the first mark is again wet, and with this she rubs the trunk at the place indicated by the owner. The old man now takes the tomahawk and notches the bark. The next thing to be done is to get the log straight and in the most convenient position for the workmen. This is done in a very skilful manner by means of wood crowbars (*aipau*), which are used as levers. A good number of these are stuck into the ground under the log, at an angle of seventy-five degrees ; to the ends above ground long rattan canes are tied ; these are passed over the log, and some ten or twenty men haul upon each line of cane, so that the whole strength of this number is exerted upon one crowbar. With ten such crowbars one or two hundred men will drag the log into position, after which the whole company return to the village, when a great feast is held. There is no dancing.

The first thing to be done is to adze off the bark and the sapwood. In olden times this was accomplished by using a *gubumutu*—that is, a stone tomahawk. These are not in use on the Fly river to-day. I have, however, seen two in use on the island of Samogi, but that was nearly twenty years ago. I have also seen one used on the Woiwoi, a tributary of the Bamu river, where iron was unknown. I had the pleasure of seeing natives sharpening one of these tools. They had no stones to grind the implement upon, and the banks of the river were nothing but mud. I wonder how the reader would proceed to sharpen such an instrument without either stone or iron at hand. The method adopted was as follows. When the tide was out a crowd of natives walked into the mud, took quantities into their hands, rubbed them together and took out all the grit. Each person produced a little, and in the end they had quite a decent handful of sand. This was put into a basket made of bark, and the stone tomahawk head was rubbed in the sand in order to sharpen it. One man rubbed a little, soon got tired, and then passed on the stone to another person sitting near, and so in time all the assembled company took their turn. I examined the stone after about an hour's rubbing but it did not seem to my untrained eye to be any sharper than it was when they started.

After the bark and sapwood have been removed, about two inches of the real timber is cut away, after which an expert comes upon the scene in the person of the designer, who very carefully proceeds to form a plan of the vessel.

1. A Canoe manned by Ten Men on the Fly River.
2. A Canoe on the Fly River with two Children.
3. A Canoe decorated and being got ready for Launching, Iasa, Fly River.

The thick end of the log of wood is always the bow of the ship and the thin end the stern. The bow is shaped by laying a piece of rattan cane upon the levelled surface, or almost levelled, which was produced by cutting away the bark, sapwood and the two inches of timber mentioned above; this is moved about until the desired shape is acquired. A piece of charcoal is used for the purpose of making the marks on the log. The process of hollowing or digging out the heart of the tree is then commenced under the superintendence of the owner or the expert canoe-maker. Any friends coming along and giving a hand in the work are fed by the owner, and when the canoe is sold a small present will be given to each one who has rendered assistance.

When the work which is done in the forest is near completion the casual labourers are not employed. The canoe expert takes full charge and puts the finishing touches to both the inside and outside of the boat. Arrangements are then made for hauling the vessel to the coast. Trees are felled and laid as sleepers on the ground all the way from the tree to the bank of the river. Two long pieces of rattan cane are fastened to a peg on the bow of the canoe, which has been left for this purpose by the carpenters. When these details are completed neighbours are again invited to come along and assist in dragging the canoe from the forest. This is regarded as a day of festivity. The two pieces of rattan cane are held in the hands of a crowd of men, women and children; twenty or thirty men are placed on each side of the canoe, each carrying a wooden crowbar. Four elderly men, abaft, abeam, attend to the steering of the canoe with their crowbars; the men on the sides look after the sleepers and help to steady the canoe when necessary. The vessel is not dragged on an even keel, but first on one side and then on the other. The people pulling in front do not put the vine rope over their shoulders, as one might have expected; the rope is kept in the hands the whole time. When it reaches the bank of the river there is great jubilation and another great feast takes place, much greater than the previous one, and large quantities of *gamada* are provided for all present.

The final smartening up, which occupies about two or three weeks, now begins. The canoe is burnt with fire made of coco-nut leaves both inside and outside. If this were not done the life of the vessel would be short. Burning is said by the natives to preserve the wood, prevent water penetrating the timber, and is a protection against both the borer on land and the *teredo navalis* at sea. *Tutu* or thwarts are now put into the canoe. Holes are bored through both sides of the gunwale and sticks put into these holes which are lashed to the vessel with strong cane. The delta folks place *upa* (made from the vegetable kingdom) in the bow of the canoe, whilst the people higher up the river place a carved piece of wood, shield-shaped, as an ornament or decoration. The outrigger is fixed on the canoe before the decorations are commenced. The vessel is painted red, white and black in any design the owner or the chief expert may determine. The ship is then said to be finished.

The *motomoto* or double outrigger sailing canoe is by far the most important native craft in the Fly river district. It consists of an ordinary large dugout, the hull of which is built up so that a greater amount of freeboard may be obtained. The first operation in making or building the *motomoto* is to bore a number of holes, near the top, on both sides of the hull. A number of planks are then procured from nine to twelve inches broad and two inches thick. Holes are also bored through these, an inch or so from the edge, to correspond with the holes in the hull. These timbers are named *bodo*, and are fitted on to the top edge of the canoe. Long pieces of split bamboo (*maumaro*) are laid, both inside and outside, upon the joint made by the board and the edge of the canoe. Strong lashings of rattan cane are passed through the holes of both the canoe and planks and also over the bamboos, which are made as tight as possible. This makes a good joint and prevents water entering the vessel. Both sides of the canoe are treated in the same way. A piece of crooked timber is obtained from the bush and forms the bow of the canoe. This is about two feet in length. To increase the height of the bow out of the water another piece of timber, the *sabi gabo*, is placed upon the top of the *bodo* and securely fastened. The *awaro* or platform upon which the man stands to spear turtle and dugong is fixed transversely upon the *sabi bodo*. Two booms thirty-six or forty feet long are laid across the canoe amidships, six feet apart. These are tied to the *bodo* on both sides of the craft. Fastened to the ends of these booms by means of a number of *tugu* or spokes, diverging upwards, are two *sosome* or pointed floats. A platform (*patora*) of adzed planks is made on the top of the booms in the centre of the canoe. Two large boxes or crates, open at the top, are built on the platform and project about eighteen inches over the sides of the vessel, one being on the starboard and the other on the port side. Two masts are stepped in the bottom of the ship and kept in position by strong rattan rigging or wire rope. Only two sails are carried, a mainsail and foresail. There is no jib.

The method of steering these canoes is by means of a board about twelve or fourteen inches broad and about six feet long. Rattan canes are lashed on the outside of both sides of the vessel and the steering-board is placed between the hull and the rattan. When the canoe goes about the steering-board has to be taken out from one side and placed on the lee-side of the craft. In the centre of the platform amidships there are two holes, twelve inches long and about two inches wide, just above the sides of the canoe. When the vessel is going to windward a board or paddle is placed through one of these holes and pushed as far as is necessary into the water and acts as a centre board, and is very effective for the purpose. When the wind is aft two steering-boards are used, one on each side of the vessel at the stern.

I have often travelled in these craft and they are very comfortable, if the weather is good and the sea calm. When the wind is fairly strong the lee float often sinks into the sea, whilst the windward float rises from the water in an alarming manner. To counteract this the crew, always on the alert, rush along the two booms on the windward side and by their weight bring the float again into the water.

Hunting.—The only animals that it is possible for the Kiwai men to hunt are the pig, the cassowary and the wallaby. Sometimes one man will go alone with his bow and arrows, accompanied by one or more dogs; sometimes two or more may go together. Often, however, a whole village will go hunting and make a grand drive of a certain district. They will proceed to the place arranged and as far as possible surround it, then set fire to the grass all the way round. The hunters stand outside the fire with their arms ready to fire and their dogs standing by. The animals are of course driven out by the fire, and as they rush through the burning grass both dogs and men, ever on the alert, bring them down to the ground, when they are dispatched. Sometimes these drives are very successful, at other times they are not. I have been present at a score at least and have seen only one really successful drive.

The making of a water-bottle from a coco-nut is an interesting bit of work. The coco-nut is first skinned and the water is poured out from a hole made at the point where the nut sprouts when beginning to grow. A stick is then used as a lever; the nut inside is broken into small pieces by the pointed stick and shaken out of the hole. When the whole of the flesh has been removed the shell is dried and is then fit for use. A piece of stout string about a yard long is obtained and the two ends tied together into a knot, which is pushed through the hole into the empty shell. A cork is then made by rolling a leaflet from a coco-nut leaf big enough to fit the hole. This is inserted alongside the string, which prevents the latter from being withdrawn whilst the cork is in its place. The loop of the string is thrown over the shoulder and the water-bottle carried under the arm.

CHAPTER IX

TURTLE FISHING

THE turtle fishing commences about the beginning of October. The ritual to be described was in vogue when all the canoes were propelled by paddles, and before the advent of the sailing canoe, and was as follows.

The day before the fleet put to sea all the canoes were hauled out of the water, placed upon the beach and a small log of wood laid under the bow of each vessel. These were all decorated with perfumed leaves and grasses, which were regarded as charms. A mat was spread out on the sand in front of the bow of each craft. A large quantity of food was placed on the mats. Alongside this the wooden figure of a man or a bird, with carvings of turtles upon it, was set up. This image was a charm called *Kubai*, and in it was embodied the spirit which would bring good fortune to the particular canoe.

Each commander stood in front of his canoe with a basin of *gamada* in his left hand and a few leaves from the same plant in his right. The leaves were dipped in the fluid, which was then sprinkled on the image and food, each man saying: " This is for good luck to the canoe." The image and canoe were then addressed as follows : " To-morrow we shall go to the reef; we want you to bring plenty of turtles alongside this canoe." The spirits of their ancestors were

Turtle Fishing

afterwards called upon to aid the vessels on the projected expedition.

Each officer then took a short stick about twelve inches long in one hand and an old coco-nut in the other. At a given signal the nuts were struck with the stick and the water from the nut was poured upon the image and food. The crew and commander of each canoe divided the nut among themselves and ate it. No one was permitted to partake of a nut belonging to another vessel. The food was also distributed among the crews.

The following regulations were strictly observed:—

(1) No member of any crew was allowed to sleep in the men's club-house or to occupy the same quarters as his wife during the fishing season. Transgression of this law prevented a man from taking any further part in the fishing.

(2) No man whose wife was in a certain condition or whose wife was suffering from a characteristic ailment could join the fleet. If such a one were to do so the turtle on seeing him would know about him and would sink to the bottom of the sea. When, however, the ailment was over the man was free to join the expedition, but before doing so he had first to rub his body with a root of a certain plant and bathe in salt water.

(3) The above-named people could not partake of the first turtle or turtles caught.

(4) When out at sea the crew of one clan could not take either fire or water from the crew or canoe of another clan, but might do so from the crew or canoe of their own clan, but even then the fire or water might not be handed to the

applicant, but must be placed on the platform amidships, from which the one in need would remove it. The spirits under these circumstances would not be angry.

(5) One ship's crew might not render any assistance to the crew of another vessel at sea or ashore unless it were a case of life or death.

(6) No vessel might carry the charm belonging to another vessel.

(7) No person might strike a canoe or hit it with a stick, except when doing necessary repairs; should this be disregarded, no turtle would be obtained by the crew of that canoe.

(8) Only red paint might be used for painting a vessel. In 1923 quite a sensation was caused at a neighbouring village by a South Sea man tarring the bottom of his canoe. All kinds of misfortune were prophesied. The owner could not get any old hands to sail with him. A few young men, however, made the venture and soon returned with three turtles, much to the joy of the crew and the dismay of the old men.

(9) No plant or tree with thorns upon it, no woman, boy or girl, might go aboard any canoe. The thorn would make the turtle go down.

(10) No tops might be spun, no cat's-cradles be made during the turtle season, in fact no games of any kind might be indulged in by the people in the village, lest the noise should disturb the turtle on the reef.

(11) No boy might speak to any girl in the settlement, not even to his own sister, or the members of the family would be unfortunate.

DOUBLE OUTRIGGER SAILING CANOE

The man in the bow is ready to spear turtle or dugong.

Turtle Fishing

(12) No women or children might put food, firewood or water on any vessel. No woman might witness the fleet's departure from, or arrival in, port; in fact she may not even walk on the sea-beach.

When all was ready the grand fleet put to sea as the night tide was about to ebb. This enabled the canoes to reach the reef about half ebb. The paddlers bent to their task with strong arms and willing minds. They struck the water with their paddle blades in unison, and steered a direct course for the reef where they hoped to find the turtles. On the bows of each canoe, on both its sides on the water-line and in its wake, as each paddle entered the sea and was again withdrawn, streaks of pale blue and white phosphorescent foam shot up all round the craft, compared with which the Milky Way in the heavens seemed dull and insignificant, when at its very brightest.

Ritual at Sea.—The fleet anchored at the reef before daylight. At the first streak of dawn each commander broke a coco-nut over the bows of his canoe and poured the water from it upon the charms of leaves, each member of the crew repeating the word "*Sarasara*," which means good luck to the turtle fishing.

The Agumakai.—One member of each canoe was in charge of a small kind of bull-roarer, called *agumakai*. It was used only once a day. As the sun appeared on the horizon one of these instruments was swung daily on each canoe, first from the right to the left and back again from the left to the right, producing two loud, weird and uncanny blasts which I have no language to describe. The first movement indicated the plunging of the harpoon into the body of a turtle; the movement backwards indicated the withdrawal of the harpoon from the turtle which has been speared.

The Kubai.—Whilst at sea the *kubai* received marked attention. After the thunderings of the *agumakai* had subsided, he was taken from his basket and his feet were dipped into the sea. The image was drawn alongside the canoe in the direction of the incoming tide, so that turtle might be attracted and decoyed to their doom. He was then taken from the water and tied to the platform amidships. Food, water and a bamboo tobacco pipe were placed in front of him. The lighted pipe was held to his lips from time to time so that he might have a smoke. At the conclusion of this ceremony the image was addressed as follows: " We have given you plenty of food, good water and a smoke; we want you to bring us plenty of good turtles; we have looked after you, you should now look after us."

Sometimes when the canoes were paddling round the *kubais* were tied to the bows of the canoes, so that the images might attract and draw the turtles toward them. When the prey was discovered the image was removed from the bow, restored to his mat and returned to the comfort of the basket in which he was kept.

The person in charge of the *kubai*, usually the cook, was often somewhat disrespectful to so important and powerful a dignitary. He often used abusive and threatening language to him, and went so far as to say that if he did not bring along turtle dire punishment would follow. If no turtles were caught that day, his food, water and tobacco would be stopped, he would be thrown into the sea and not escape with a mere wetting of the feet. One old man quite seriously informed me that he never found it necessary to have to speak roughly to his *kubai* more than once a month. That was sufficient.

The First Turtle.—The first turtle to be caught must be a female. A male would be scorned. The female is much more valuable than a male because of the hundreds of eggs and the large amount of green fat she contains. The green fat is a great luxury when cooked and it is surprising what a great amount a native can consume without feeling sick.

Turtles may be caught in one of three ways. Sometimes they are found on sandy beaches at night, where they go to lay their eggs in the sand; under such circumstances they are simply turned over on their backs, when they are utterly helpless. They make a hole two feet deep and six inches wide and deposit their eggs in it. I have seen over two hundred eggs taken from one nest.

Another method is employed to catch the animals by hand. Two or three boys will jump into the sea, having a looped rope over the left shoulder, seize the flipper of the turtle with the left hand and with the right slip the rope from the shoulder on to the flipper.

A third method is to spear the turtles from the canoe bow with a harpoon or from a platform erected on the reef. When a turtle is speared it rushes off into deep water like the dugong, but does not travel so far, and is more easily hauled aboard or made fast to the canoe side.

When the fleet returns home with the first turtle there is no singing, drumming or dancing. The catch is thrown overboard on its back and is at once surrounded by the old men waiting to receive it. A rope is attached to the two fore flippers and the animal dragged from the water on to the beach.

The Ritual Ashore.—An old man advanced carrying in his hand a piece of a vine. This contains peculiar properties, and is said to produce an uneasy, irritating feeling when rubbed on the skin. The old man chewed a root, spat upon the piece of vine and then inserted it into the body of the turtle for a few seconds. This was said to render senseless or to stupefy all the turtles in the sea, and would make them incapable of sinking when they saw the fishermen at sea. After the medicine vine had been withdrawn a hooked stick was put in its place. A procession was then formed and the turtle was dragged on its back to the spot where it would be killed. Immediately behind the procession walked four men holding a large mat which was trailed along the ground. These men obliterated with their feet all the marks which the turtle's back had made on the sand.

The hooked medicine-stick was said to be the charm which would bring a large number of turtles to this particular village. The purpose of the mat was to shut other villages out from sharing the turtles in the ocean, and to confine them to their own community. Early next morning preparations were made for a somewhat imposing ceremony. The officers and crews of the canoes were dressed for the occasion with teased coco-nut and other kinds of leaves. When their toilet was completed a signal was given and another procession was formed. The captain of the canoe which caught the first turtle walked in front, carrying in his right hand a dancing ornament, and in the left a pole about twelve feet long, called a *dadu*, on the top of which was a bundle of cassowary feathers and several cowrie shells. This was used for signalling at sea. Each canoe captain carried his long pole and a member of each crew brought along the *kubai*.

The procession marched round the turtle two or three times, every man with bent body and head inclined forward. Each long pole was inserted into the turtle's body as were the vine and crooked stick; after this the *kubais* were also treated in the same way.

The long poles were then placed into the ground in an upright position all round the body of the turtle, and alongside these the wooden images were set up. The crews took off their dancing finery and placed it on the turtle's body. After a time the turtle was killed and shared out amongst all who could partake of it. The poles and wooden images were removed by their respective custodians and carried to a safe place.

Canoes returning Empty.—If a particular canoe were unsuccessful in fishing it would never return home until the sun had set. The captain and crew were too much ashamed to make port in daylight. When they arrived home empty-handed they were often the subject of much good-humoured raillery. I have heard a woman ask her husband if he had been away in the forest seeking turtle. Such banter is generally taken in good part.

If one canoe were constantly unfortunate the commander was suspected of having broken the first of the regulations.

An unsuccessful crew would put their vessel ashore, rub it all over with leaves from the *auhi* plant, then go into the bush and clean the grave of the captain's father. The captain would make six *gogobe* (coco-nut leaflets turned up at one end), and put two on his head, two below the knees, one on each leg, one round each ankle, and shredded coco-nut leaflets on his body. All these were put on whilst standing on the grave. He would then take a very young coco-nut, without any flesh inside, and pour the water from the nut on the grave. The empty shell (*kako*) was put on the grave over the place where the head lay. He then chewed a piece of *manababa* root, spat upon the grave and addressed his father's spirit as follows: "We have cleaned your grave and given you a drink of water. You come with us and drink some *gamada*." The captain and his crew then returned to their village and made three *kareas*, one for the dead man, one for the canoe and another for the *kubai*. Next morning the canoe returned to the fishing grounds and had much success.

The ritual connected with the wood image is now a thing of the past; the regulations, or most of them, are still faithfully carried out, but are rapidly losing their hold upon the rising generation.

One night I was anchored off the village of Sumai, some thirty miles from the mouth of the Fly river. Captain Mitchell, who was in charge of my vessel, and I had turned in about nine-thirty and were dozing off to sleep when we were aroused by a stampede of the crew on deck. Some ran from the stern forward and yelled at the top of their voices in the native language, "Bring that tomahawk quickly!" whilst the chief officer, Bama, could be heard calling, "Hold him! Hold him!" (or it). Thinking that there was some trouble we rushed up the gangway from the cabin, and to our intense relief found that the tomahawk was not to be used for any warlike purpose upon a human being,

Turtle Fishing

but to dispatch a Fly river turtle which had been caught by hook and line. This turtle is the *Carettochelys Insculpta* and is found only in the Fly. The eggs of this turtle are perfectly round, and have a hard shell unlike the usual marine turtles, which in addition to having a soft shell have a kind of dent in them.

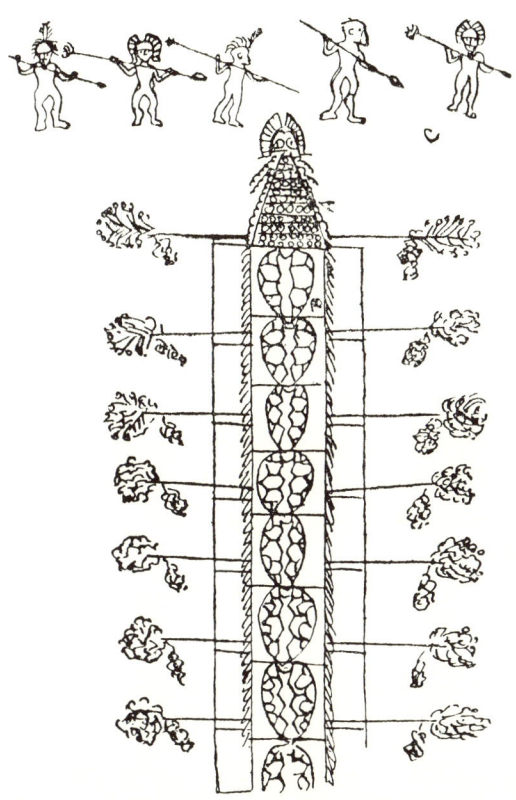

THE *Agu*, UPON WHICH TURTLE SHELLS ARE PLACED TO SHOW THE NUMBER CAUGHT IN ONE SEASON

A represents the heads of the turtles; B the shells; C the figures of dancers in the *Woibu* dance which the women perform. This dance is in honour of the shells of the *Agu*.

CHAPTER X

DUGONG FISHING

A BRIEF description of the dugong may not be out of place here. It is one of the two existing generic representatives of the Sirenia, or herbivorous aquatic mammals. In the upper jaw of the male is a pair of large tusks which in the female are arrested in their growth and remain concealed. There are never more than five molar teeth on each side of either jaw, or twenty in all, and these are flat on the grinding surface. The flippers are unprovided with nails and the tail is broad and crescent-shaped. They browse on submarine pastures of seaweed, for which the thick obtuse lips and truncated snout pre-eminently fit them. The female produces a single one at birth, and is remarkable for the great affection it shows for its offspring, so that when the young dugong is caught there is no difficulty in capturing the mother. The meat is splendid eating, especially that of a young calf. The best cut is from the breast. It may be boiled or roasted just as an ordinary joint of beef. I think it is much better roasted. It is not unlike beef, but there is a faint fishy taste which rather detracts from its value. In shape the dugong is something like a porpoise, but much larger. (I once measured one which was thirteen feet long, and I estimated the girth at seven or eight feet.) The skin is light brown in colour, and in an old male is an inch thick.

READY TO STRIKE.

Dugong Fishing

Dugong are speared on moonlight nights and at other times when the sea is very calm and there is a great amount of phosphorescence in the sea-water. The presence of the animals is easily detected as they rush through the water leaving a long white shining light in their wakes.

The instrument used for spearing the dugong is a long pole fifteen feet in length. This is made of hardwood and one end is much thicker than the other. The thin end is decorated with a number of cassowary feathers, over the top of which are four cowrie shells and seven gora nuts. In the middle of the thick end is a hole, into which is

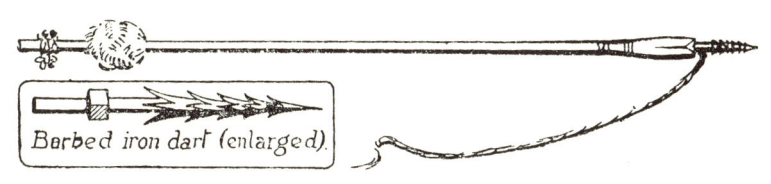

NATIVE HARPOON, OR *WAPO*, AND BARBED-IRON DART

inserted a barbed-iron dart five inches long, which is used for spearing the dugong.

A good harpoon is a great treasure and is very valuable. I bought two many years ago and paid two pounds each for them.

A rope eighty or a hundred yards long, made from vines, five strands, and two vines to each strand, neatly plaited, is essential for dugong fishing, to give play to the animal after it has been speared. This floats in the water.

The most important part of the outfit is not the harpoon or the barbed dart or the rope, as one might perhaps expect, but a piece of string, one end of which is tied to the barbed dart and the other end to the long rope. This string is made of teased coco-nut skin fibre, five or six strands, plaited by hand and very carefully made. It is regarded as the most vital part of the equipment.

The initial ceremony connected with dugong fishing is not always the same. A series of ceremonies and dances

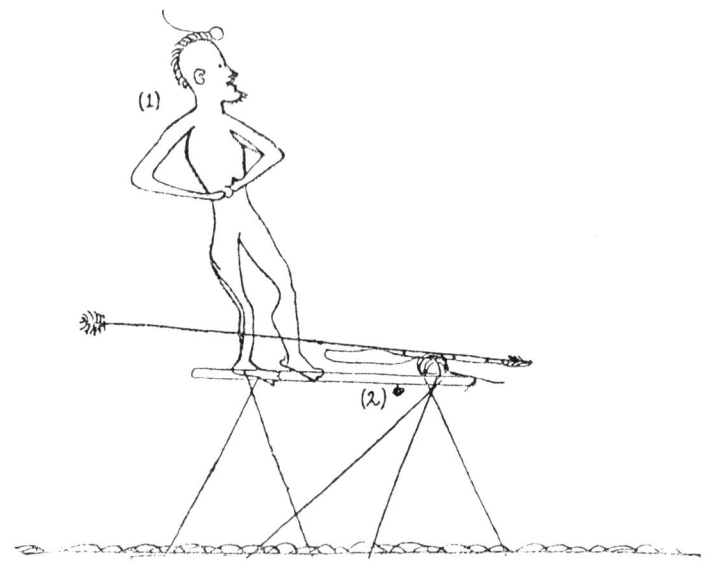

(1) Standing on the *narato* waiting for the dugong to appear. (2) A stone tied under the *warega*, or the plank where the man stands. This is to charm the dugong and attract them towards the particular stand. The coil of rope is of native make and is of five strands, with two vines to a strand.
(*From a Native Drawing.*)

which are held only every four or five years, named *taera*, leads up to a special opening ceremony for the dugong fishing, which I will now describe.

When the *taera* ceremony begins all the harpoons are placed inside the sacred enclosure and remain there until the end of the ceremony. This ensures good luck for the following season.

Dugong Fishing

The whole of the gear used in fishing, together with the roots of plants, sweet-scented leaves and stones, all of which are used as charms, are laid alongside the harpoons. Each clan makes its own good-luck ceremony and the various articles are all sprinkled with *gamada*. As the leader dashes the fluid upon the objects he says: " This is for good luck; we have danced for you; we have given you good food; give us women dugong, fat dugong." The spirits of their fathers and forefathers are next invoked: " Bring

The harpoonist is not permitted to sit on the platform. The man represented is sitting on his heels. (*From a Native Drawing.*)

the dugong along for us to-morrow and do not let them return again to the sea."

After this ceremony *gamada* is drunk; the small articles are put in baskets and carried into the houses; the harpoons remain in the sacred ground.

On the following day wood, water, food and *sadi* (a root used for stupefying fish on the reef), and dried coco-nut leaves for torches, are put aboard the canoes by the men. The vessels are all brought opposite the sacred place. The head man of the Gurai clan enters the enclosure, places on his head an ornament made from a coco-nut leaflet and another on his right wrist, takes up his harpoon and marches from the ground straight to his canoe. All the rest of the spearmen, similarly attired, follow his example. Each man makes his way to the bow of the canoe, holds up the harpoon, and then all jump into the water at one time, swing their instruments round in the sea and imitate the noise made by the dugong. The dugong fishing following the *taera* is the only time the harpoonists wear any ornaments. All the men's bodies are covered with charcoal.

Most of the regulations given under turtle fishing apply also to dugong fishing. The following are additional :—

No man may sit down on the top of the spearing platform when the tide is flooding or all the dugong would go seawards and not come near the reef. He may, however, sit on his heels.

No man may throw a fire-stick into the sea. This would make the water hot and the dugong would not come near the reef.

Bones of fish eaten on the canoe at sea must not be thrown into the water, lest sharks be attracted and the dugong driven off by them.

Building the Narato or Spearing Platform.—The first thing to be done when the canoes reach the reef is for the commander to walk round and fix upon a suitable place for the erection of the spearing platform. He is able to see where the dugong have been nibbling the grass on the reef, and having made his observations, selects his position and builds across one of the tracks, knowing that at the next flood-tide the animals will return for food. Each commander must build his own platform and may not receive any help whatever from his crew.

Dugong Fishing

The Narato.—This is not an elaborate affair. When I first came here it consisted of five pieces of wood or sticks and a board, with a few vines for tying these together. To-day it consists of six pieces of wood. Four of the above-mentioned sticks are called *suru* and the fifth *masi*. Before the *suru* are put into the ground on the reef they are rubbed

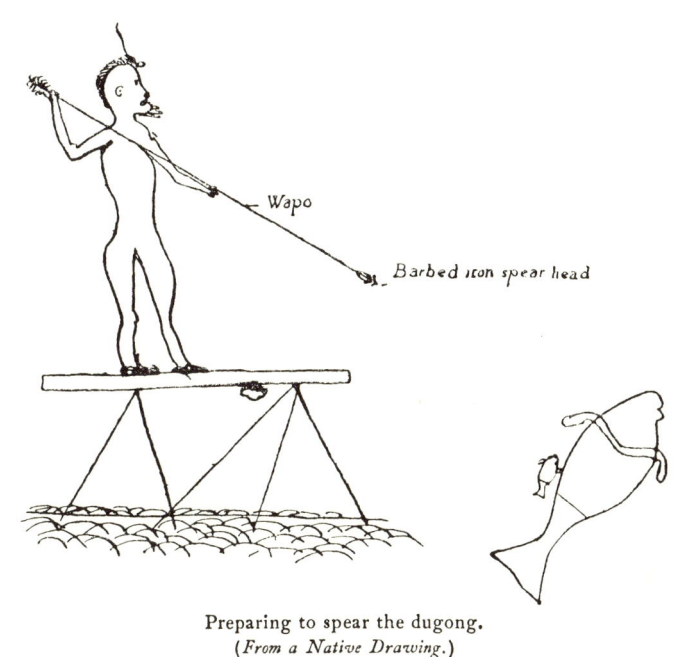

Preparing to spear the dugong.
(*From a Native Drawing.*)

all over with leaves of the *tibeio plant*. Two of these sticks are put into the sand a distance of six feet apart and crossed at the opposite ends like the letter **X**; at a distance of eight feet the other two are similarly placed and tied together with a rope called *iga*. Upon the top of these two **X**'s a board, a piece of an old canoe, is laid and made fast. This board is called *warega*. It is also rubbed with *tibeio* leaves. The builder bites off a piece of *manababa* root, chews it up and spits into the water previous to tying the rope which secures it in position. There now remains the *masi*. This is not fixed in any haphazard way. Its position depends entirely upon the situation of the deep water into which it is considered likely the animal will rush after it has been speared. This acts as a stay and is generally put at the end where the rope is placed and where the man stands, so that when the animal rushes seaward the *narato* will not carry away and the *masi* will be driven farther into the ground. This stick also receives a special rubbing down with *tibeio* leaves and chewed *manababa* root. The idea is that the perfumed leaves impart their nature to the sticks and board of the *narato*, and that this perfume attracts the animal and lures it to certain destruction. After the operation of building is finished the harpoonist mounts his *narato* and tests it in every way. If any adjustments are needed they are immediately executed. The crews in the meantime have been fishing on the reef and when the tide begins to flood they return to their ships.

When the tide is considered sufficiently high the harpoon men, with head-dress on head, all mount the *naratos* or platforms at one time. The barbed dart is made fast to the rope and is then put into the hole at the end of the harpoon pole. This has to be adjusted with great care. It must not be put in too tightly, or it will not come out of the pole when the dugong is struck, or too loosely, or it will not get a firm grip in the dugong hide. Leaves from the *kauwaro* tree are used as packing, and unless this is properly arranged misfortune will follow. The *ede* is then fastened to the *amu* or long rope and the harpoon pole laid on the top of the

Dugong Fishing

narato. The harpoonist now stands erect and calls upon the spirits of his forbears to send along the animals and to give good fishing.

When the sea-cow has been speared it rushes off seawards at a tremendous speed, but soon shows signs of exhaustion—that is, as a general rule. The natives follow after it in a

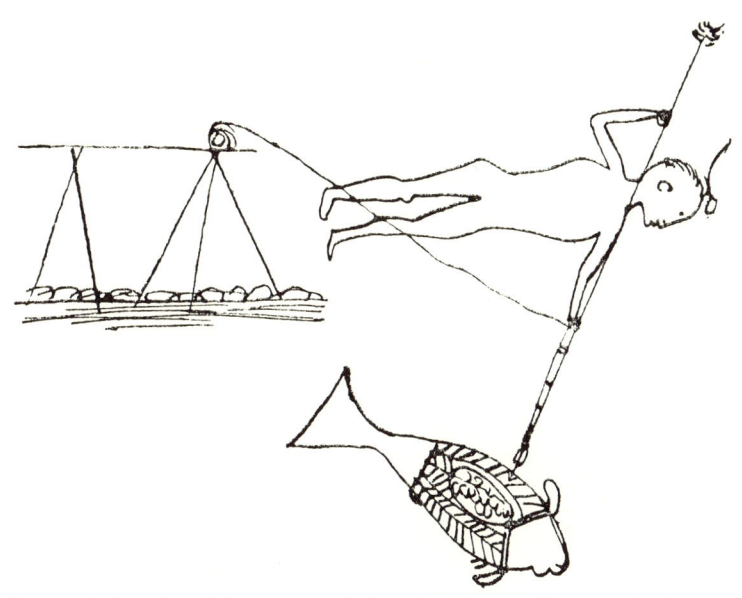

Harpoonist jumping off the *narato*, or platform, into the sea. He spears the dugong and withdraws the pole, leaving the barbed dart in the body of the animal.
(*From a Native Drawing.*)

canoe and fasten a rope round its tail as soon as possible. They haul upon this rope and endeavour to raise the tail out of the water. The effect of this is to cause the head of the animal to sink and the dugong in consequence dies by drowning. In the days of the single outrigger canoe the captive was made fast to the side of the canoe, the head of the animal was made fast to the bow, and the tail to the stern of the vessel. When two were caught, one was carried on the starboard and the other on the port side. Progress was only slow with such a load, but as the canoes always returned home with the tide and were often able to use their mat sails there was not much difficulty on the return trip.

When the fleet is ready for returning during the *taera* time only one man may blow the *tuture* or conch shell as a

A man spearing a dugong close to the *narato*.
(*From a Native Drawing.*)

signal on the reef. On other occasions anyone may do this. On the journey home there is much blowing of trumpets, which is heard by the village long before the canoes come in sight, if the wind is favourable. The folks ashore do not respond by blowing their instruments. On arrival at the port an old man goes down to the beach to receive the report from the different ships. Each commander gives him one small fish and reports what has been caught. He then takes these fish to the club-house and on his way there informs the

Dugong Fishing

women and children what the respective boats have caught. At *taera* time the first dugong is taken near the sacred enclosure, but is not put inside, and cut up there. The man who caught the dugong is not permitted to do this. The work falls to the lot of his wife's relatives, either the father-in-law or brother-in-law. Should there have been many caught on the first day out, all would be brought and laid in a line opposite the sacred ground. Coco-nut leaves are spread out on the soil and all the dugong washed with salt water before being cut up. The animals caught by each clan are all put together in one place. When all have been set in order, the captain of the first canoe which arrived at port takes a bamboo knife and comes from the inside of the sacred ground, dancing all the way, until he reaches the animals. He then pretends to cut each in turn, and as he takes the knife from the different animals he places it against his nose and smells to see if all are good. He then withdraws behind the dancing screens.

The captain and crew of the first canoe now put coco-nut leaves on their bodies and wear the *poriso* head-dress, with the addition of a *kaikai* or ornament of white feathers. The captain carries his dugong spear and one of the crew has part of a *bogo* tied on to his back. This *bogo* is fifteen feet long and is part of the midrib of the coco-nut leaf with some six or eight leaves left upon it. The women are sitting in their accustomed places, and the wife of the commander advances and kneels with a yam in her hands. The husband advances, with the crew behind him, all dancing, and strikes the yam with the end of the dugong harpoon. This is repeated by all the captains, their wives and the respective crews. This is carried on all night. At daylight the first captain and his wife are upon the stage again. She kneels with the yam as before. Her husband advances and smashes it into two halves. The women take one half and eat it themselves. No girl may partake of it. The other half of the yam goes to the first captain. This is taken out to the reef, cooked and eaten at sea.

About ten years ago a Mawata man that I knew well, named Dadia, met his death after jumping from the *narato* and spearing his dugong. It was a very dark night and there were many dugong about, but no *sagu* or phosphorescence in the water. At four A.M. the moon came up, and as an animal was near the platform he attempted to spear it but failed. About six A.M. another came along; he jumped and succeeded in his object. The crew were quite near and did not hear him call his son's name, as is the usual custom, nor did they hear him call for them. They immediately paddled to the *narato* and seized the rope and pulled along it until they reached the dugong. Nothing whatever was seen of the missing man, nor were any remains found. The native theory is that the rope got round the man's neck and the dugong rushing off caused the head to be severed from the body. They further say that had his legs got caught in the rope it would have remained fast long enough for them to have reached him and rendered assistance.

After the first dugong has been caught the fat is cooked, and before the canoes leave for the reef again each *wapo* is well rubbed with dugong fat. If this were not done the harpoon would be angry and refuse to do its work. *Gamada* is sprinkled upon the *wapos* and also drunk for good luck

Dugong Fishing

for the next trip. Should the hole which holds the barbed dart be enlarged, another *karea* or good-luck ceremony is made. These are made mostly in the men's club-house, but occasionally outside in the open.

Every dugong brought ashore has a *wodi mutu* or nose-stick put through its snout. This is not done for decoration, but to enable the head of the dugong to be made fast to the side of the canoe. A rope is put round the nose-stick, then passed round the head, or rather neck, and made fast to the *tubu* (Kiwai, *piu*) timber of the outrigger. The tail is secured by another rope which is lashed to the stern part of the outrigger. The animal is thus fastened to the body of the canoe.

When an animal is speared the natives assert that it does not open its mouth again. If it is not dead when brought alongside the canoe, coco-nut skin is often used for blocking the nasal air passages to hasten death. This is inserted by means of a stick.

This chapter will conclude with the personal experience of a Mawata man named Adagi, the drawer of the sketches, who almost lost his life by being carried out to sea by a speared dugong, as illustrated in the sketch on page 140. This was written at my request, and the following is a near translation of the orginal.

Adagi's Story.—" A few years ago I had a *narato* on the reef named Karabai. I went to look for dugong. It was a very dark night, not long after the sun had set. I saw a dugong coming towards me. It was a very big one. There was a little phosphorescence in the water but not much. The tide was coming in and the water was not deep near me. It would reach to the middle of the back. I heard the animal call and I answered. It came close alongside my *narato*. I then jumped into the sea and at the same time speared the dugong and called out: '*Mo Waiba abera! Waiba, Waiba!*' [I am the father of Waiba Waiba, Waiba.] I threw the harpoon near the platform and seized the rope with both hands

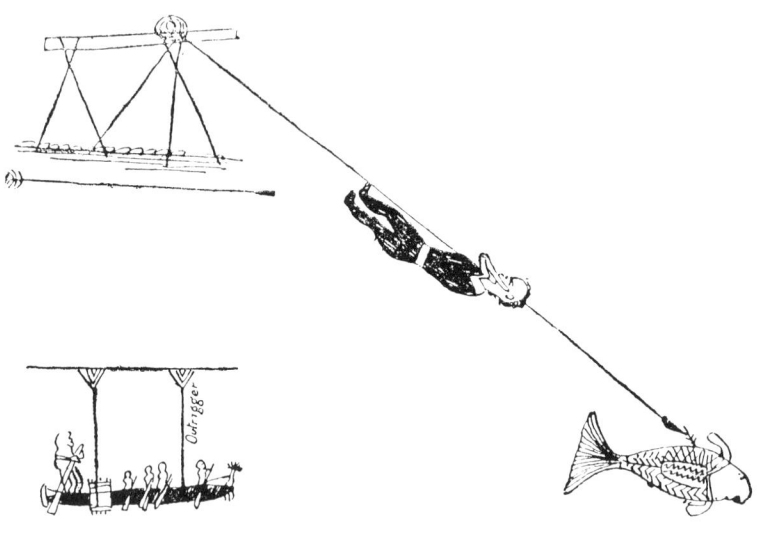

An old method of spearing dugong. The man speared the cow, left his *wapo*, or spear, and seized the rope and was dragged out to sea in deep water. This was done so that the rope should not be lost. He frequently called out to his crew so that they might know where he was. The rope was not fastened to the framework. The inset shows the crew setting off to pick up the man taken out to sea.

(*From a Native Drawing.*)

and placed it behind the right ear. My head and mouth were out of the water. The animal was very fierce and carried me out to sea, rushing first to one side and then to the other. Its tail turned like the propeller of your launch. It ran very quickly. As soon as I had called my boy's name I called for my crew. I thought I was finished, and that I should not see the sun rise again. I called again and again for the canoe

Dugong Fishing 141

to come quickly. I got no answer. I heard some birds making a noise and thought it was my crew. About midnight my strength was nearly finished. I held on to the rope with what strength I had. I then heard a noise which was a long way off. I called out as loudly as I could and saw the canoe some distance away bearing down upon me. They soon got alongside and picked me up more than half dead. I was very glad when they took me from the water as I could not have held on much longer. The names of my crew were Abai, Bagi, Saima and Kopa. It was daylight before we had the dugong tied up to the canoe."

The distance he was carried out I think must have been about a mile. He mentions two places on Daru which are about a mile apart. He is able to fix upon these owing to the position of another reef and its distance from his *narato*. This account has been confirmed by the man Abai.

CHAPTER XI

GAMES & AMUSEMENTS

THE study of Kiwai games and amusements will show that the natives are possessed of considerable skill or ingenuity in devising different toys and games for the entertainment of the children, all of which are provided without cost of money and with very little labour.

The Game of Aniopu.—This takes its name from a tree named *ani*, *iopu* being the fruit of the tree. The fruit is almost round, and about the size of half-a-crown, and half or three-quarters of an inch in thickness. The sides of the players are drawn up in two ranks facing each other, the space between being eighteen feet, both toeing lines marked on the ground. The *iopu* or nut is placed on the surface of the soil between the two lines. The members of both teams pick up two handfuls of sand, squeeze this between the palms of the hands and throw it at the fruit on the ground. Each side tries to drive it over the enemy line, and when this is accomplished one point is scored. The side scoring the greater number of points wins the game. Sometimes the game is played without any line or mark on the ground, and in such a case one side tries to drive the other back and back until they are in the sea or up against some obstacle which cannot be passed. The nut must not be touched with either the hands or feet.

Games & Amusements

Sailing Baby Canoes.—This is played by boys only and is a favourite pastime amongst them. They make splendid imitations of canoes in a few minutes and without much effort. The material used consists of the midrib of the sago-palm leaf, which is very pithy and easily worked. The body of the toy canoe is about two feet long, four inches broad, and about three inches deep; a single or double outrigger may be attached. One or more masts of the same material may be placed in the hull with sails of nipa-palm leaves or bits of old rags fastened to them, with the necessary booms and gaffs. When the crafts are finished they are put into the water and raced one against the other. They are generally lost by being carried out to sea.

Dancing.—Every native child has an aptitude for dancing, from which they derive much pleasure and recreation. It is no unusual sight, and a very amusing one, to see little toddlers of three and four years of age dancing and imitating all the various movements of their elders. Children a few years older are quite skilled in the art. They supply their own music and are independent of the drums used by the men. With an ipa shell in each hand, convex side uppermost, they strike the hands together, and the noise of the shells produces as high a quality of music as the grown-ups with their conch shells, drums or empty kerosene tins. They will amuse themselves by the hour in this simple way.

Epoo Koroio.—An *epoo* is a mound of earth built by a bird named *kamuka*—generally known by the name of brush turkey or scrub hen—which is about the size of a common fowl.

In this game two mounds of earth are heaped up some

six or eight yards apart. Two or more boys, according to the number playing, are appointed as guards of the mounds—that is, two or more to guard each mound. The rest of the players form two attacking parties whose duty it is to get past the guards and destroy the mounds. Their positions are thus: mound, guards, attackers (two parties), guards, mound. The attack on the two mounds is made by the two opposing parties simultaneously, and the guards may use their hands to push back the attacking party, but the attackers are not supposed to use theirs to push the guards. From what I have seen of this game the defenders cannot possibly win, as they are outnumbered by two or three to one by the attackers. It develops into a rough-and-tumble, and there does not appear to be any degree of skill required.

Guda.—This is a spinning-top game. A large round nut of the *guda* tree, an inch and a half in diameter and an inch or more in thickness, is procured from the forest. A hole is bored through the centre of this and a piece of wood, named *tere iopu*, four inches long, is inserted, one half inch, or a smaller amount, being pushed through the nut and acting as a pivot upon which the top spins. This leaves a length of two and a half inches above the nut on the other side, which is twirled between the palms of the hands, when the top spins rapidly round for a short time. This is very entertaining.

Mere Eremeberisi.—This is a very simple game which gives much pleasure and amusement to the children. A ball is made from leaflets of a coco-nut neatly interlaced, about the size of an ordinary cricket ball. This is knocked into the air with the palm of the hand, and the player who makes

Games & Amusements

the most hits without dropping the ball on the ground is declared the winner.

Another game in which young children of both sexes find great enjoyment is the making up of damp earth into

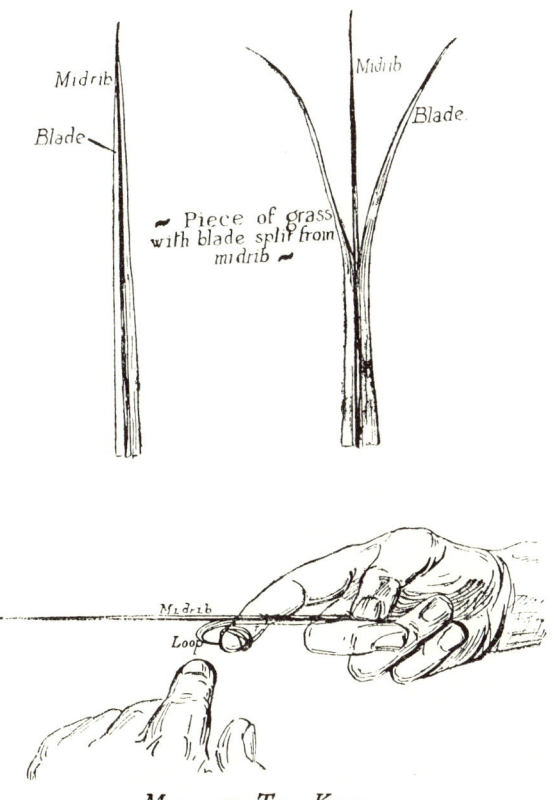

MOSIBO OR TEA KOROIO

bundles similar to those made by the women with sago. What is made one day is left till the next, when it is cut up in portions ready for cooking and afterwards thrown away.

Mosibo or Tea Koroio.—This consists in shooting the midrib of a piece of lalang grass. A native takes a piece of grass nine inches long. He splits off the blade from each side of the midrib for about half its length. The two pieces of the blade are then wrapped round the end of the index finger on the right hand. The direction of winding is very important and must be from without towards the body. The grass is held between the thumb and long finger, the midrib passing over the index finger. The next step is the most important part of the proceedings, as it supplies the momentum which will send the midrib, with the speed of an arrow, a distance of fifty or sixty yards. The first finger of the left hand is placed in the loop on the top of the right index finger. It is then jerked violently outward, stripping off the remainder of the blade from the midrib, which is shot forward at a tremendous pace, the blade only remaining in the hand.

Nuku Koroio.—Another game of this name will be later described (p. 150), which is quite different from this one. A group of children or grown-ups sit round in a ring, each person having the half of a coco-nut shell in his hand (from which the husk has been removed). With these they tap the floor, or the flooring-boards, in unison, singing meanwhile. After this has been going on for a short time the leader passes his shell to his next-door neighbour; all follow his example. He may pass his shell five or six times in succession, the other players doing likewise; this is carried on *ad lib.* It is a very interesting game and any number may sit down and take part in it. I am inclined to think that this has been imported into Papua from the South Seas via Torres Straits. There are Samoan words in the song as sung on the Fly river and in the coastal villages.

Outi Gagari.—This game is mostly confined to boys and youths. It is simply a shooting game with very small bows and the thick stems of long grass about twelve or sixteen inches long, which are used as arrows, and are named *kokoba*. Companies of boys go out on shooting expeditions; the objects shot are chiefly small birds. I have seen a boy at thirty yards send one of these grass arrows clean through the body of a bird walking on the ground. When the boys go out in companies there is a shooting match. There is a scorer on each side who carries a young coco-nut leaf, and each time a bird is shot a portion of one of the leaves is broken off. At the end of the match the side which has the greater number of broken leaves wins the game. No boy eats any bird he may happen to shoot; he gives his bag to others so that they can bear witness to his prowess should the number be called in question.

Another game with the small bow and grass arrows is played at night-time. Small pieces of wood are put into one end of the grass arrows; these are placed in the ground and the wood end lighted. When the wind has blown these alight or made them red like fire they are shot into the air, when their brilliance is increased, and they appear like small meteors travelling through the atmosphere.

A third game with the toy bow, but with a different kind of arrow, which is made from the midrib of the sago-palm leaflet, and is much stronger than the grass one, provides practice at shooting at a moving object. A number of boys go into hiding on each side of the playing-ground, whilst one boy walks or runs down the lane between the two sides, pulling after him by means of a long piece of string a long piece of the midrib of the sago leaf. As he runs down the lane the boys on both sides shoot at the moving object. The side which shoots most arrows into the midrib wins the game. The arrows are withdrawn and another contest commences.

A fourth game provides practice for shooting at a stationary object. A young sapling named *gamogogamogo* is obtained from the woods and put into the ground in a perpendicular position. The players sit on the ground and fire with the grass arrows at the sapling. The greatest number of hits wins the game.

Kuke Koroio, or the Game of the Flying-Fox.—Six or eight persons may take part in this, some sitting and some standing. One couple cross hands, and each with thumb and index finger seizes a portion of skin on the back of his partner's hand. If six play there will be twelve hands in one column, each hand pinching up the skin on the back of another hand. The whole column of hands is moved up and down, and during this time the players sing,

" *Kuke, kuke, kuke,*
Kuke, kuke, kuke,"

when the hands are all thrown up into the air at one time and a loud *gir-r-r-r* issues from every throat. The pinching up of the skin represents the flying-fox hanging on the branch of a tree, the throwing up of the hands the flying away of the bat, and the *gir-r-r-r* the noise made when the bats take to the wing.

A few very simple toys are made of leaves, of which one is spun or whirled round by the wind—a whirligig (called

Games & Amusements

by the Mawata people *oborope*, bushman's canoe; Kiwai, *tururube*).

A wind instrument is manufactured from the leaflet of a coco-nut leaf which is wound round in the shape of a funnel. In the middle of the funnel there is a narrow piece of the leaf projecting from the top about a quarter or half an inch, forming a kind of reed instrument. This is called *konitoto* (*koni* is the name of a grub; *toto*, a nest). A rattle (*sawaria*), which is swung round and round, is made from the midrib of a coco-nut leaflet and a part of the leaf.

CHAPTER XII

INDOOR & OUTDOOR GAMES

*N**UKU KOROIO*, or the game of *nuku*, is a very popular game amongst young boys. The only materials required for playing it are a *nuku*, a stick about twelve or eighteen inches long, and a block of wood upon which the *nuku* may be placed. A *nuku* is the half shell of an old coco-nut from which the flesh has been extracted, or it may be the shell of a young nut. An enamel plate is often used in place of the empty shell when such can be obtained; it is no doubt a great improvement, and adds more interest to the game, because it can be thrown a much greater distance than the coco-nut shell.

Any number of persons or players may take part. This game is played only on bright moonlight nights. Before a start is made all the players assemble together to arrange who is to take the first turn as guardian of the *nuku* or plate. When the choice of custodian has been made, that person takes up the stick and *nuku*, then rushes out into an open space with these articles in his hand. He sits on the ground and places the *nuku* on a block of wood twelve or eighteen inches high, or if there is not one at hand he places it on the ground in front of him, and begins to beat it violently with the stick. His eyes must be closed whilst this operation is in progress. Another boy stands by his side to see that he does not open them. In the meantime the rest of

Indoor & Outdoor Games

the players are hiding themselves in any nook or cranny that they can find. When the boy who is standing by sees that all the players are in hiding, he takes the *nuku* from the hand of the custodian and throws it away as far as he possibly can. The *nuku* guardian upon opening his eyes finds neither the *nuku* nor the boy, who vanishes at top speed to some secret corner. The custodian immediately stands up and begins to look round for the missing *nuku*, and when this is found he takes it back to its original position and lays it on the block of wood. He then begins to search for the boys in hiding, keeping one eye upon the *nuku* continually, lest some boy should rush out and throw the *nuku* away. When the guard discovers one of the boys in hiding he calls his name, runs back to the *nuku* and commences to beat it with the stick. If he has called the right name of the boy, the latter comes from his hiding-place into the open and is for the time being out of the game. If he has called the wrong name no one appears and the custodian must proceed with his search.

When a number of names have been correctly called, all stand round ready, in case they are released, to go into hiding again. Release is only possible when one of the undiscovered players can steal out from his place of concealment, unobserved by the *nuku* guardian, seize the *nuku* and hurl it in the opposite direction from that in which the custodian may be standing, walking or running. The game proceeds until all the names are correctly called; when this is accomplished, another boy acts as custodian and a fresh game begins.

It is a very fast, exciting and enjoyable game. It is

surprising what a distance a boy can hurl the *nuku* skimming through the air; a plate, however, can be skimmed much farther on account of its shape. The most astonishing thing in the game is the silent manner in which a large group of boys can vanish when one of their number manages to slip out unseen and succeeds in throwing the *nuku* away and at the same time releasing those who have been temporarily out of the game. A group of boys are standing together, away goes the *nuku* and before a spectator knows what has actually happened there is a silence like that of the grave, and not a soul visible except the one chasing the *nuku*. It is nothing short of marvellous the manner in which the youngsters can disappear from sight.

I have never seen the custodian, however much he may have been harassed, lose his temper, or give up the search until he has won through.

Another game is called *paru koroio*, or the game of ball. This is something like hockey, but the rules under which it is played are quite different. There may be any number of players on each side, from ten to forty, or even more. When there are not more than ten or a dozen a side it is an enjoyable game to watch and is very amusing, but when there are forty or more in each team the field of play looks like a shapeless mass of humanity rushing hither and thither in the greatest disorder and without any definite object before them.

It is a favourite game for squaring an old cause of quarrel or secret enmity. It is quite an easy thing when striking at a ball, which may be near or may be some distance away, to miss the ball and hit an opponent on the shins or on the head.

I have seen many nasty scars on the heads of boys which one would have difficulty in believing had been accidentally inflicted. When great numbers are engaged in a game there is nothing entertaining (that is, after seeing the first one) in the sense of true sport. There is abundance of yelling, screaming, laughter, often quarrels, and a rare amount of brandishing of the bats or sticks with which they strike the ball. The dominant note of the game is confusion.

The field of play is set out as follows. Two long parallel lines are marked on the ground, one at each end of the field of play; or another style may be adopted which is very popular in the coastal villages—two sticks or posts may be placed in the ground, just like the posts on a football ground. The two lines are called *gowo* or creeks. When posts are used, a bunch of leaves, a twig, or a handful of grass or flowers, representing a flag, is fastened to the sticks as an ornament.

The instruments used for striking the ball are crooked sticks, chiefly hardened rattan cane, an inch or so in thickness and curved at one end, something like an ordinary hockey stick. The ball is, of course, home-made. One kind of ball is obtained from the root of *po'o* tree. It is, when green, nodule-shaped and is called *bo'o*, which means lump. It would be impossible to play with it when freshly cut from the root of the tree, on account of its shape, as it would not roll. This defect, however, is soon remedied. The natives will go into the bush to find a suitable root, and when this has been found the nodule is cut out and afterwards placed in the fire to harden it. When sufficiently burnt it is removed from the fire and whilst hot is scraped with an ipa shell (which is about the size of an ordinary oyster shell) and is with ease made fairly round. When the cooking and scraping operations are finished it is called a *paru* or ball.

Another method of making a ball is to take a lump or a nodule-shaped piece of wood from the wild mango-tree and treat it in the same way as the *bo'o*. This is said to make a better ball than the former. Both kinds will stand a considerable amount of knocking about and will last a good long time. They are much cheaper than the real hockey balls of civilization and for the purpose required are just as serviceable as the more expensive article.

The object of the game is for one side to drive the ball past the line representing a *gowo* or creek, or past the upright stick of the opposing side. The ball must not be handled or touched with the hands in any way. Should this rule be broken the ball is again placed in the centre of the field and a fresh start made. When the ball is driven past the goal-line or stick a point is scored by the side accomplishing the feat.

There is no such thing as a goalkeeper, no linesmen and no touch-lines. The ball is in reality never out of play, except when a point is scored by one of the sides.

It is supposed to be a passing game, in which art, judging from the games I have seen, the natives cannot be said to have attained a very high degree of skill. Passing in the real sense of the term is conspicuous by its absence, the policy generally adopted being to drive the ball toward the enemy goal and try to score by rushing the ball past the mark or post.

I once attempted to act as referee in a game when there

were about forty players on each side. I never knew what chaos was till then. Some were playing for both sides at once. It did not matter in the slightest degree which way the ball travelled, the point was to hit the ball and hit hard; others did not know which side they were playing for when the game was five minutes old. The confused sound of many voices shouting at the same time, together with the laughter of the men and the clashing of the clubs, made it impossible for anyone, except those standing near the umpire, to hear the whistle when it was blown for some breach of the rules; the result was, no one took the slightest notice of the whistle or referee. The game never stopped. The official retired a sadder if not a wiser man. A very amusing part of the game is the manner in which the full backs behave. I tried hard to instil into them the necessity of keeping in their respective positions, but it was useless—the full backs on both sides were for the most part of the game waiting quite near the goal of the opposing side, on the offchance of making a score.

This game used to be played in old times at the beginning of the *taera* ceremonies, which are described in another chapter.

Obo koroio, or the game of water, is played on a ground which is marked into a number of courts, each court being about twenty by twenty-four feet. The courts must be large enough for one of the players to be able to stand in the middle without being touched by any of the four players who may be guarding the lines of the court when their arms are stretched at full length—that is to say, when there are four players, one on each of the four lines of the court, they must not be able with their outstretched arms at one and the same time to touch the one in the centre. The number of courts depends upon the number of players. If there are six players on each side there will be eight courts, and so on in proportion.

On the base-line of the courts there are two marks, one

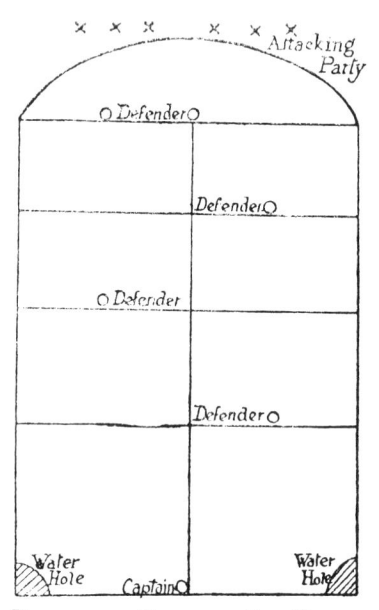

PLAN OF THE FIELD FOR *OBO KOROIO,* OR THE GAME OF WATER

at each corner; these represent water holes or wells. The object of the game is for the attacking party to reach one of these water holes, where they are supposed to have a drink, then to return the whole length of the courts, without being touched with the hands of any of the defenders. The latter have to try to prevent their opponents from reaching the water holes and quenching their parched throats, but should they be unsuccessful in doing so, they are to endeavour to prevent their return through the courts by touching one or more of them with the hand.

The master or captain of the side defending the water holes has much more freedom of action and movement than any of the other players who are defending with him. He may travel all along the base-line and also along both side-lines of the court from one end to the other. There is one defender on each of the lines parallel with the base-line, another defender on the line running down the middle of the courts, whilst the captain defends the two outer lines. None of these defenders may run along any other line than his own. The only exception is the captain, who may run along three lines.

Before the game starts all the attackers stand in a body outside the courts, at the opposite end to where the water holes are situated. The defenders stand on their respective lines. The captain of the defenders calls out in a loud voice: "*Obo!*"—that is, water—then the game begins. The attackers rush for the first court. The first line of defence makes every effort to prevent the enemy getting past his line. He may do so only if he succeeds in touching one of the attackers with his hand. Should he manage to touch only one of the attacking party, the game is over and sides are changed. The defenders become the attackers and the latter the defenders.

Should one of the attackers get through the defence and reach one of the water holes, he must return through all the courts to the point from which he originally started before a point is scored. It is not an easy matter to get through twice without being touched, but it is frequently done.

Another most interesting and enjoyable game is called *sio boromo koroio*, which being translated is the game of dog and pig. Any number of players can take part in this game; about fifteen or twenty is near the usual figure engaged.

It is played in the following manner. A ring is formed by all the players, except two, joining hands. One of the two not forming the ring stands in the middle of it, the other stands outside. The one in the centre of the ring is said to represent a pig; the player outside the circle represents a dog. The people forming the ring represent a fence or wall surrounding the pig.

The object of the game is for the dog to break through the fence, enter the ring and seize and worry the pig. The players forming the ring endeavour to prevent the dog entering, but they may not use their hands for this purpose or take hold of him in any way. Their hands must remain clasped the whole time. They may, however, try to prevent him with their arms—namely, by lowering the clasped hands—or they may prevent the dog entering by moving their legs, which are put in front of the dog in whatever manner they please. It is no easy matter for the dog to break through the pig fence when there are a lot of determined players taking part. Should the dog make his way into the enclosure either by strategy or force, the pig quickly slips out of the fence on the opposite side to that where the dog entered, passing between the legs of those guarding him. The dog immediately also slips out of the fence in the hope of seizing his prey, but in the twinkling of an eye the pig is back inside the fence. The game proceeds in this manner until the pig is caught. Two others will then take the places of the pig and dog respectively, when another game is commenced. It is very amusing and most entertaining to watch the dog, who after much hard work has managed to get inside the enclosure, trying to slip out again after his prey, which has made an unostentatious exit on the other side. The dog is no sooner out again than the pig is safe within the fold.

The game of water-melon (*waiati koroio*) is very similar to that of the dog and pig. A ring is formed by a number of people which represents a fence enclosing a garden where water-melons are growing. The water-melon is represented by a boy who lies down on the ground. A second youth outside the garden wall is supposed to be a thief, who is prowling round seeking an opportunity of getting through the fence into the garden to steal the melons. The thief tries the fence here, there and everywhere, and may be prevented from entering only by the arms and legs of those forming the ring. When the thief does eventually get inside the garden, he kneels beside the water-melon, then with the nail of his forefinger gently taps the head of the boy, just as he would do when testing a water-melon to see if it is ripe. This is the recognized method of testing coco-nuts when one desires a young one for drinking purposes, also to see if pumpkins and melons are ready for eating.

After the thief has succeeded in obtaining the prize another game is commenced with two new performers.

Korowatio koroio, the game of touching, is the old-fashioned game of tig, in which one person chases another with the object of touching the body of the person pursued. When one player is touched by another, the former takes the place of the latter and begins to pursue the other members taking part in the game.

Geni koroio is another game of tig, but quite different from *korowatio*. In this game there are two sides, generally one of boys and another of girls, though the game may be played by a party of either sex.

The plan of the playing-field is as follows. Two sticks are placed in the ground about a hundred and fifty or two hundred yards apart. These serve as touching posts or goals, one belonging to each side taking part. Before the game starts all the players assemble in the middle of the field of play between the two posts or sticks. A member of one team will then touch a member of the opposing team and the game begins. The former then endeavours to reach the goal on the opposite side of the field without being touched by any of the team playing against him. Should he be successful in doing so, a point is scored and the teams again line up in the middle of the field. If, however, he is not successful and is touched by one of the enemy, the latter makes tracks for the other goal with all speed. The side scoring the greater number of points wins the game. I have seen some really fine running by boys when playing this game. It is the most taxing of all the games I have seen the Kiwais play.

Obokare is a game played by children on the sea-beach, or on the banks of a river, when the tide is flooding or coming in, and the waves are breaking on the land. The point of the game is simply to dodge the waves without getting the feet wet.

Indoor & Outdoor Games   161

Sairokare is the name given to what we should call a hopping match. A number of players line up and at a given signal start off, hopping on one foot to a fixed point or goal. The first person to reach the end of the journey without placing the other foot on the ground is declared the winner of the game. Any player putting both feet to the ground during the trial is disqualified from any further participation in the hop.

Doropodaramidi is a peculiar game. I have not been able to discover anything instructive, interesting or amusing in it. This, however, may not be the fault of the game or the skill of the players, but may be due to the inability of the observer to appreciate the finer elements of sport.

In this game a number of persons stand in a line and clasp each other's hands. One player at the end of the line remains stationary, holding the hand of the next person to him. He acts as a pivot, and around him winds the whole line of players. The line gets less and less until the whole of the players stand together in a single mass. To illustrate the game more clearly, one might say that it is just like a person making one end of a rope fast to a tree, stretching the rope full length, taking the other end in the hand, then marching round the tree until the whole of the rope is wound round the body of the tree.

When the first movement of the players is completed an unwinding process begins; the line then moves backwards until it is in its original position. Still holding hands, all the players sit on the grass. The stationary member of the team, or the man who acted as pivot, then releases the hand of the person next to him, stands up, walks in front of

L

the sitting line, and with the side of his hand strikes the clasped hands of every couple, thus separating them. When the last pair of hands has been severed the game is ended. The children seem to get a fair amount of pleasure out of it.

Wao is the name of a jumping game, in which each player takes a long stick or pole, eight or nine feet long, which is used as a lever when jumping. The players stand on a fallen tree trunk or on the ground, and the person jumping the greatest distance with the help of the pole is declared the winner.

Waiowaio is a game which consists in turning round and round until one gets dizzy and has to retire. The winner is the one who can carry on the greatest length of time without getting too giddy.

The game of *kokadi* is played with a ball (named also *kokadi*) which is made from the leaflets of a coco-nut leaf. Along the coast *kokadi* is the ordinary game of rounders, which is probably an introduced game.

Cat's-cradles—if such can be called a game—is played both inside and outside the house. It is quite a usual thing to see a group of people, men, women and children, young and old, sitting on the ground or on the floor of the house deeply engrossed in making cat's-cradles of an extraordinary character, with nothing more than a piece of string or cord. It is very interesting to see the skilful manner in which the hands, fingers, knees, feet, toes and mouth are brought into operation.

There is one part of the year when the making of cat's-cradles can hardly be called a game, and that is when the yam gardens are finished being planted. It is much more than a game. It is nothing less than magic. The object in making the cat's-cradles is to ensure the yam shoots twining themselves round the sticks put in the garden for this purpose. In the Old Country you would make cat's-cradles so that the sweet-peas would climb round the twigs stuck in the soil. Just as the string in the cat's-cradle is twined round the hands of the makers, it is desired that the yam shoots shall imitate the string and climb round the sticks.

There is a cat's-cradle time and there is a period when they may not be made. At the commencement of the turtle-fishing season cat's-cradles are prohibited. This law is strictly observed to-day in the coastal villages. A person making them would bring misfortune upon the turtle fishers.

Cat's-cradles are often made to the accompaniment of music. As I write this a man is engaged, two yards away, making a pig and is grunting away like a hungry boar. He has just made another figure representing a sea-serpent (*gera*), when he made a hissing noise exactly like a snake.

As examples of the figures made by the Kiwais I will give a few only : a bird ; a boy paddling a canoe ; a canoe ; a crab ; a crayfish ; dogs fighting ; an eel ; a frog ; a messenger ; people going to the garden ; people returning from the garden ; a pig ; a snake ; a shell ; an ipa ; a starfish. Cat's-cradles may only be made in the daytime ; it is not permissible to make them after the sun has set.

Oropiriti koroio, the game of hiding, is nothing more nor less than the well-known game of hide-and-seek. One or more players will go outside the house so that they cannot see where the remainder of the players hide themselves. When the latter have safely stowed themselves away, the two searchers come into the house and begin to look round for those in hiding. When found, the names are called as in the game of *nuku*, and the play is carried on in like manner.

Owaraidiro, the game of swinging, is carried on inside the house at nights. A swing is made by fastening two ends of a long piece of rattan cane to two separate rafters in the roof of the house. In the loop made a native will sit and swing to his heart's content. There is no board for the person to sit upon. He must sit upon the bare cane or cover it with grass. I have seen old men and women enjoy a swing just as much as the young children do.

CHAPTER XIII

DEATH & BURIAL

WHEN a Kiwai man is considered to be on the threshold of death his mother and wife (if he has more than one it would be the first woman he married) take charge, nurse and supply all his bodily wants. The wife, however, is not allowed to remain with her husband during the night. Her place is taken by the man's eldest sister, but if no such person exists, a younger sister would act as nurse; if there is no sister, some woman from the mother's clan would be called in to assist.

In olden times life or death of a sick man was foretold by an omen, the nature of which cannot be here related. If the omen were unfavourable, the patient was never left alone; if favourable, the relatives did not trouble much about him.

When it is realized that a man is actually dying, all friends and relatives assemble to show their sympathy for the family and respect for the one laid aside. The wife sits on the left-hand side of her husband so that she may be able to massage the head without having to lean over the body. If there is severe pain, the affected parts may be cut with a piece of shell until blood flows freely.

When the husband is dead the wife throws herself full length across the prostrate body, showing her grief and sorrow by the shedding of tears and by cries of mournful lamentation. Every member of the clan takes up the dirge set by the wife. The most mournful dirges for the dead are sung without a moment's intermission until the body is removed for burial.

I have passed many sleepless nights under such circumstances. After a time the man's mother will tell the relatives of the wife to proceed with the ceremony. The body is prepared by placing the feet together and laying the arms along the sides. The corpse is rolled up in a *tiro*—that is, a sewn mat and not a plaited one—and tied round with cane. In olden times the head was not covered with the mat, the reason for which will be seen later on. The body is then put into the side of an old canoe and is carried to the place of burial. The master of ceremonies takes a long stick, measures the mat, and marks out the length of grave required. The stick is not thrown away. The grave is dug deeper at the feet than the head. When completed, sticks are laid at the bottom, some lengthwise and some across, so that the corpse will not have to lie upon the cold earth. Prior to the body being put into the grave the mat is untied so that the relatives may look upon the form for the last time. After being tied up again it is reverently laid upon the sticks in a slanting position, the head, which is not buried, pointing toward the west and the feet to the east. The canoe is left alongside the grave so that the spirit of the departed will have means of reaching its final destination.

A forked stick, with the fork uppermost, is driven into the ground at the head of the grave. On that of a man an arrow is tied to the stick. On the top of the fork is placed the man's *adigo* or gauntlet. If the deceased be

Death & Burial

a woman, her basket and grass petticoat are hung upon the stick.

On the evening of the burial food is placed upon the grave by members of the clan to which the person belonged. When this is completed a fire is lighted upon the grave. The person supplying the food addresses the spirit of the departed as follows: " This food is for you. We leave it here. We have also made a fire for you." At sundown all houses in the village are closed and doors securely fastened, to keep out the spirit which wanders round for several days. If anyone goes out at night the spirit, like the white light of a fire, may be seen going towards the west. Food is placed on the grave for five consecutive days, during which time no work is done in the gardens except such as is absolutely necessary.

On the sixth day the director of the sacred rites, having first covered his body with charcoal and placed a white cockatoo feather in his hair, takes a lot of young plants, lays them on the west side of the mound, and addressing the unseen spirit says: " These plants are for you. This is the last day we shall make food for you. *Auto ogu*, go."

Special Cases of Burial.—Should a woman die in childbirth, or should both mother and child die, it is not deemed fitting that any male relative, or in fact any male member of the community whatever, should take any part in the funeral rites and ceremonies connected with the burial. The women of her clan immediately take charge of the body, perform all duties, dig the grave, bury the body, fill in the grave, place the forked stick at the grave head, and her basket and grass petticoat on the fork of the stick, without receiving the slightest assistance from any of the men. Should a man touch the body, he would be stricken with some terrible disease, sicken and die.

In 1903, after a very trying trip round Torres Straits and the Fly river, I returned to Daru at eleven P.M. Weary and tired, I retired supperless to bed; my last meal was at eight A.M. At two o'clock next morning I was wakened by hearing a footstep on the steps of my house. I raised my head from the pillow and saw the light from a lantern and called, " Who is there ? " first in English and then in Kiwai, but received no answer. I then got out of bed and went towards the light, calling several times : " Who's there ? " The light vanished. When I reached the top of the steps a second light was seen coming up another lot of steps at the other end of the house. I went towards it and invited the bearer of the lamp to come forward. It immediately retreated as the first had done. I went into the house and got an old gun (I had no ammunition), and then stood on the top of the steps and informed the persons under the house that I had a gun and that they had better come forward. There was no response, so I went to the bottom of the steps, and on arriving there heard a weak voice say: " *Misi pepa.*" I told the unknown person to bring the paper to me and then two youths stepped forward and handed me a large sheet of blotting-paper. This was a note from a Frenchman living on Daru. This gentleman had a countryman of his staying as a guest in his house, whose wife had been confined the day before, and serious complications existed. I was requested to go down and see the person needing assistance, and went almost immediately. I was not long in doing what was required and setting things straight. I asked for water, soap and towel, which were provided, and when I was about to leave, the wife of the resident Frenchman, a native Kiwai woman, politely told me that she and the rest of the women present were very sorry for me and that I should be dead before another day dawned as I had done things which no man could do and live. I called upon the patient the day after and found her sitting up smoking. The native women were much surprised to see me alive. This was a staggering blow to one of their superstitions, which, however, is not yet dead.

If a man or woman is killed and carried off by a crocodile there cannot of course be any burial of his or her body. Should any person have witnessed the crocodile carrying off the body, a small platform is erected on the edge of the water where the person was taken. If no one saw the accident and a person should be missing, the cause of death would be one of conjecture only, and would be put down to the ferocious crocodile: in such a case the platform would be erected near the place where the missing person was last seen on the edge of the water. Food is placed on this platform for a period of five days as on an ordinary grave and the same ceremonies are observed. The men here play a very cowardly part which is intended to terrify the women and children. Some of them dress as ghosts and at sundown may be seen near the platform just coming out of the water and taking the food which has been placed there. The women and children have their attention drawn to the presence of the apparition or apparitions, and run off to their homes screaming with terror.

Burial of a Distinguished Person or of an Only Child.—A

chief or a person who has been highly respected in the settlement, or the only child of one of the heads of a clan, may not be buried in the manner already described. It may be desired that the memory of such should be handed down to future generations, and to this end some more spectacular and more telling method was formerly employed, which will now be described, even though it be somewhat gruesome.

After the death of the man of high degree, or of the child as stated above, the body was not buried, but taken away some little distance from the village into a small cleared place in the woods. Here a small platform made of sticks about three or four inches in diameter was erected, about five feet from the ground. This platform was called a *tai*. The body was carried to the platform in a sewn mat and placed upon it, and exposed to the sun. There was no covering over the body. It was absolutely naked. After the corpse had been in this position for two days, the leader of the clan to which the person belonged went to the platform, carrying water and a coco-nut shell in his hands, and poured the water upon the body, first upon the head and then upon the rest of the corpse. This was said to make the flesh soft and to assist considerably in the decomposition. This was continued daily for fourteen days. At the end of that period the master of ceremonies brought his beheading knife with him into the woods, stood near the head of the platform, on the left-hand side of the body, and removed the skull, no force being required to do so.

It is somewhat strange that this operation was delayed so much longer than in the case of a burial. One cannot

Death & Burial

imagine that much cutting was required to get through the tissues, which must have been in a very putrid state after so long an exposure under a tropical sun.

The mass of decaying matter was left on the platform and the skull was taken to the seaside to be washed. One or more assistants might take a hand in the washing. The Kiwais did not remove the brain in the same way as the Dorro head-hunters, who inserted a stick into the foramen magnum, under water, and whirled the stick round until the brain was washed out; they just simply shook and shook and shook in the salt water, looking from time to time to see how the operation was progressing. When the washing was satisfactorily finished the skull was rubbed with several kinds of sweet-smelling leaves, named *manababa, iware* and *tibeio*, which helped to remove the grease and the offensive smell from the skull. The operators then bathed and rubbed themselves down with the above-named leaves.

The skull was next taken into a small outbuilding, near the house where the person lived, which had been erected for the purpose, where it remained for some days until it was suitably decorated. No women or children might go near or enter the hut where the bony structure was kept, only the male members of the clan were allowed to enter. The reason for this was that the object had "no eyes, no nose," and in consequence of this was not presentable or fit to be seen by the female community.

Before being put into the hut the skull was dried in the sun for a short time until all smell had been removed. Preparations were then made for supplying artificial eyes and nose. A kind of beeswax, called *wamo*, was obtained from the trees in the forest, which was placed round the eyes and into which small red and black berries were set as an ornamentation. A false nose was constructed of the same material and a nose-stick inserted in it; pieces of pearl shell, named *pinare*, were inserted in the orbits of the eyes and made secure by the aid of beeswax. Every day the M.C. might be seen with his staff of helpers walking in single file to the little hut to their task of the decoration of the skull, so that it might be made fit for the eyes of the mother and other women to see. After the beautifying had been completed by the artists, and the desired perfection obtained, arrangements were made, as soon as possible, for a great feast and dance. All the food that could be procured from the native gardens, every clan contributing, was brought into the village and stacked in two great heaps a few yards apart. A new mat was laid on the ground by the wife or mother, as the case may be, between the two piles of food.

On the appointed day for the feast many guests from neighbouring tribes arrived, invitations having been sent by special messengers to them by the M.C. or father of the child. When all were gathered together the M.C. issued from the hut with the decorated skull, which he carried to the empty place between the heaps of food and handed to the widow or the father and mother, who were seated on the mat. The wife took the skull in her hands and wept bitterly, or the mother hugged the remains of her little one and pressed it to her breast. Relatives, friends and guests gathered round to see the object, amid much crying and lamentation. The wife or parents remained with the skull until after the dance, which began at sundown and finished at daylight next day. The skull was taken into the house and placed in a basket, which was hung from one of the rafters of the house, above where the mother slept. Should the mother go to her garden for one day, she carried the basket with her. Should she go for several days, or on a fishing expedition for more than one day, the basket was left with some old woman living in the same house, who received some of the produce of the garden or fish for her trouble.

We have seen what became of the skull taken from the body laid on the platform, but what of the body that remained? This, it is said, lay on the *tai* for twelve months. The bones by that time were well bleached. The widow or the mother then suggested that it was time the bones were buried. The M.C. gathered them together, rolled them up in a mat and then quietly buried them in a little grave.

Another feast, much greater than the last one, then followed. When I asked the reason why another feast was held the answer was "because it is the last thing we can do to recall the dead." The Mawata people inform me that they never had more than one body on the *tai* at one time, as they feared some disease or sickness might break out on account of the smell.

After my experiences at Goaribari I am not surprised that the Mawata tribe of the Kiwais did not care to have more than one corpse laid out on the *tai* at one time on account of the smell, from fear of sickness and death. The language which would adequately describe the Goaribari scene does not exist.

The following is a translation of an account, written at my request by Adagi of Mabadauwane, of a curious custom formerly practised in the bush village of Togo, some forty miles from Daru as the crow flies. An old man named Uria vouches for the accuracy of the statements herein contained :

"When it was discovered that a *togo* (man) was very sick and likely to die, his family and friends went to the gardens and brought in a quantity of food, which was placed alongside the sick man. If any of this went bad before the man died fresh supplies were procured. If the patient recovered, the food was divided amongst the relatives and friends. When the man died, the corpse was carried to the burial ground, a grave dug and the dead body laid alongside the grave. The trunk of a banana plant was placed in the grave and covered with earth.

"At one end of the grave a fire was kindled and upon this a piece of bamboo about six feet long was laid. When bamboo was put on the top of a fire and became very hot, a loud report took place which sounded like an explosion. As soon as the bamboo exploded the *urio* or spirit of the dead man was said to have ascended into the air. The body was then cooked and eaten. Some of the bones were buried in the gardens, which were said to make the garden prolific; others were burnt; the residue was rubbed on the bodies or trunks of fruit trees to make them more productive."

CHAPTER XIV

THE *KAIKAI OBORO*

KIWAI tradition says that this dance and ceremony first originated on the island of Daru. Its beginning was due to the ready invention of children whilst at play. The fathers and mothers of these boys and girls were accustomed to go into the woods to make their gardens, and to make dances which they did not wish their children to see. Food was left behind by the parents for their offspring when they departed from the village. The youngsters were left to their own resources and had to contrive some kind of amusement to while away the time. Children all the world over are quick at making contrivances for games, and these Kiwais showed great inventive ability and produced a new play. They talked matters over and decided that the boys should dress up and dance, each dancer to be the representative spirit of a brother or sister who had recently died. It was, of course, only a make-believe. The girls went fishing, brought back their catch, and each child laid aside one fish for the boy who was to represent the spirit of a brother or sister. That particular fish was then *tarena* (sacred) to the person who had given it, and who would not eat that particular kind of fish again, because it had been given to the spirit. As they had no drums, they provided an excellent substitute: every child taking an ipa shell in each hand, used them as clappers and so supplied the necessary music for the dancers.

Some time afterwards two middle-aged men, feigning sickness, remained behind in the house to watch the unsuspecting children at play. They were suspicious that the bairns were concealing something from their parents. From their hiding-place they saw the little drama and related what they had witnessed to the other members of the community upon their arrival in the village at sundown. Some believed the report, others disbelieved, and some doubted. It was considered a serious matter, and arrangements were made for a few of the older men to remain behind and inquire more fully into what was going on. These spies saw the whole of the performance and were much impressed. They reported to the rest of the elders in council and made certain suggestions, which, after further deliberation, were accepted. It was decided, first, that the new play was excellent in character, but quite unsuitable for young children living with their mothers; secondly, that the bigger boys who were connected with the play should cease to live with their mothers and should go to live in the men's house; thirdly, that only those residing in the said house should be permitted to take part in such plays in future. The elders thus robbed the young children of their newly invented game and took permanent possession of it.

As time advanced this play became one of the most important functions in the life of the community. The representative spirits of the dead were soon believed to be the real spirits of the departed. The ritual employed became more complex as time went on, and the men, always keeping

1. THE GOGOBE HEADDRESS.   2. A FLY RIVER NATIVE.
Worn at the Initiation Ceremony.   With cassowary-feather headdress.
3. Dead body drying on a wooden platform at Goaribari.

The *Kaikai Oboro*

these matters in their own hands, added to the mysteries which so interested and yet perplexed the women and children. By degrees it developed into a sacred ceremony and spread from Daru to all the coastal villages.

In all these a portion of land was set apart for the observance of this ceremony. These portions of land were soon regarded as hallowed spots. They came to be reverenced, loved and feared. Reverenced, because they were reserved for the performance of sacred rites; loved, because of the historic associations which memory recalled; feared, by the women and children, because of the uncanny and weird performances enacted therein.

Women and children were not allowed under any circumstances to enter the sacred precincts. The men who represented the spirits of the recent departed did their utmost to make the flesh of the female part of the community creep. The brightest moments of their lives were when they could assume the appearance of some wild, ferocious spirit, meander round the settlement and sacred enclosure, and cause a shiver to run down the spines of the onlookers. The dresses assumed by the spirits are grotesque, and are sufficient to instil fear into the heart of any woman and child. The men are nothing more nor less than scaremongers, and make good use of every opportunity to terrify the weaker sex, who are informed that the dancers are real spirits who have come from Adiri, the land of the departed. The statement is swallowed wholesale without any questioning whatever. I shall never forget the first time I saw one of these strange apparitions who represent the departed spirits. I was walking from Dirimu, more than twenty years ago, to the village of Tureture via Kunini, and had to pass the sacred ground of the former place. I was quite unaware of its existence, and was walking along the track when all at once a strange figure came from the bushes about thirty yards ahead of me. There was no face or head to be seen and I stopped dead for a few seconds, and seeing two black feet on the ground guessed that the natives were having a little fun at my expense. As I drew nearer the figure mysteriously vanished into the bushes again. Some months after, the man came and admitted that he was the culprit. He had much enjoyed the joke. I cannot say that I did at the time.

The little simple memorial service invented by the children became degraded into an exhibition of wild, fierce dancing and feasting by the men. By their deceptions they imposed upon the credulity of the women and children and obtained large quantities of food, which were brought as presents for the spirits and which the men ate in secret.

The Horiomu.—To understand the ceremonial of the Kiwai dancing and its ritual it is necessary to get a clear idea of the dancing ground, and the meaning of the word *horiomu*. This is a coastal word, and means a feast. The word used on Kiwai island is *soriomu*.

In the old fishing days, when a turtle or dugong was brought ashore at Daru, it was customary, and still is to-day, to cut it up in a small enclosed space of ground, the walls of which are made of coco-nut leaves and which stand about five feet above ground. The meat was for a feast, and soon the term *horiomu* or feast was used to signify the little shanty or screened-off place. Now when the children produced their little opera they laid out the ground according to their

The *Kaikai Oboro*

own ideas, and to produce a good stage effect, and provide a background for the performers, they erected a similar screen to that which enclosed the place where the meat was cut up. The boys ate the food provided by the girls behind the two screens, which then were also termed *horiomu*.

Originally the word meant a feast, then the place for making a feast, then was used to denote a screen for the dancers to dance in front of, and behind which they could retire when their turns were finished; later the word *horiomu* was used to designate the ground round about the screens where the sacred ritual takes place, if such it can be called. As already stated, the boys ate their food behind the screens, and the men do the very same at the present time when ceremonies are observed.

The native name for the dance in memory of the dead is not called the *horiomu* ceremony, as stated by some recent writers (in fact there is no such thing as a *horiomu* ceremony), but *kaikai oboro*.

The word *kaikai* needs a little explanation. It must not be confused with the word *kaikai* which means either "food" or "to eat." There is no connection whatever between the two words. In Kiwai the word *kaikai* means an ornament of white feathers tied round a stick about sixteen inches long.

The night before the dance in memory of the dead takes place, an interesting little ceremony is enacted in the men's club-house. Two men from each clan in the village assemble in solemn conclave at three P.M. At Mawata there are five clans, so that there would be ten all told. One of these feathered sticks (*kaikai*) (at one end there are no feathers for about two inches) is placed or put through the stalk of a

180   The *Kaikai Oboro*

leaf from a tree named *warakara*—no other leaf can be used for this purpose—the end without feathers is pushed

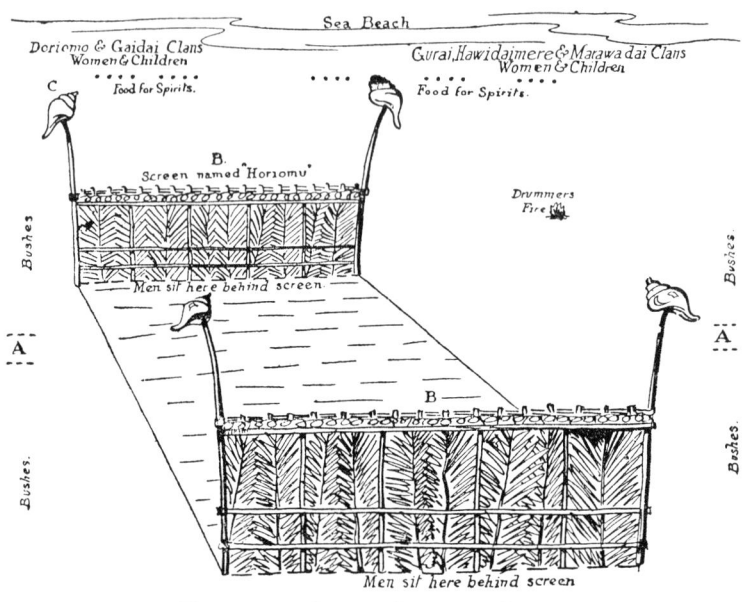

Horiomu, or Sacred Dancing Ground

> A shows two passages leading into the bush where the men acting as spirit dancers dress, and from which they make their way into the dancing ground. B shows the places where the spirits dance. The right-hand screen is reserved for the three clans, Gurai, Hawidaimere and Marawadai, and only the spirits of these clans may dance there. The left-hand screen is for the spirits of the two clans Doriomo and Gaidai. When a dancer has finished his turn he retires from the stage, passing between the two screens. He is then able to get back into the dressing or green room through another passage in the bushes. C shows conch shells placed upon the top of posts for decorations. The screens are about five feet six inches high and are made of coco-nut leaves.

into the flooring-board of the house and the *kaikai* stands erect upon the broad leaf. This is to represent or symbolize the spirits of the recent dead who are to appear during the coming ceremony. All the dresses which the spirits are to wear on the following day are laid in a line along the floor of the house in front of the feathered stick. Then *karea* is made by an elder, who takes the coco-nut shell containing *gamada* in one hand and a few green *gamada* leaves in the other, dips these into the liquid and sprinkles the *kaikai* or stick of feathers and says: " This is for good luck. We have waited until the north-west was finished to make this dance for you. We shall meet you to-morrow. We want you to come early in the morning." The elders then partake of liquid refreshments (*gamada*), and liberal quantities are consumed. The feathered stick is picked off the flooring-boards and wrapped up in a mat and put in a safe place. The spirit dancing costumes are gathered together, taken outside the house and hidden, so that the men may dress without being seen by the women and children. They are carefully laid out in the same order as they were in the house. At about three A.M. the ten dancing men are up and dressed for the first act of the dance in memory of the dead.

The Kaikai Oboro, or the Spirit Dance with the White Feathers.—The *kaikai oboro* (*oboro* is the spirit which exists after the death of the body) can take place only during the south-east season of the year. Should a person die in the north-west season, the ceremony cannot be held until the following south-east season. There are two reasons for this: first, the initiation ceremonies take place in the north-west, and to add more ceremonies to those of that season would overburden the programme; and secondly, there is a much greater supply of food during the south-east season than during the north-west. Both reasons are weighty ones in the minds of the natives. The dance takes place in the month of *Keke*, or June.

As already stated above, the entertainment begins at three A.M. There are no spectators present and the performers are not seen by the audience, who at the time of the rising of the curtain are all asleep in their homes. The spirits dress in the place where their costumes were left after the " good luck " ceremony. The dress will be briefly described. The head is adorned with a kind of mat made from the yellow leaflets of young coco-nut trees, which are sewn together, thirty inches long and twelve inches broad. This is named *poriso* and is not used again after the opening performance. The body of the dancer is covered with shredded leaves of the young coco-nut, and a kind of petticoat made of the same material is worn which reaches below the knees and hangs very gracefully on the hips. One man carries a piece of the midrib of an old coco-nut leaf. When the ten men are fully attired they advance with slow and solemn steps towards the women's houses, bows and arrows in hands and a bundle of arrows under one arm. When a few yards distant from the houses the leader lays down his bow and arrows and with the stick strikes the ground with all his strength—bang, then a pause; bang again, and another pause; bang again, and a third and longer pause. The men sleeping in the clubhouse give the spirits a hearty greeting by calling in a loud voice: " *O-O-Ogu-o!   O-O-Ogu-o!   O-O-Ogu-o!* " The capital O is simply an exclamation; the word *ogu* means come. The elders have taken good care to have a few of their number sleeping with their own families in the women's houses ready for this particular scene. Upon the spirits striking the ground the first time the men welcome the guests in the same way as the club-men, by calling " *O-O-Ogu-o! O-O-Ogu-o! O-O-Ogu-o!* " and then kindly inform the women that the spirits are just arriving from the west. The poor souls are terrified, except the very old women, who know part of the truth but dare not reveal what they know for fear of black magic, and soon all the fires are burning—their only method of light in the house—and all are sitting up in anticipation of something, they know not what, coming upon them. After the spirits have had a long pause the ground is struck a fourth time. This is followed by a long drawling whistle in which all the spirits take part. This is continued for some minutes, and, taking place in the very early morning, produces cold shivers down the backs of the women and children. After prowling round the village the spirits quietly walk away, whistling till they are some distance from the settlement, and make straight for the sacred enclosure named the *horiomu*. Here all disrobe.

The old men have now assembled in this place and lighted fires for the purpose of warming the spirits and adding a little to their comfort. Then follow songs of welcome and much beating of drums, which is kept up till the rays of the sun are seen shooting from the horizon. Then all return to the village. One of the elders then publicly calls upon the women to extend hospitality to the spirit guests, their own people, who have just arrived from the west after a trying voyage, and who need a little sustenance, and that if any of them have a little dugong or turtle meat, or fish or crabs, let them bring it along, with a plentiful supply of yams, bananas, sweet potatoes, young coco-nuts for drinking, and any other food-stuffs available. The coastal Kiwais do not wish to be considered mean and inhospitable when dealing with spirits from another world, so a large amount of food is soon forthcoming, that their guests may be entertained with honour, and future favours obtained. The food is cooked by the women and carried by them to a place near the sacred ground and laid upon the earth. Other younger men remove this into the sacred enclosure and place it in front of the place where the different tribes sit during the performance.

The spirits of the recent dead are given breakfast, but the spirits of those who have been dead many years are not so provided. The families of the former will always have on hand a supply of cooked food for their spirit. Breakfast is partaken of in the sacred enclosure.

At two P.M. the second act of the opera is staged. The orchestra takes up its position outside the sacred ground and an overture on the drums is rendered with vocal music, and during this musical introduction the spirits are adorning themselves with their dancing costumes.

There may be four kinds of spirits represented, man, boy, woman or girl. The bodies of the representative spirits are dressed differently; all are, however, covered with charcoal. The costume of the man consists of bird of paradise head-dresses, or head-dresses made of cassowary feathers, one standing erect on the forehead and another hanging down across the face, both being tied at the back of the head. Twigs and leaves are added until the face is absolutely shut in. Into the head-gear of all recent spirits are placed *kaikai*, or sticks covered with white feathers. Older spirits generally

The *Kaikai Oboro*

have them, but may be without, which would be unusual. These are placed in the head-dress just above the ears at right angles to the face. The body is covered with the shredded leaflets of the young coco-nut leaves, as already described. There are always a number of old spirits who appear with the new ones, and they are all dressed alike, but not armed alike. The spirit of the man who died last northwest season carries a bow and five or six arrows in his left hand and one arrow in the right hand to which is tied a split croton leaf. The old spirits carry a quiver of arrows under the left arm in addition to the bow in the left hand, and a single arrow in the right. On the left fore-arm a gauntlet is worn to which is fastened a bunch of cassowary feathers which project beyond the elbow. A beheading-knife is worn on the chest, armlets on wrists and upper arm, leglets (*makamaka*), made from the leaflets of young coco-nut leaves, are tied round the ankles and below the knees. The bodies of all the male spirits are covered with shredded coco-nut leaflets from young trees. Belts and sashes are worn by all.

The costume of the women spirits is different. They do not carry arms of any description, only a kind of walking-stick. They wear long grass petticoats which reach to the ankles, giving them the appearance of widows. Two green coco-nut leaves are held against the breast and kept in position with the hands, one passing over the right shoulder and the other over the left. Their faces are covered with *pia*, highly coloured red leaves, and other ornamental plant leaves. The backs are bare, or rather covered with charcoal, while round the waist croton leaves are worn. The spirit of a girl is attired in the same or similar garb to that of a woman.

The boy spirit on his first appearance does not wear either bird of paradise or cassowary plumes. His head is covered by a *poriso* and a mass of leaves. He does not carry arms of any kind. In each hand he carries small bundles of *terege*, the midrib of the leaflets of coco-nut leaves. These are carried in a horizontal position.

During the dressing operations, which take a considerable length of time, the orchestra takes a rest and liquid refreshment—from a young coco-nut, of course—talks and smokes. A messenger at length arrives and informs the musicians that the spirits are toileted, and they then proceed inside the sacred enclosure and take up their positions round a fire, all standing. A few old spirits first emerge from the bush dressing ground, run about hither and thither and finally enter the *horiomu*. The *pupi rubi* (signallers) wave a coco-nut leaf intimating to the women that they may approach. Then a *kau oboro*, a spirit that turns round and round when they appear, vanishes into the dressing-place, and the women and children take up their positions and sit in clans outside the sacred ground.

Before the spirits appear on the stage the stone or wood club of the deceased, together with his beheading-knife and *wapo* (the long wooden harpoon handle), are placed inside the dancing place, between the drummers and the food of the spirits.

A signal is made to the spirits in the dressing ground that all is ready, and the drummers begin with a very slow measure. The spirits then appear in the arena, six old spirits with one new one, the latter walking between the six. The slow beating of the drums is for the benefit of the new spirits,

The *Kaikai Oboro*

who are not strong and cannot walk fast. The mother, wife and sister of the deceased now come forward and recline on the ground with their faces upon their hands. The men are dancing meanwhile. The new spirit jumps over the prostrate bodies of the women again and again, whilst the drums beat a quicker measure. After a time the spirit picks up the stone club, turns to the points of the compass where deceased captured human heads, and brandishes the instrument, imitating its use in war. Then follows the harpoon, which is taken in both hands, and the dancer imitates a man looking out to sea for dugong, and finally finishes the performance by the spearing of an imaginary sea-cow. This is now laid aside and the dancer takes up a *moisa* and *gora* (dancing ornaments) and dances for some time. He then pours water on the father, mother, wife and sister, who up to this time have not bathed or washed their bodies since the son and husband died. They have been able to wash only their faces, hands and feet, after which they have smeared them again with charcoal. They are now at liberty to bathe regularly, if they so desire. The women, trembling, weeping and terrified, fully believe that the real spirit of their dead has been dancing by their side.

The women spirits, personated by men, are led into the arena by some old spirits, as, being new arrivals, they do not know the way into the dancing ground. The old spirits form a half-circle and the female spirits occupy the stage for a time and then retire. This is said by the natives to be the most appreciated of the dances.

The spirits of children also appear led by older ones. A piece of native-made rope about six feet long is fastened to the belt of the old spirit, the other end is held in the hand of the boy spirit. "Being only a child, he needs special guidance and help, and so holds the rope that he may not make a mistake and take the wrong turning."

I have inquired how the men manage to convince the women that a grown man who is personating the child spirit is the spirit of the child. The man from whom I inquired smiled and said: "That is easy enough: we always appoint the smallest man to dance for a child's spirit, and when he or it appears we tell the mother that the spirit has grown very quickly since the body died, and they are satisfied." The child spirit dance is much quieter in tone. There is not the rough jumping about such as there is by the men and women spirits. They are weak children and too much cannot be expected of them.

The great song of the opening of the dance is as follows:—

"*Piamasara piamataeba,
Iwaro goina piamataeba,
Iwaro kima piamataeba.*"

I have copied the above from a copy made me by a native at my request. I was unable to pick up the words as they were sung for me, so I got a man to write it down. I had got the first line correctly, but the speed and intonation of the second and third lines were beyond me.

This dance is now almost a thing of the past. It is never practised as in the old days, but is enacted as a kind of pageant in some of the villages during Christmas week.

CHAPTER XV

MUGURU, OR FIRST INITIATION CEREMONIES

THE word *muguru* was used to designate a number of very important ceremonies which were held in olden times by the Kiwai natives. All youths who were just entering upon the threshold of manhood were compelled to pass through these ceremonies in order that they might gain a knowledge of the mysteries and inner secrets of the tribe. Certain ceremonies were held for children but I am not including these under the term *muguru*. The period occupied in putting a youth through the initiation ceremonies was two, three or more years. An initiate was called a *kowea mere* (the word *kowea* means finding or seeing; *mere*, a boy; a *kowea mere* was therefore a finding or seeing boy). There were no less than six of these ceremonies—namely (1) the *kaikai oboro*, the spirit with white feathers which danced in memory of the dead; (2) the *yam muguru*; (3) the *gamabibi* dance; (4) the *mimia*; (5) the *uruba*; (6) the *taera*. These will be described in detail in separate chapters. The ordeal of some of these was very trying for the youths, and possibly more so for their mothers and sisters, who suffered much vicariously during the time they were in progress.

Before the ceremonies commenced the names of all the youths who were to be initiated were publicly announced. Then followed a short period of anxious waiting, during which the initiates were in a state of high nervous tension, not knowing what was before them. The mothers and sisters of the youths wept. They realized that the initiation of the boys meant a great break in the family life. The child practically passed out of the mother's life and there was a very great wrench and a tugging at the heart-strings. From this date the son began to grow apart from his mother and sisters. There could not be any confidences between them in future. The boy was not permitted to hold converse with them or any other female in the community. The mother's eldest brother now took absolute charge of the youth, and directed all his doings until the ceremonies were concluded. The lad was very carefully watched and always suspected when not in the company of the uncle. Should the latter find his ward sitting with his mother or sisters, or holding conversation with any of the opposite sex, he would be very severely reprimanded and sent off to the men's club-house without a moment's delay.

At the conclusion of the initiation ceremonies the youth returned to his home an altered being. He was in possession of the secrets of the tribe, which he dared not divulge; were he to do so his life would be forfeit.

The First Ceremony.—The preliminary arrangements for holding the first initiation ceremony were made in the men's club-house. The elders of the tribe convened an assembly of the men-folks, who talked matters over, and decided upon the day when the ceremony should commence. At this meeting it was proposed to hold what they called a *giradaro*—that is, an inspection by the members who lived in the club-house—of all the gardens owned by the different

First Initiation Ceremonies

members of the settlement. *Karea,* or a good luck ceremony, was made, during which the *ororaorora* (the spirits of the bush) were requested to leave the gardens, as their task of guarding the same was at an end. A plentiful supply of *gamada* was consumed after the *karea* was concluded.

On the following morning one of the old men went into the village and made an announcement as follows: " Women, women, we are going to make *giradaro*; you had better go out and get some fish." The object of this announcement was to prevent the women going into the bush to work in their gardens during the period of inspection. It was an unwritten law that no women should be present or near the gardens when this function took place.

All the men proceeded in a body, walking in single file, to the garden land for the inspection. Every garden was visited. The plots of land planted and owned by each individual citizen were pointed out to the whole company. A garden might be the property of one man or of twenty or thirty men. In the communal gardens, which were very large, the ground was divided into allotments, and these were again divided into plots or beds. One man may have three or more plots, all depends upon the size; his wife will have one plot less; then there is one or more for every child in the family, however young they may be; none is omitted.

During the garden inspection the whole community knew exactly what amount of food each individual had in his garden. This varied much. A man with three or more wives and several daughters had, of course, the greatest amount of food; another with only one wife and no daughters had not as much wealth and often felt a little envious of the former.

After the examination of the gardens a large space of ground was cleared near the garden fence. The young men who had been initiated during the last few years were sent to gather coco-nut leaves. These were brought to the newly cleared spot and laid upon the ground. The men were sent away a second time to procure a quantity of food, a long forked pole (*kago*), a planting-stick, named *woto*, and a number of *togo* (from twelve to eighteen inches in length)—these are the midribs of the leaflets of the coconut-palm leaf.

The forked pole was placed in the centre of the meeting ground, which was circular, the forked portions being above the surface. Each clan put a portion of food on the forks of the pole, such as yams, taro, sugar-cane, coco-nuts, etc.

Whilst the above was in progress members of the various clans cooked the breakfast, and when the decoration of the forked pole was finished food was partaken of by all. The clans sat apart round their own fires, and after their repast smoked and carried on a general conversation.

After a time an old man advanced into the middle of the ring and stood near the central post. As he did so a solemn stillness fell upon the whole assembly. Taking the planting-stick, which had been laid on the ground, in his left hand, he addressed the assembly and announced the names of the different ceremonies which his clan desired to observe during the coming or present south-east season, such as the *madia, wete, gaera* and *apeiriho*. Having enumerated these, he stooped and picked up the *togo*, and, speaking again, informed the audience that he had a grandson who was

First Initiation Ceremonies

old enough to be shown the mysteries of the *kaikai oboro*. He then called the name of his own son (the father of the boy) and afterwards the name of his grandchild. As he pronounced the lad's name he lifted the planting-stick from the ground and gently replaced it in the hole he had originally made when first he put it in the earth. He then picked out one of the *togo* and most reverently stuck it into the soil in an upright position. In like manner he named every boy in his clan who was considered old enough to be initiated, and, as he did so, put a *togo* into the ground for each one. The planting-stick was raised every time a name was called and put back into the same hole on each occasion. The old man, having completed his task, took up all the *togos* he had put into the ground, placed them alongside those he had not used, laid them on the earth, and retired to the place where his own clan was sitting.

In a similar way the leaders of each clan advanced to the centre of the circle, announced the names of all the minor ceremonies their people wished to hold, and finished up by calling the names of those who were to be initiated. This was a quiet, dignified, solemn and impressive ceremony.

A consultation was next held as to who should have the honour of conveying the information of what had been decided at the meeting to the people in the village. The two oldest men present were generally selected for this purpose.

A division of the food which had been hung on the forked poles was then made amongst the various clans, and the meeting terminated. On the arrival of the men in the village all the women's houses were closed and the doors fastened. The two old men went, stood outside each house in turn, and announced the substance of what had been determined at the meeting held in the bush. The names of the youths who were to be initiated were called, together with the names of their fathers and the clan to which each belonged. The message having been delivered, the women were commanded to open the doors of the houses, and upon this being done the men entered and partook of food with their wives and children.

After an interval of two or three days, during which great preparations were made by the men who were to dance as representatives of the recent dead, the initiates were taken from their mothers' care by their uncles and lodged in the men's club-house. The old men made *karea* and spent the night drinking *gamada*.

Early next morning the first part of the *kaikai oboro* dance took place. This being concluded, the guardians of the initiates seized their charges and carried them on their shoulders to the sea-beach, where all were washed in salt water. When the ablutions were completed the youths were again carried by their uncles, shoulder-high, to a fire which had been lighted near one of the houses, so that their bodies might be kept warm.

A large stack of food, collected by the mothers and sisters of the youths, had been piled up near the fire. A portion of food was given to each boy, and after eating this the sisters carried the candidate on their shoulders about a hundred yards from the house and back again.

When the sun was just coming over the horizon the old

First Initiation Ceremonies

men left the club-house with their drums, lighted a fire, then began to drum and sing:

> "*Kamaida iaba matara,*
> *Igiwoinara kamaida*
> *Wakaiara pamisa*
> *Rarapamisa pamisa.*"

There is no translation of these words.

This was continued for half-an-hour, and the orchestra then took a rest and smoked.

During the following performance it was thought necessary that the guardians of the boys should have assistance so that their charges might not have an opportunity of running away. Each boy was now guarded by two men. The initiates were carried to a place on the beach where for a time they witnessed the evolutions of the spirit dancers. The mothers and sisters of the youths are said to have wept as their children and brothers were carried off. At the end of the dance the performers went into the *horiomu* or sacred enclosure. The boys were also carried there and permitted to stand outside, a guardian on each side holding an arm. One of these guardians covered the boy's eyes with his hand so that he was unable to see. Whilst thus blindfolded, another person came behind with a sharp-pointed stick and dug it into the boy's legs again and again until blood was drawn. The youths were informed that a sting-ray fish had bitten them, or that a centipede had wounded them. The lads screamed and yelled, calling upon their mothers to come and rescue them from such tortures. The women-folks were, however, confined to their houses and not permitted to leave them. Whilst the yelling and screaming of the terrified initiates was going on the drummers did their best to drown the noise, and the rest of the men sang their loudest, with the same object in view. This concluded the first act. At the commencement of the second act the boys were allowed the use of their eyes and were led, for the first time in their lives, inside the sacred enclosure. All singing ceased; the drums were beaten most furiously.

As soon as the initiates had entered the *horiomu* they were overcome with fright, caused by a mad rush of the ghostly apparitions, who yelled, danced and jumped before them, threatening violence to all. The dancers knelt in front of them, performing many insane antics and so scaring the youths that they would have fled had they not been held by their guardians. Suddenly the drumming ceased. The dancers then drew aside with their hands the coverings of the faces so that the initiates could recognize them, and said to the boys, " I am your father " or " I am your brother," as the case might be. " I am not a spirit. When men die their spirits go to Adiri and never return. In the past you have been deceived, along with your mother and sisters. To-day you have learnt the truth. You are not to tell what you have now seen to your mother or sisters; if you do, we shall kill you." The spirits then removed their head-dresses and dancing costumes, that the initiates might fully realize they were not again being deceived.

In this manner the youths were initiated into the secrets of the *kaikai oboro* and learnt for the first time that their own fathers and brothers danced as spirits of the dead. From early childhood the youths had been taught by their own

First Initiation Ceremonies

parents, relatives and friends that the dancers in the dance in memory of the recent dead were real spirits who had come from the west, Adiri, to see the old home again. Now that the truth had been revealed to them they were freed from a terror which had haunted them all their days. Thus ended the second act.

The third act was begun by one of the *pupi rubi* (a signaller) waving a coco-nut leaf as a signal to the man on guard between the *horiomu* and the settlement that the women should come to see the last part of the ceremony. This information was communicated to the female community, who were hidden in their houses. They lost no time in responding to the call, and took large quantities of food for the dancers, which they left outside the *horiomu*. As they walked along the seashore they were met by one of the dancers, a kind of clown, who conducted them to the position they usually occupied near the sacred ground. As soon as the women and children were seated some of the young men advanced, took up the food the women had brought and carried it to the dancers behind the screens. Other spirits appeared and danced for the women. Three good turns were done on their behalf.

Whilst the dancing was going on the initiates inside the *horiomu*, who could not be seen by the spectators, were being rubbed all over with charcoal and water and were made as black as possible. Armlets were placed on the biceps muscles of both arms of every boy; a belt (*eporo bagi*) was presented to each initiate. This had to be put on by placing the belt on the ground, stepping into it, then pulling it over the legs and body until the waist was reached. A bunch of grass, named *gana*, was stuck between the belt and the body as a decoration; a small basket was given to every boy, which contained a *uwere*, or small knife for the purpose of cutting fish, an *oboia*, or water-bottle (this was a coco-nut shell with a small hole in the top, the whole of the fleshy part having been extracted), an ipa shell, for the purpose of scraping coco-nuts; a bone from a sting-ray fish, four or five inches long, was inserted in the septum of each boy's nose—these, together with the head-dress mentioned above, completed the initiate's first outfit, of which he was very proud.

After the dressing operations were completed the initiates were again carried, sitting on their guardians' shoulders, with one leg on each side of the uncle's neck, to the place where their mothers and sisters were assembled, so that they might see their offspring and brothers and admire their new attire. We might compare the initiate with the British boy wearing his first suit of clothes and finding two pockets in his pants, a threepenny piece, two marbles, a few bits of string and a knife with two blades; or rather we might compare him with the youth wearing his cap and gown on degree day. But this is a digression. Some of the Kiwai mothers, upon seeing their sons in the garb described, wept, feeling sad at heart, and realizing more than before that a yawning gulf existed between them and their bairns. Other women were pleased and thankful that the ordeal was over and that nothing serious had happened to their children. After the mothers' inspection the women-folk returned to their own homes and the initiates to the *horiomu*, where they were given a little food, but were not permitted to eat either fish or coco-nut. When the frugal meal was finished the boys were carried back to the men's club-house by their guardians.

On the following day the youths returned to the *horiomu* in charge of their guards and were allowed a certain amount of liberty, and might walk outside the sacred ground provided there were no women in the immediate vicinity.

During the two following days the initiates spent their days in the *horiomu* and their nights in the men's club-house. On the third day the women of the village went to fish and get crabs. They returned about two o'clock and cooked what they had caught. *Tiro* mats were now laid along the beach in a single line, one mat for each boy. Upon these mats the women laid the crabs, fish, a young coco-nut and other kinds of vegetables. When these preparations were finished, the guardians of the initiates emerged from the *horiomu* with their wards sitting on their shoulders and carried them to their respective mats. The former sat down with the latter. The uncles then took a wee bit of crab and a wee bit of every kind of fish which was on the mat, rolled this into a ball, told the youths to open their mouths and then threw the fish into them, after which they picked up the young coco-nut and gave the boys a sip of the water only. When I inquired from my informants the reason why such a small fish ball was given, the reply was: "It is to teach them that if they would eat fish they must first learn to catch them."

The women, adorned with dancing ornaments of various kinds, performed what was called the *hete* or *sese* dance, which was of a festive character and very humorous. This was only of short duration, and at the conclusion of it they returned to the village, when the food was distributed amongst the different members of each clan. The old men spent the night drinking *gamada*. This was the end of the first initiation ceremony.

No boy could take part in a dugong expedition until he had passed through this order. The elderly men proceeded without delay to arrange for the dugong fishing, when the initiates were taken by their guardians to the reef and instructed in the science and art of erecting a *narato* and the various charms necessary to ensure a successful day's fishing.

CHAPTER XVI

YAM MUGURU, OR SECOND & THIRD INITIATION CEREMONIES

THE *yam muguru* is one of the Kiwai initiation ceremonies in which the youths are instructed in the correct method of planting yams, the secrets of making medicine for these tubers and the mysterious powers of the bull-roarer, which they see for the first time, and which is believed to be effective in producing an abundant harvest. Like all the other *muguru* ceremonies, every effort is made to terrify and frighten the initiates. This is by no means so trying as the *gamabibi* and *mimia* ceremonies, but is quite as exciting, for a time at least—so those who have passed through these orders inform me.

Origin of the Bull-Roarer.—The bull-roarer is said to have originated at a place some seventy or eighty miles west of Daru, somewhere in the vicinity of Bugi. According to the legend, two women went out into the forest to collect firewood. They were gathering white mangrove, named *otoro*. Whilst one of them was splitting a rather large piece, by striking it against another, a portion flew off and went buzzing through the air, making a very strange noise which frightened both the women; the sound was, *bububububububu* (let the reader repeat or sing this very quickly and he will get a sound similar to that produced by the bull-roarer). After the women had filled their baskets with wood, one of them was bold enough to pick up the piece that had made the strange noise. It was about nine inches long, four broad and egg-shaped. She placed it on the top of her basket and carried it to the village. On her arrival there she called her husband and related the marvellous story of what had happened in the forest. He was much impressed by the account, took charge of the piece of wood and told his wife that she was not, under any circumstances, to make public what she had revealed to him, as he felt sure there was some great secret connected with it. This foreboding turned out to be correct, as will be seen from the events which followed. Now when the husband retired for the night he took the piece of wood with him to bed. In the early morning he had a dream in which the spirit of the piece of wood appeared before him and said : " My name is *madubu* [*madubu* means I am a man]; my language is *bubububububububu*. I am the father and mother of all yams. Whenever you make a yam garden you must make *muguru*. You must make a *madubu* like me, decorate it [namely, carve it], make a hole in one end and through this hole pass a piece of string, then tie this to the wood. You must tell the people to make a lot of *madubus*. They must be made in the men's club-house. No woman or child may see them; they are *tarena* [sacred]. When you have planted your yams, you must swing the *madubus* round your head in the gardens, then bury them until the yams are almost ready for taking out of the ground; afterwards take them into the men's club-house and keep them there until the next planting season." Such is the coastal story.

Another legend says that the men from Kiwai Island went

Second & Third Initiation Ceremonies

to Boigu, an island some three miles off the coast of Bugi, and brought the bull-roarer from the men of that island, and they called it the *umamomaramu*—namely, the mother of yams.

Up to the time of a youth's initiation he had not been permitted to plant any yams or even to see them planted. He had assisted his father to make the garden fence and there his work had ended. He was now permitted for the first time to view the ritual connected with the yam-planting ceremony. The first part of this initiation took place in the men's club-house. Each initiate was provided with four yam tops, which he would be taught how to plant after he had seen the bull-roarer. The method of planting will be found in the chapter on Gardening and need not be repeated here. The boys were told what the medicine was made from, and were shown how to mix the various ingredients. They were kept in the club-house all night whilst the bull-roarers were whirled by the men outside the house.

Early next morning, before the initiates were awake, the majority of the men were away from the house to make preparations for the *muguru*. The few old men who remained behind took charge of the initiates. When the latter woke up the old men asked them in very subdued tones the reason why all was so quiet, and inquired of them with bated breath the whereabouts of the rest of the men. After a time one of the number would tell the youths that he feared they had gone away to prepare for a fight against them. By these means they got the boys unnerved and frightened. The boys were then led to some spot within sight of the garden where the rest of the men from the village were assembled, all armed with bows, arrows, stone clubs, beheading-knives and head-carriers, bodies painted, and all in full war dress. When they arrived at the place the men were sitting on the ground in an egg-shaped formation or in the form of a bull-roarer. The boys and old men entered at the open end. Immediately they got inside, the end was closed by the men standing near, so that the initiates might not be able to run away. There was no talking, all was quiet; then at a given signal every man rose; some put an arrow on the bow-string and threatened to shoot the initiates, whilst others brandished

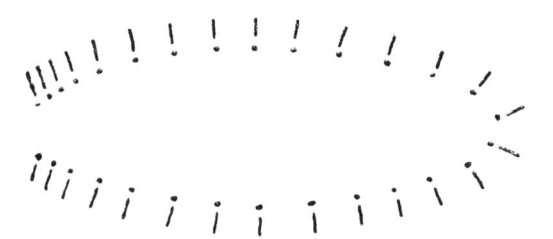

MEN SEATED IN THE SHAPE OF A BULL-ROARER
The dots represent men and the strokes their bull-roarers.

stone clubs about in a menacing manner. This performance lasted for several minutes, during which the initiates howled and called for their mothers. The bull-roarers were then picked up, the arms first being laid on the ground, and whirled round the heads of the men with deafening noise. The youths were then shown the bull-roarer and told its name. The guardian of each boy then presented his ward with a newly made instrument. This was followed by the usual instruction and threat of the penalty of death if any of them should divulge the secrets they have just learned to the women or children. The guardians next led the youths

Second & Third Initiation Ceremonies

into the garden and instructed them in the method of planting, and the use of the medicine which was given them the night before. They then saw all the ritual described in the chapter on Gardening. In the coastal villages the initiates saw the bull-roarer when the yams were planted, but on Kiwai Island they did not see it until the yam harvest. There are slight differences in the ritual of the Fly river people and those living on the coast.

During the afternoon of this day the third great *karea* of the year was held (the other two being the *nigori gamo* or north-east turtle and the dugong *karea*); the initiates were in the care of their respective guardians, who gave instructions and explanations whenever they deemed it necessary. The diagram on page 206 will show the arrangement of the interior of the house, the bull-roarers being in the centre of the passage or hall of the house; on either side of these were many dancing ornaments, bird-of-paradise and cassowary-feather head-dresses, *adigos* or gauntlets with the *koima* or cassowary feathers fastened on a stick which protrudes beyond the elbow, armlets and other things; on the outside of the dancing gear were a large number of coco-nut shells, or rather half-shells, like small basins; opposite every line of bull-roarers were two of these basins, one containing water and the other *gamada*. A bunch of leaves from the last-named plant was laid between the two cups. These leaves were dipped into the water, which was sprinkled north, south, east and west, when all the spirits of the forest were called upon, together with the ancestral spirits, to come and produce a great yam harvest. The story of the origin of the bull-roarer was told to each initiate by his particular guardian.

All were exhorted to " be strong when making gardens " and when made to look after them well; should any enemies come near the village they were not to be afraid of fighting or killing them; they were always to be on their guard when away from home and not give another village any opportunity of killing them; they were exhorted to look after their fathers and mothers, and after they were married

THE *YAM MUGURU*

Ground plan of the central hall or passage in the middle of the men's club-house during the *yam muguru* or initiation ceremony (Mawata). The egg-shaped figures in the centre represent the bull-roarers, which are laid on mats on the floor. The lines represent dancing ornaments. The dots represent coco-nut shells (halves), one with *gamada* and the other containing water. The men sat with their backs to the sides of the house, facing the cups and each other.

In every bull-roarer there was a small hole at one end for the purpose of putting a string through so that it could be whirled round the head. Before the bull-roarers were laid upon the mats the string was taken off and croton leaves inserted in the hole. This was done for decorative purposes.

to look after their children, make gardens for them and take good care of their wives.

The following regulations were strictly carried out in the old days:—

(1) A man and wife who had collected medicine for the yam garden must live apart until the yams were ready for taking out of the ground.

(2) One man might not take the bull-roarer of another man and swing it over his own yam patch.

Second & Third Initiation Ceremonies

(3) A son might not borrow his father's bull-roarer to swing over his own garden, nor might he swing his own bull-roarer over his father's patch.

(4) The guardian of an initiate might swing the instrument over the yam patch of his ward should the latter be away fishing when the yams were planted, but it must be the instrument belonging to the ward.

(5) Women and children might not walk near the garden the first planting day lest the spirits of the bush should be offended and clear off.

CHAPTER XVII

THE *GAMABIBI MUGURU*

THE initiation ceremony known by the name of *gamabibi* (*gama*, a drum; *bibi*, to hit—the drum-hitting ceremony) was by far the most important, the most cruel and the most revolting of the whole series of ceremonies included in the term *muguru*.

This was, however, much more than an initiation ceremony. It was also an indispensable preliminary to every sanguinary raid or warlike expedition undertaken during the north-west season of the year. It was often held three or four times during that period. The men would never have dreamed of going to war without making the *gamabibi* in the north-west, but strange to say the ceremony was not made in the south-east season should any fighting take place. No youth or young man could bear arms on the field of battle who had not gone through the rites or been initiated into the secrets of the *gamabibi*. It was an awful ordeal for a youth to experience. There was a very definite object aimed at in this ceremony—namely, to make the initiate fierce, strong, and courageous in war.

The word *gamabibi* was only one of the many names used to designate this ceremony. It was sometimes called the *muguru*; the *aruwa* or *ede muguru* (the snake ceremony); the *kewori muguru*; and amongst the men in the club-house it was generally spoken of as the *boromo* (pig) *muguru*. I

A DANCER'S DRESS FOR THE OROMO RUBI OBORO.

asked an old man why they used so many different names for one ceremony, and he replied: "We have these names so that the women may not know what we are doing; if we used only one name, they would know as much as we do." There does not appear to have been any other reason than the wish to mystify the women in the village; none of the names conveys any idea of what the ceremony really was.

The head men of the village decided when the *gamabibi* was to be held. At four A.M. on the appointed day several parties of young men were sent into the bush, each party accompanied by a number of hunting dogs, to procure a wild pig, without which the ceremony could not be held. These parties went in different directions. It was their object to take the pig alive if possible, but if not, to bring one in dead. If a small animal were caught it was generally taken alive, but a large one, being more difficult to handle, was generally killed. The first party to obtain a pig blew their conch shells most furiously as a signal to the other hunting parties, and to the old men who had remained behind in the men's club-house, and who anxiously awaited news of their success. The elders on hearing the signal became much excited, and sent an answering shrill blast from the conch shells in their possession. The women and children were panic-stricken and remained in their houses. Whilst the hunt was in progress all coco-nuts were taboo; when the conch shell sounded the taboo was removed.

The pig was carried to a place named *maubo* (every village has its *maubo*). If alive, its mouth was securely tied with strong rattan cane, and its legs were fastened to pieces of wood so that it could not move in any way. A small platform (*dodo*) was built in the *maubo* and the pig placed upon it so that dogs could not get near the animal. No women or children would dare to go near the place where the pig was concealed. For two or three hours the excitement was intense; the men kept up the blowing of the conch shells and sang without intermission until close on eight o'clock, when they returned to the village, received their food from their wives and then retired into the club-house to eat it.

After breakfast the women went to work in their gardens, and as soon as they were gone the men marched in single file from their club to the place in the bush where the pig had been left, every man dressed as if going out to fight. Here the most diabolical of ceremonies was enacted.

The Decoration of the Pig.—When the men arrived at the *maubo* the pig was taken from the platform, where it had been previously placed, and laid upon the ground, facing the north-east, its abdomen being on the earth. Its head was decorated with two head-dresses, one made of the plumes of the bird of paradise and the other of cassowary feathers, its back painted red with burnt earth, and if alive it was securely lashed down.

The Initiates arrive.—When the above preparations were completed the guardians of the initiates returned to the village, painted their charges with charcoal and water, and dressed them as if for active service in war. They were then marched into the bush to the *maubo*. On arriving there they were compelled to lay down their bows and arrows.

The Ceremony.—All the men present, with the exception of the initiates and their guardians, lined up in single file and stood about two yards apart, with their faces towards

The *Gamabibi Muguru*

the hind-quarters of the pig. They then stooped, or rather bent double, placing their hands upon their knees and their legs wide apart. One at a time the terrified youths crawled on their hands and knees between the outstretched legs of their elders. The particular guardian of each candidate walked outside the line of men, carefully watching his ward for any signs of faltering or loss of courage. On arriving at the end of the line the boy was startled to find a pig. The guardian made his way to the head of the animal and commanded his charge to lie down on the pig's back, then to bite it on the nose or one corner of its mouth. This feat being accomplished, the youth was told to get up, and just as he was raising himself from the pig's back his guardian said: "Open your mouth." The boy complied with the request. The guardian thereupon placed in the lad's mouth a most vile concoction named *bisare*. This was made up like a pill and was about the size of an ordinary marble. He was asked if he had swallowed it, and whatever his answer might be, he received a dig in the back by his uncle, so that, taken by surprise, he would swallow the pill if he had not already done so. All the initiates were treated in the same way.

When the last of the candidates who were to be initiated had swallowed his pill, they were all lined up, one half of them on each side of the animal and facing it. An elder, standing at the pig's head, harangued the youths, and grave warnings were given as to what would happen to them if they made known to any person the secrets which had just been revealed to them. The initiates were then permitted to pick up their bows and arrows, which they had been compelled to lay down on their arrival at the *maubo*.

Until midday the time was spent in the vicinity of the *maubo*. The men sang, beat their drums, blew the conch shells and made as much noise as they could. There was no dancing. They sang sitting:

> "*Dorobaime agibe dorobaime busere ramu,
> dorobaime busere ramu.*"

Another song was:

> "*Dowomioimo agibe dowomoimo
> agibe busere ramu.*"

It is impossible to get any sense out of the above jumble of words. The Mawata tribe sang the songs very slowly, whereas the Kiwai men in the Fly delta sang them much quicker. I have heard both lots of vocalists sing these songs but am unable to say whether they sang the same tune or not. I hardly think they did.

It must not be thought that because I have heard the above songs sung that I have seen the ceremony, for such is not the case. The natives would never allow any white man to be present at such a ceremony as the *gamabibi*. The information herein contained has been obtained from men who have actually passed through the order, and whose confidence I happen to possess.

To return to the ceremony. At noon a procession was formed which marched from the *maubo* to the men's club-house. The initiates, with their guardians in attendance, walked first; then followed the youths who were initiated the previous year; after these the young married men (*orio rubi*); behind them came the middle-aged men; then the

The *Gamabibi Muguru*

old men of the community; four strong men brought up the rear, carrying the precious pig, one trumpeter marching in front of the animal, which had been carefully covered up with leaves of different kinds lest the women, who had already returned from their gardens, should be bold enough to peep through any cracks or holes in the side or walls of their houses—a not unlikely contingency—and see what was being carried into the men's club-house.

On entering the building the pig was laid near the sacred post, which was in the centre of the house. The men stood round the post and sang to the accompaniment of the drum and conch shell.

Before the procession entered the men's club a rather unusual proceeding took place. Two masked women, wearing plumes of the bird of paradise and cassowary feathers, their bodies enclosed in coco-nut leaves, mounted the steps of the house in front of the initiates and danced from one end of the house to the other. On reaching the end veranda both jumped to the ground, ran to one of the women's houses and entered therein. Both must enter the same abode. I had great difficulty in accepting this piece of information on account of the fact that no women were permitted to enter the men's club during the *muguru* ceremonies. This statement has been confirmed by several old men, who say that an exception was made in this case and in one or two others.

After sundown the men again assembled in the club, when the pig was cut up by the person who had caught it and distributed amongst the various clans. It was cooked and eaten inside the house. The initiates, for the first time, had the pleasure of tasting a very small piece of the *muguru* pig, which they had always thought to be a snake. The women, however, did not have the opportunity of sharing the luxury of pig's flesh with their husbands and sons. The men spent the night singing and dancing. The drummers remained sitting throughout.

The Bisare.—I have spoken of the *bisare* or pill which was given to the boys during the ceremony which took place in the bush. What were the ingredients of this compound? Every father mixed the pill for his own son. The contents depended to a certain extent upon the character of the father. Under ordinary circumstances the pill contained the following:—

A portion of scraped finger-nail—the father's.

A small portion of dried human eye.

Small portions of certain organs of human bodies, which have been dried in the house and put away until required.

A portion of a *mamani*.

A portion of an *oriogoruso*.

The human nail was given so that the youth would be able to hold an enemy with his hands; the rest of the ingredients were given to make the initiate fierce and strong.

Such was the ordinary compound. This, however, was not considered by some of the fathers to be capable of producing the desired results and making the boy an efficient fighter, so a stronger potion was sought by the fond parent. Such a father went off into the bush, long before his offspring was to be initiated, to procure the most poisonous snake he could possibly find. To secure such a prize the man carried a two or three pronged arrow. On discovering the object he sought, he pinned the animal's head to the ground by means of the pronged instrument, in such a way that it was unable to move or do him any injury. He then cut a piece of skin from the middle of the forehead of the snake, using an ipa shell or a beheading-knife for the operation, after which the snake was set free. The skin was taken home, hung up in the house until it was dry, then put away in some secret place until it should be required for the *bisare*. As like produces like, the boy partaking of a pill containing this particular ingredient would naturally be a more formidable enemy than the one who had taken a weaker compound. The mixture was sometimes given compounded with beeswax, sometimes it was wrapped in the snake skin, before being administered.

Some of the more warlike men, in addition to having a special *bisare* made for their own offspring, were not satisfied to have the ceremony conducted in the bush, where the *ororaorora*, the goblins in the trees and other spirits were lurking about, which might distract the attention of the initiate or affect the efficacy of the *bisare*, but preferred to have their sons initiated into the mysteries of the *gamabibi* inside the men's club-house, where the ceremony could be conducted without any disturbing elements, and where the best results could be obtained from the medicine—namely, a pure and unadulterated spirit of ferocity. In such cases the desires of the men were granted, and the boys were put through in the club-house; as a result of this they were said to become more powerful and ferocious, far more so than the boys who went through the ordeal in the forest.

Part of the ritual has not been related; it is simply unprintable. It may be stated, however, that it is not concerned with the incident of the pig.

A day or two after the *gamabibi* ceremony a dance of a festive character was held, in which men, women and children took part; this was called *wabea*.

After a short interval the men assembled in the club and made arrangements for raiding some neighbouring village to give the newly initiated youths an opportunity of obtaining a human head as a trophy, and to show their prowess in war. The elders spent the night drinking *gamada*, but only small portions were drunk by those who were to take part in the expedition. I carefully inquired the reasons for the moderation and was told that the big fighting men did not drink much or smoke much, lest their heads should be heavy and their fighting powers decreased; they would be less alert and might lose their own heads. These words are mine, but the arguments are from the lips of natives themselves. After the council of war the men spent the afternoon with their wives and families and the evening in the club singing and dancing.

Preparations for an Expedition.—Early next morning the men-folk bustled round the settlement collecting their arms and equipment. All bows and arrows were taken to the club to be overhauled. New strings were put on every bow; every quiver of arrows was unstrung and each arrow separately examined; any defective ones were passed out and the crooked ones made straight by warming at the fire. The fathers of the youths who were to go out for the first time took great pains with their sons' arms and saw that none

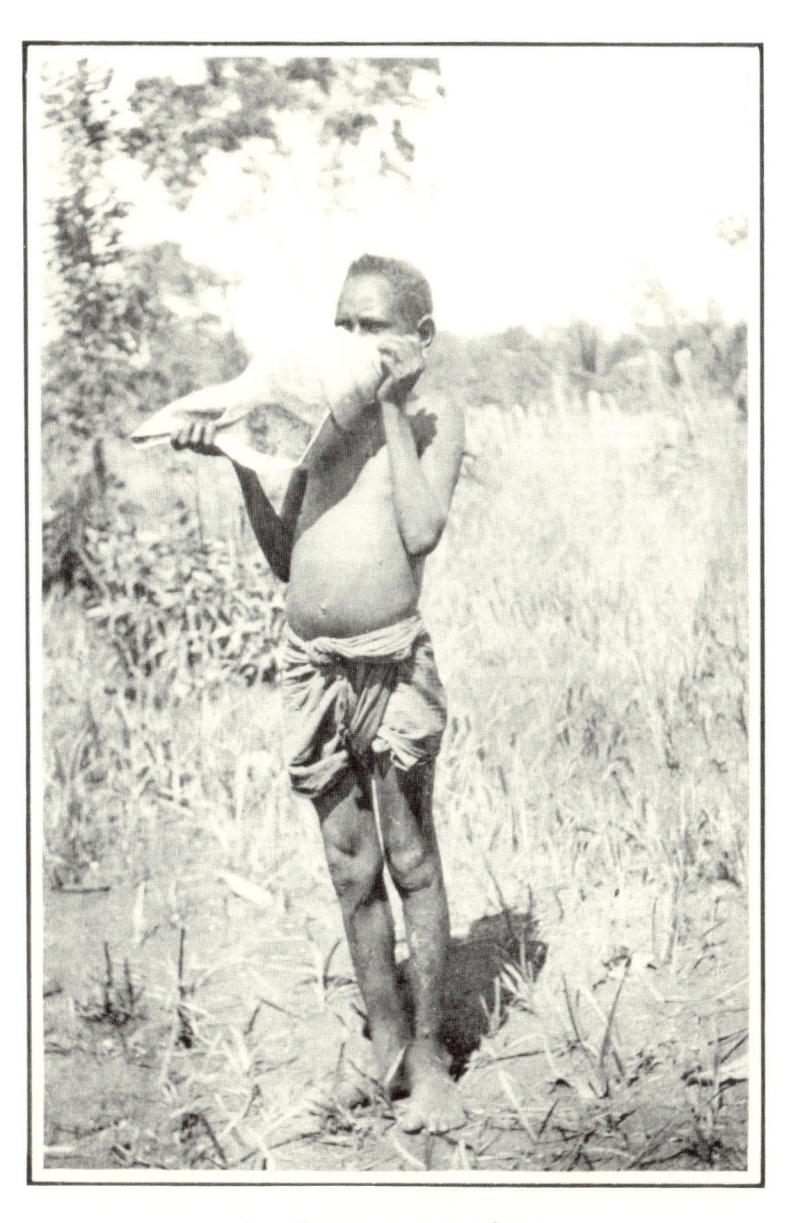

BOY BLOWING A CONCH SHELL.

The *Gamabibi Muguru*

was defective. After the examination was concluded a feast was held.

Next morning other arms were carried to the club-house, stone clubs, wood clubs, beheading-knives and head-carriers. These weapons were all laid out in a row on the floor of the house, each warrior being seated on the floor opposite his own arms. Whilst the men were sitting a young man brought a coco-nut, which he had just skinned, a stick named *hemoro gubu*, a coco-nut shell containing *gamada*, and a few leaves from an ornamental tree named *pia*. The man who was to lead the expedition took the stick in one hand and the coco-nut in the other, struck the nut with the stick, broke the shell and poured the water into the basin of *gamada*. He then took the *pia* leaves and stirred up the coco-nut water with them. He then raised his right hand and, turning to the point of the compass where the village lay which was to be attacked, shook the leaves, and said, "*Karea goi*" (This is for good luck), the *gamada* falling in drops on the floor of the house. If the object of the expedition was a village named Badu, the leaves were again dipped in the *gamada*, and the leader said: "*Waroito Baduwato ainimoiwotoiri*" (To-morrow in Badu we will slay the Badu bushmen). He then sprinkled the arms which lay on the floor, and said, "*Karea goi*" (Good luck to the arms). After a short pause the leader made *karea* for each clan which was to take part in the fight, calling the name of the clan's totem (*nurumara*) as he did so, in the following manner:—

"*Sibara aiwerebairi* (The crocodile will catch them).
"*Baidamo aiwotoairi* (The shark will slay them).
"*Edei aiworuhori* (The snake will bite them).

"*Diware airaramuhiodoiri* (The cassowary will kick them).
"*Umu aiwerebairi* (The dogs will catch them)."

The ceremony closed with the words: "To-morrow we shall go to fight."

Any stranger or strangers arriving at a village during the time the *gamabibi* ceremony was in progress would not have been allowed to leave the village again alive. All would have been put out of the way.

I have mentioned the terror of the women and children when the conch shell announced that a pig had been caught. The most pitiful scene I have ever witnessed was at the village of Gesoa, on the island of Wabuda in the Fly delta in 1902. I landed on the beach soon after six A.M., when there was a furious blowing of conch shells from the bush. This was answered by an old man near the club-house. I do not know what the ceremony was except that it was one connected with the *muguru*. The women rushed from their houses to a number of canoes on the beach, screaming and yelling as they ran, took their paddles and children into the canoes and paddled across a very rough sea to a neighbouring island. Those who could not get into the canoes fled back to their houses panic-stricken. It was a pitiful sight and made one's heart ache to see such distress. I made my way back to my boat, not wishing to obtrude upon their sacred ceremony, for such I believe they consider the *muguru* to be.

CHAPTER XVIII

THE *MIMIA ABERE*

*M*IMIA is the name of an edible plant something like sugar-cane, but is not sweet. It is cooked before being eaten. This plant begins to flower about the end of February or the beginning of March. This ceremony must be held in the north-west season, but cannot take place until the plants are in flower.

The word *abere* means old woman. On Kiwai Island there are two wooden figures carved out of wood, one representing a man and the other a woman. The coastal tribes do not use such figures, but have two stones, one larger than the other. These are specially endowed with spirits.

After the conclusion of the *gamabibi* ceremony, and when the *mimia* plants are in bloom, the elders in council decide upon the date for holding the *mimia*.

When describing the *gamabibi* we saw that the object was to make the youths who were being initiated more vigorous and ferocious. In the *mimia* the object is to continue the education of the youths and instil into their minds the quality of self-control, to test their physical vigour, to teach them how to endure suffering and pain, how to fight, to give blow for blow with added interest whenever possible, and to infuse into their natures the traditions of the elders—" an eye for an eye and a tooth for a tooth."

The ceremony commences in the afternoon and lasts for

six or more days. A number of young men are sent out into the gardens to procure a quantity of green or young coco-nuts. These are brought and placed in the men's club-house. When all the men have returned, the elders assemble and drink the water from the young nuts and then lay them on one side for a short time whilst the men talk and smoke and rest. About five P.M. a game is commenced in the club. The men sitting at one end begin to throw the empty nuts at those who are at the other end, and vice versa. This is done merely for fun, but no loud laughter would be permitted lest the women should hear and conclude that they were not engaged on the *mimia* ceremony, and the more serious matters of the state connected with the education of the young men. After the coco-nut shying has gone on for some time a signal is given for it to cease. The players remain sitting throughout the whole of the game.

Each man has provided himself with two sticks; some of these are wrapped inside a small piece of mat so that one cannot see what it contains. Other sticks are made from the *te* tree. A piece of wood two feet six inches or three feet long is split three-quarters of the length of the stick, down the middle; the unslit portion serves as the handle, shaped like a tuning-fork. Every man has two sticks, and when all are ready the signal is given, when they proceed to hit the floor of the club-house with the two sticks, one in each hand, producing a very peculiar rumbling noise which tends to make one somewhat nervy. I have seen this part of the *mimia* ceremony at Sumai and must confess that I have never heard anything so weird. After a time the rumbling noises are followed by an intense stillness. There is a feeling in the air that something is about to happen which makes one uneasy. I can well understand these proceedings striking terror into the hearts of the youths who are being initiated.

During this stillness the men in the club have all stood up and formed into a procession. They emerge from the house in single file and then form a company ten or more abreast. Crouching double, they jump about on the beach or near the village, continually striking the ground with their sticks, which, being slit in the middle, sound like clappers. The procession is followed by two men carrying long thin poles which they strike one against the other all along the route. These are the only persons walking on their feet. When sitting on the veranda of the house this part seemed even more uncanny than the rumblings which had come from the men's club. The company were wandering round at least half-an-hour and it was impossible to see any of their bodies so intense was the darkness. At last they came past my place of observation, where I was permitted to have a light, and saw quite clearly the naked bodies and faces of the performers, with grim determination written on their faces. They then entered the club-house and the performance closed for the day.

A quiet night follows. Next morning, before daybreak, the tap, tap, tap, followed by the rumbling noise, starts again, and lasts till eight A.M. The women's houses, which have been closed since the *mimia* commenced, are now opened. They have already cooked their husbands' food and upon the arrival of the men breakfast is laid before them. When the repast is over the women go to their gardens and the men just wander round until the time for the next act, or rather for the repetition of the previous one. The same thing is gone over for two, and sometimes three, nights in succession.

On the third day the opera opens at ten A.M. The young men commence by throwing the coco-nuts about as on the first day. The elders come along from the women's quarters and pick up any stray bones or pieces of wood which they may find on the way, and throw them into the club-house through the open door. This develops into horse-play and lasts till noon. After a light refreshment, play begins at three P.M. until five P.M. At six there is a new turn in the programme which is very pretty when seen for the first time. Every man has a torch in his hand. These torches are lighted at the different fires burning on the *momogo* or fireplaces in the respective apartments. These lighted torches are sent skimming along the floor of the house, all ablaze, from one end of the house to the other; the elderly men are quite experts at making them travel, and much more dexterous than the younger men, who have not had the same amount of practice. At nine the show closes. Another day follows with the clappers in the morning, and torches in the afternoon and evening.

Next day a council meeting is held and arrangements are made for the whole village to proceed to the woods for the purpose of obtaining some of the *mimia* plants which are in blossom. After breakfast all take their departure for this purpose. Each individual plucks one stem only of the plant. In addition to this, each one brings from his garden a little food, a yam, banana, etc.; banana leaves, yam leaves, and leaves from other food plants are also carried back to the village. As the procession wends its way back they sing in merry strain:

> "*Ubia ubia bogera,
> Bogera mimia ubia.*"

On reaching the village all the women's houses are decorated with the banana, yam and other leaves, which are hung over the door. As these are placed in position they utter an invocation to the unseen as follows: " May our gardens grow quickly and have plenty of food in them."

The food is carried to the men's quarters, and at Mawata, where stones are used in place of the wooden images (these stones are laid at the bottom of the main post of the house, the *haro*), the food is laid along the sides of the stones and on the top. The *mimia* blossoms which have been collected are laid upon the food, covering both it and the stones. Singing is then indulged in by the elders.

The young men then rush off to the women's houses and take charge of all the boys they can find over about eight years of age. The very small ones are seized, told to open their mouths, and upon their doing so receive a small portion of ginger from the person's mouth who holds him. The older boys are commanded to open their mouths and the portion of ginger falling to them is thrown into the open mouth. They then return to their club and the rest of the day is spent very quietly.

Early next day the whole settlement again goes to the forest, and each one carries back as much *mimia* as he and she can possibly carry with comfort. This is cooked by the women. After cooking, it is brought into the men's club-house by both women and children. The *mimia abera* is covered up with mats so that the women and children may not see it, and so that no evil consequences will follow.

At six P.M. the initiation candidates are brought into the club-house by their guardians, one to each boy, who hold them firmly by the arm. These guardians have during the day caught a snake and extracted its teeth. It is then tied up to a post in the house with a long piece of string or rope, and as soon as the candidates are placed standing in the middle of the house the snake is thrown towards them without any warning whatever. They are ignorant of the fact that it is toothless and cannot do any harm. This is looked upon as a great test of the boys' character: if a boy is fearless and stands his ground he is said to be all right, courageous and strong, but if he jumps about and shows signs of fear he is thought weak and lacking in courage.

Then follows what is perhaps the most trying of all ordeals in the *mimia* ceremony. The boys are kept standing after the snake trial whilst the elders fasten coco-nut skins to the midrib of the nipa palm. Half of the men are on one side of the boys and half on the other side. They are not close to them, but thirty or forty yards away on each side (the houses being 400 feet long). The torches are all ready, the signal given, and all are lighted at the fire. The torches are then skimmed along the floor right in amongst the boys, who have to dodge them as best they can. This is somewhat difficult, since torches are coming in both directions at one and the same time. This *sagu* or torch is said to resemble the phosphorescence which is seen in the sea as a fish rushes through the water. The name for phosphorescence

The *Mimia Abere*

is *sagu*, hence the name of the torch. This act lasts about an hour. Then all lights, except those on the fireplaces, are extinguished, and the house is very dark. The boys are still standing as before. Other torches are now being prepared, which when completed, at a sign from the leader, are all lighted and held aloft. The men now begin to advance towards the middle of the house where the boys are standing, who, seeing the blazing torches bearing down upon them from two different directions, become terrified, and cry aloud for their mothers to come to their rescue. The fire draws nearer and nearer until the sparks begin to fall upon the naked bodies of the boys and their guardians. I have not seen this act, but from what I have learnt from men who have been through the order, the boys' terror is indescribable. They scream and howl, and it is with great difficulty that the guardians prevent some of them from running away. These men do their utmost to shield the boys by leaning over them and receiving the falling sparks upon their own bodies. I have seen this performance minus the boys, and was much astonished at the fortitude displayed by the men whilst the burning embers from the coco-nut skins were dropping upon their naked bodies. Not a man flinched. The boys, however, could not be expected on a first occasion to display the same stamina as their elders. The conduct of each boy is closely scrutinized during the fire scene, and his character summed up according to his conduct under trying circumstances. At the close of this scene the guardians and their wards are provided with a special house for their night's repose.

During the day, quite unknown to the *kowea mere*,

or initiates, all the canoes have been brought to a spot on the beach as near as possible to the men's house, and anchored near the beach. The object of this will be seen later.

A huge pile of faggots is also piled high upon the beach with much ostentation, deliberately planned, to draw the attention of the women to what is being done, to whom dark hints are dropped that the boys will be put on the top and then the faggots will be fired, and their children will be burnt alive. This of course is never done, and some good excuse is always offered, and a promise that the affair will be carried through the following year. It is simply postponed. The one object of this is to terrorize the women and initiates, so the old men inform me. The boys are also informed that they will be thrown on the top. This fills them with fear, and sends a shudder down the backs of the youths. It thus serves a double purpose, filling both women and initiates with alarm and dread.

At midnight on the same day as the last torch scene the women are up and about cooking food for the coming day. The men do not rise until about three A.M. The younger of the men now decorate themselves with all kinds of head-gear and other decorations. Each one carries a stone or wooden club in his hand. They enter the canoes and conceal themselves as best they can.

A messenger is sent to the house occupied by the guardians and their charges, informing them that all is now ready. Immediately on receipt of this message the boys are wakened. Each one is given a wood club and told that they are now going out to fight the bushmen, and that all the rest of the men in the village have already gone, and that they are now to follow. The clubs are handed to them with these words: "Here is a club; if any man hits you, hit him back again as hard as you can. Don't be afraid to strike back, and when you do, strike hard." As soon as the boys come from the house they hear, rather than see, two men dressed as clowns talking all kinds of gibberish and performing all kinds of antics. It is not yet daylight, and apart from the noise made by these clowns all is still and quiet.

The boys are now led toward the beach where the canoes are anchored. The occupants of these craft have now put their heads above the edge of the canoes and begin tapping the sides and making a low mournful cry as if in great pain. The guardians point out these strange figures to their charges, whose hearts are already palpitating. As they slowly advance in the faint light before sunrise the horrid grotesque figures in the canoes jump overboard and with a frantic yell rush upon the boys, drag them to the *otahiro* or pile of wood, seize them somewhat roughly and pretend to throw them on the top. The boys scream, and call upon their mothers for help, who, hearing the helpless offspring's terror, shed tears of sympathy for them.

Several men are standing by with long sticks hitting the pile of wood to make the youths imagine that the twigs have been lighted and the noise is the crackling of the twigs of the pyre. The pandemonium now increases as the men from the canoes begin to belabour the initiates (with their wooden clubs), who howl and shriek in a pitiful manner. The guardians encourage them to hit back, and show them a good example by striking as often as opportunity presents itself. Sometimes a boy is singled out and unmercifully beaten; the boy's father upon seeing this rushes to his son's aid and gives blow for blow or two for one.

I must digress here for a moment. This scene is one in which men in the village pay off old scores and settle old unforgiven offences. A man may have acted dishonourably towards another, or towards his wife or daughter. Such an offence is not forgotten. The injured man is ever on the look-out for an opportunity of squaring the account, in a nice quiet way, when no punishment is likely to fall upon his own head, even should he cause the death of his opponent. Some of these men not only carry stone or wooden clubs, but other terrible weapons, such as the whip-like tail of the sting-ray, often two yards long, with a biserrated spine, which is capable of inflicting a most ghastly wound, or sharks' serrated teeth fastened on a stick representing a saw. These weapons are used without mercy by any man having an enmity against his brother man who has wronged him. As I write these words I have a man sitting before me who bears the marks upon his abdomen of a terrible gash he received from one of these shark-teeth implements. It was no unusual thing for one or two men to be killed in either the fire scene or the sham fight held on the beach, with which we have just been dealing. If one man killed another the relatives of the slain did not seek vengeance. The death was laid at the door of the spirit of the *mimia abere*, and this was accepted as a satisfactory explanation of death. This fact may possibly account for men nursing grievances in their hearts for months, and even years, and then inflicting a malicious injury in return for an injury received, at such

The *Mimia Abere*

a time when no punishment would fall upon the head of the one who avenges.

We will now return to the fight on the beach. This lasts a considerable length of time, according to the statements made by men who have been through many a hard battle. The women have been sent away from home, and are now occupying a *tiro moto*, or a small house covered with mats, half-a-mile from the settlement, to be out of hearing of their children's appeals for help, and the devilish yells of those thirsting for vengeance.

On the cessation of hostilities the wounded are attended to by their friends and relatives on the male side, and their wounds dressed in some simple way. The person alluded to above who was gashed with the shark's teeth informs me that he dressed his own wound. He chewed a piece of ginger, lay down on the floor and put the gingered saliva upon it—nothing more. The flow of blood was checked, and he was able to get about in a few weeks' time.

The initiation youths are led by their *aberamigo* (fathers) and *naramigo* (brothers) into the sea, where they are washed from head to foot, after which they undergo a further test of their power of endurance. The youths are taken by the head and feet. The head is held under water and the feet raised out of the water. If a boy can remain under for what they consider a reasonable time, about a minute, without kicking and struggling he is considered quite satisfactory. If, on the other hand, he begins to kick and struggle, and endeavours to release himself after only a few seconds, he is considered short-winded and lacking in the power of endurance. A big fire is lighted so that the boys may be warmed immediately they are permitted to leave the water. This kind act is performed by the old and infirm men of the tribe. Each youth is then compelled to drink from a coco-nut shell, and is told that the fluid is *bamu obo*, and that it will make him strong in battle. They are told immediately after drinking the fluid that it is urine, and are cautioned not to tell the women-folks under penalty of death.

The young and middle-aged men then begin to dance and play round the fire and endeavour to make the poor youths with their sore bodies and aching limbs look a little more cheerful, and in their simple way to comfort them in the hour of trial. With this object in view they indulge in all kinds of antics and dancing without restraint.

The food which was cooked by the women at midnight is now divided amongst the different clans, and subdivided again among the families of the clans. This food consists of the *mimia* plants and flowers cut up and mixed with sago and scraped coco-nut, and cooked in the leaves of the nipa or coco-nut palm. Part of the food is consumed by the men and boys, and part put aside for the women and children. There is an exchange of food between the clans before the repast. Each man in every clan gives a portion of food to a member of another clan, and in return receives a like present. The object in thus exchanging food is said to be " to show friendship to each other."

After the morning meal all the male population, except the small boys who have been with their mothers during the *mimia* ceremony, now go into the woods and cut bamboo, from which small toy bows are made. A great quantity of *kokoba* is cut : this is a kind of rush, from the stem of which small arrows are made and are called *kokoba*. Large quantities of branches with variegated leaves are also cut down. All these are carried into the village, which was cleaned and swept by the men previous to their going into the woods. All the houses are decorated by the men.

The initiates are now dressed with a cassowary head-dress and a string of white feathers on the higher part of the forehead, and bunches of variegated leaves in their armlets. The guardians of these youths, also fully dressed in the same manner as their wards, then lead their charges from the women's houses, where they have spent a little time resting, to the men's club. Each boy is presented with a bow and arrow made by their respective keepers. These are regarded as presents. On entering the club they are led with all solemnity to the chief post of the house (Mawata, *haro*; Fly river, *saro*) to see the *mimia abera*, or sacred stones or wooden figures, as the case may be. The stones are carefully uncovered, and the initiates for the first time behold one of the most sacred treasures of the tribe—two old stones brought in from the sea, with rough sketches of human faces painted upon them. They are then told that "this is the *mimia abere*." The usual warning is given that should they divulge what they have now seen, or give any information whatever about it, they will be killed. The stones are again respectfully covered over with *mimia* plants.

Five men next appear in costumes made from leaves, and dance. They call upon the south-east wind to come and ripen the food in the gardens. The rest of the men leave the club with their bows in their hands. One foot is placed inside the bow-string, a few inches from the ground, and in this attitude they hop towards the beach, a distance of thirty or forty yards. On reaching the beach they swing the foot which is in the bow-string towards the south-east and backwards towards the north-west, calling in unison upon the south-east to come that the harvest may soon be fit for use. The dance is called the *uro komodori*.

Early the following morning a small feast is made in honour of the *abere*—that is, the stones. After partaking of breakfast all the village, men, women and children, assemble in the men's club. They then form two lines from one end of the house to the other, something like an amphitheatre in form, mothers and fathers standing together in the lines. Two men with sticks six feet long, two inches broad at one end and three inches at the other, which are garden spades, named *ea*, walk behind the two lines, one on one side of the house and the other on the opposite side. With these sticks the two men press the calves of the legs of all the community, causing the knees slightly to bend forward. This is to keep sickness away. These garden spades are then carried to the long post where the stones are lodged and put inside the mats which cover the latter and hide them from the women's and children's eyes. This concludes the ceremony until noon next day, when only the men assemble in the club-house. The two stones are to be removed from the building. *Karea* is made—good luck to the undertaking. One of the elders addresses the stones as follows: " We have made this feast for you. We have decorated all the houses for you. We want you to see to it that we do not get sick. We want you to look out for our good. You are now going to stop under the house." At this point the mat is removed

1. Knives used for severing heads. In the Author's possession.
2. The Gora. A most important dancing ornament.
3. Bamu River native with pubic shell.
4. A Dancer at the ceremony in memory of the Dead.

The *Mimia Abere*

from the stones, two planks of the floor are displaced, and the two old stones are pushed through the hole in the floor and fall upon the earth under the house. The speaker continues: " You sleep under the house now. Take care we do not get any sickness. We have danced for you, and the next time we make *mimia* we will bring you into the house again." Men are immediately sent under the house to cover up the stones with any rubbish they may find near at hand.

I omitted to mention one interesting feature which takes place on the day the *mimia* plants are brought from the woods. After these are cooked and divided out each mother gives some to her children. Before doing so, however, she takes one of the flowers of this plant and rubs the child's elbows, wrists, knees, ankles, ears, forehead, shoulders and the lumbar region. This is to ensure the children against all kinds of sickness.

From what has been said above it appears that this ceremony is not only connected with the initiation of the boys, but also with the idea and purpose of ensuring good health to the community.

Since writing the above I have gone over this chapter with two old men, who say that the snake incident ought to have been put in the *gamabibi* ceremony. My original informants stick to the point that it is correct.

CHAPTER XIX

THE *URUBA MUGURU*

THE *uruba* ceremony was held but once a year. It was celebrated a fortnight after the last dance of the season in memory of the recent dead. It is quite easy to fix the time of the *uruba*, as it took place at the close of the turtle and dugong fishing season, which is about the end of December.

There were three important features or salient points in the ceremony. In the first place, it was a kind of memorial service in honour of those members of the tribe who had passed away since the previous *uruba*. In the second place, it was a time when both men and women surveyed the past and speculated upon what the future might have in store for them. The names of all who had fallen by the way during the preceding twelve months were reverently recalled; their virtues and deeds of valour were also related. When speaking of the future one old man would say to another: " I wonder if I shall be here when the next *uruba* is held." During these serious meditations the men ate their food, drank *gamada* and wept tears of sorrow for their departed loved ones. In the third place, it was a farewell of the spirits of the dead, who, at the conclusion of the ceremony, were to return to their home in the west until the wet season, which was just about to commence, should be finished.

The *Uruba Muguru*

The natives say that the *uruba* was *pai muguruia*—that is, not a proper *muguru* like the *gamabibi* or the *mimia*. They place it under the head of "*muguru* ceremonies" because the initiates were permitted for the first time to witness the ritual and take part in the proceedings.

Two days before the celebration of the *uruba* commenced the women were informed when the ceremony was to be held, so that they, with the help of the girls, could get in a huge supply of food for the festival. When this had been collected from the gardens it was carried in baskets to the men's club-house, where the most important events took place, and handed over to the male members of the community.

Let the reader recall the ground plan of the *darimo*, or men's club-house, given in a previous chapter and the following particulars will be easily understood. Some of the baskets of food were placed near the central post of the house (which was called the *bobo omabu*, *haro* or *saro*); other baskets were laid along both sides of the broad passage running down the middle of the building. These were all profusely decorated with croton leaves.

Two different kinds of memorials were set up in the house, one for men and one for women; those for the former were much more elaborate than those for the latter.

Adjoining the apartment or *motee* of each deceased male a long thin pole (*suru*) about ten feet in length was fixed in an upright position close to the central passage. One end of the pole was placed in a niche in the floor and the other end fastened to one of the beams supporting the roof. On the top of the pole a bunch of croton leaves was tied.

Some four feet below these a string four or five yards long was made fast to the pole. In the middle of this string a dancing ornament named *gora* was well secured. During the ceremony the natives sat on the floor of the house and pulled the strings, when the sixty empty nut shells on the *gora*, striking against each other, made a loud jingling noise.

Under the string and at the base of the pole was a collection of other things, four pieces of sugar-cane, and a small parcel containing two pieces of sago with fish cooked inside; these were wrapped in a small *tiro* mat and tied with a *bata* or plaited cord two inches broad. This cord was looped so that it could be passed over the shoulder and the parcel carried under the arm. There was also a bundle of arrows and a bow. On the top of the bow was an *adigo* or wrist gauntlet, to which a bunch of cassowary feathers was attached. At the foot of the pole was a bunch of bananas and a number of sprouting coco-nuts. This completed the memorial for one of the males.

If there had not been any deaths in one house during the year, the inhabitants of that house would erect a number of poles and decorate them as described above, in memory of those of their number who had died in previous years.

The women's memorials were set up near the apartments of their male relatives in the club-house. *There was no pole and no gora with its white feathers and jingling nuts.* (In the death dance the same regulation was strictly observed. No man dancing as the spirit of a dead female carried a *gora* in his hand.) The memorial for a woman consisted of a basket of food, a parcel of sago, fish, sugar-cane and sprouting coco-nuts, as supplied for the men, with the addition of

The *Uruba Muguru*

two grass petticoats and a wooden spade, which were placed on the top of the basket. Croton leaves from a particular tree, which could be used only for women, were placed round the edge of the basket.

This food, which formed the memorial along with the various implements, was to supply the needs of the spirits, who next morning would commence their long journey to their residence in the west. The men were equipped for fighting and hunting, whilst the women were supplied with spades for work in the gardens in the spirit land. Such were the ideas instilled into the minds of women and children by the adult male members of the community.

After the spirits were supposed to have departed, the tasty morsels of cooked fish and sago were eaten by the men in the club-house. The rest of the food in the baskets was handed over to the women and children.

Before the celebrations commenced, the young children were all warned by their parents that they were not to wander about in the bush, as many evil spirits were roaming round who might do them harm.

The ceremony commenced just after sunrise. All the young men, together with the initiates, went out into the bush and collected huge bundles of croton leaves. A good number carried drums. Having procured the leaves, the company assembled at about two hundred yards' distance from the women's houses, when they began to beat the drums. A procession was formed, which marched towards the above-mentioned houses, each person scattering leaves on the road as the company advanced. There was no singing or dancing. The young men entered every house where there had been a death during the preceding year and pretended to search for the spirits—namely, the *urio* (not the *oboro* or spirit of the dead which had gone to Adiri)—which might be hiding in the house. The women struck the floors of the buildings with the palms of their hands or with brooms, and when doing so commanded the spirit or spirits to quit the premises. Croton leaves were thrown all over the floor of each house visited.

The spirit-hunters did not enter any house or search in the vicinity of any house which had not suffered a bereavement since the date of the last *uruba*. Such places were not likely to be troubled with roving spirits, and hence they were passed by.

At sundown the ceremony inside the club-house commenced. The men covered their bodies with earth as a sign of mourning. No fancy costumes or head-dresses of any kind were worn. They sat on the floor all night long, thinking of those who had gone before, and of their own chances of seeing another *uruba*; they sang mournful dirges and wept tears of genuine sorrow as they remembered their dead. Middle-aged men alone were permitted to beat the drums. No dancing was allowed. A long line of men, sitting on the floor opposite the memorial poles, with the string in one hand, pulled it in such a way that the *goras* danced up and down, accompanied by the musical sounds of the tinkling nut shells. As soon as one person tired of pulling the string another would take his place.

In a most solemn and impressive manner the ceremony continued from sunset till the late hours of the morning. About four A.M. the last scene, before the departure

The *Uruba Muguru*

of the spirits for their distant home, was enacted. All the middle-aged and young men took a dry coco-nut skin in each hand and lighted them at the fire. Sitting on the floor, two lines of men faced each other and, stretching from one end of the house to the other, waved the blazing coco-nut skins about, each person crossing his hands again and again to increase the fiery flames, producing a very impressive and most fascinating scene.

When the skins were well alight the men left the house stealthily in twos and threes and made their way to the sea-beach, which was quite near, where they stood for a few seconds, then gradually extinguished the flames by dipping them in salt water. As the lights died out one by one, the spirits, who were supposed to have put their food and implements aboard their canoes, which were anchored in a near creek, took their departure on their homeward journey.

The women and children came out of their houses and stood round, but dared not approach the beach, to see the last of the spirits of their own dead.

After putting out the fires the men returned to the clubhouse, carrying the remains of the unburnt coco-nut skins in their hands. Had these been thrown away on the beach and been discovered by the women and children the following day, a lot of inconvenient questions might have been asked, and doubts would have been cast upon the veracity of the head men. When the lights were put out it was a sure proof that the spirits had really gone to sea. Had not their canoe lights been seen vanishing below the horizon? To have left the coco-nut skins on the beach would have spoilt the innocent make-believe.

During the intervals for conversation in the club-house the initiates were seriously and reverently requested by their elders to continue this ceremony after their death, and never under any circumstances to neglect this sacred duty. Thus ended the *uruba* ceremony in the men's club-house.

The women, who were not permitted to enter the club-house during this ceremony, or to see what was being done there, sat round the fires in their own houses, sang, talked and wept for their dead. Like the men-folk, their bodies were covered with earth, and widows wore their full regalia of mourning; they recalled with tears the name, the virtues and good deeds of all their loved ones who during that year had entered into rest.

CHAPTER XX

THE *TAERA* CEREMONIES

TRADITION says that the *taera* ceremonies originated on the island of Daru and were devised by the Doriomo clan, which has always been, and still is, recognized as the leader in these ceremonies. If any clan desired to celebrate the *taera*, it must first consult and obtain the promise of the Doriomo clan to set the necessary machinery in motion for the holding of these dances.

The *taera* consists of a long series of ceremonial dances, which are partly religious but mostly festive in character. In olden times they were held at intervals of two, three, four or five years. The full series has not been carried out for some twenty-five years, but parts are enacted at such times as Christmas without much of the old ritual. There appears to have been three reasons for holding these ceremonies: firstly, to do honour to those who have long been dead; secondly, to ensure a good fishing season for turtle and dugong; thirdly, to provide amusement for the whole of the community. They have some connection with the initiation of the youths into the secrets of the tribe.

The opening ceremony is somewhat similar to that related in the chapter of the first initiation. *Karea* is made, and every male who is able to walk proceeds into the bush to inspect the gardens, after which a meeting is held in a cleared piece of ground near the garden fence.

A planting-stick named *woto* is taken to the meeting-place, together with a number of *terege*, like small twigs, which are placed in the middle of the assembly. One of my informants says that a *kaikai*, or stick with white feathers, is laid alongside the above, whilst another denies this statement. (This is an example of the differences in the accounts mentioned above.) A leaf from the *warakara* tree is tied to the *woto*.

After the food has been consumed an old man walks into the centre of the enclosure, takes the planting-stick in his hand, and asks another person, a brother if he has one: "What shall I say?" The brother will reply: "The canoes have been dry a long time, put them all in the water." The old man repeats: "The canoes have been dry a long time; shall we put them into the water?" During this time he is gently tapping the surface of the soil with the sharp end of the *woto*. He calls every clan by name and asks each one what they think. All remain quiet, and no answer is given. The old man halts a few moments and then asks: "Shall we put the canoes in the water, they have been dry a long time?" He lifts the planting-stick and says: "*Iga naragiwai?*" (Shall I drive it?) The whole assembly cries: "*Aragiwai! Aragiwai!*" (Drive it! Drive it!) He then drives the sharp end of the *woto* into the ground several times and repeats the words: "Let the canoes be put into the water, they have been dry a long time." Then follows a most impressive part of the ritual. The old man, who must belong to the Doriomo clan, stoops down and picks up the *terege* or small twigs with his left hand; with the right he pulls out one of the twigs, puts it into the ground and calls

The *Taera* Ceremonies

out the name of one of his own family who has died since the last *taera* was made. Another member of the same clan calls the name of his father, another the name of mother or child or some relative; as each name is solemnly spoken another twig goes into the ground. When one clan has finished the names of the dead, the leader counts the twigs, pulls them all out of the earth, the *woto* as well, and lays all reverently on the ground. He then walks back to his own clan and resumes his seat in silence. A few seconds are allowed to elapse before the leader of another clan rises, advances to the middle of the ground and repeats the same ritual as the Doriomo leader. Every clan leader does likewise. The form of words used by the leader when putting the *terege* into the ground is as follows: " This is for my father, I have not made *taera* for him before." The *taera* can be made for one person one time only.

The talk of putting the canoes in the water is just to mystify the women and children, whom they wish to keep in ignorance of what is afoot. It is not considered proper or right that the women should know the intentions of their husbands and sons. Should they by any accident hear their husbands talking about canoes going into the water they would be none the wiser.

Another illustration of the use of the word " canoe " has been given me by three of the men, which is as follows. Suppose a number of persons are visiting a village in a friendly manner, and are being hospitably entertained by their hosts, and that there is a long outstanding account to square against the visiting tribe: should one of the latter be on very friendly terms with one of the hosts, an attempt would be made to give this particular friend an opportunity to get safely away. After the elders have decided to put the visitors out of the way, a messenger would be secretly sent to the member of their clan who is entertaining the man who is to be spared. The said messenger would simply say: "The canoe will break to-morrow." The host would immediately request his friend to depart with all speed. He would not be given an opportunity of communicating with the others.

To return to our story. The men carry the food into the village, which is given to the women and children, and in return they receive quantities of fish which the women were sent to catch early that morning. The men return to the club-house, when *karea* is made in the afternoon, and the evening is spent drinking *gamada*.

The next day the *kaikai oboro*, or the ceremony in memory of the recent dead, is held. A new *horiomu* is erected—that is, two new screens—before the above-mentioned dance is held. An addition is put on to the screens named *mepai*. This is made from coco-nut leaves plaited in a special way. When the women see the *mepai* they know that the *taera* is to be held. After the *mepai* have been erected no family with children in arms may sit in the front seats as there will be a sudden rush later on from the ground, when young children might get hurt.

At the conclusion of the dance in memory of the recent dead four of the Doriomo clan, dressed as spirits, commence playing with a ball which is knocked up in the air with the hands. After a short game one of the men catches the ball, chews a portion of *manababa* root, and spits upon the ball,

The *Taera* Ceremonies

when the whole crowd yell, "*u-u, u, u!*" The women jump up with the children and run away; the man throws the ball after them; then throwing off their dancing costumes the men race after the crowd. This ball is made from a hard wood named *oni*; it has lain all day on the top of a *warakara* leaf inside the *horiomu*. In this chapter the word *horiomu* will be used to signify the sacred ground.

On the following morning the ground all round the *horiomu* is cleaned and carefully swept in preparation for a great game of hockey which is played for about ten or twelve successive days, in which men, women and children join.

After the lapse of the time stated above an order is issued by the elders that the game must be brought to an end. On the last day of the hockey game five men, one from each clan, dressed in dancing costumes, with bows and arrows in their hands, come out from the bush and sit down on the sea-beach where they can be seen by all the villagers. The hockey ball is purposely driven near these men, one of whom rushes toward it, picks it up and places it in his mouth. All the people cry out, "*u, u, u!*" The hockey sticks of every man, woman and child are lifted above their heads as they cry again, "*u, u, u!*" The women and children now return to the village. The men all wend their way into the *horiomu*.

During the afternoon food for the men, water and sleeping-mats are taken inside the sacred ground, where the men will now sleep for the next five or six weeks. The aged, infirm and sick remain in the men's club-house and act as caretakers; the women and children live in the women's houses. At six P.M. a very spectacular performance commences. The young men and youths are sent about half-a-mile on the other side of the village with instructions to collect large quantities of dry coco-nut skins, and an abundant supply of long thin poles ten to twenty feet in length. The coco-nut skins are teased, hung upon and tied to the sticks; some are carried by two men, some by a single person. A stick for the latter would not have any skins in the middle, only for the two ends, the middle part being left empty so that the person can carry it easily. The sticks carried by two persons have the ends empty but the middle covered with skins; one person then holds each end.

Soon after dark a procession is formed, and all the coco-nut skins on the long poles are set alight; with these ablaze the torch-bearers march, at a fair distance behind each other, past the village on to the sacred ground. The wind at this season of the year is blowing against the men carrying the blazing poles, and in consequence the flames and sparks are considerably increased as they forge their way along the road. These are supposed to be spirits arriving from the west on a visit to the village. The torches are carried to the *horiomu* and thrown down on the ground, where they are left to burn. The young men then return for another fireworks display. A third journey is made, which ends this part of the programme for the night. The same performance is continued for four or five nights in succession. The women and children are duly impressed by the arrival of so large a number of spirits, from the land of the blest, in their midst.

A *dodo*, or wooden framework, upon which food may be placed, is erected in front of each of the screens in the sacred enclosure, and large quantities of food are placed on each one. Whilst this is in progress the *imigi* dancers arrive and give

The *Taera* Ceremonies

instructions to those who are expert in the art of spearing turtle and dugong that they are to place their long wooden harpoons in the *horiomu*.

A large leaf named *aui'i*, some two feet long and twelve inches broad, is procured from the woods, together with a handful of grass named *esame*. *Manababa* root is chewed and spat upon these, which are then laid upon the ground in the *horiomu*, and the conch shell placed on the top. This conch shell or trumpet can be blown by only one man, and he must be a member of the Doriomo clan. He is called the *muru* man, and is the master of ceremonies until the *taera* is finished.

The Doriomo clan must provide the M.C. If for any reason the clan cannot do so, they may obtain the services of a man from another clan to fill this important office. Payment is demanded for the person before he takes over the duties of the *muru* man. This account was met with dog's-teeth necklaces, bows, bundles of arrows, and other things. The man becomes for the time being a member of the Doriomo clan. At the end of the *taera* he reverts back to his own clan, but the payment is kept.

The drums and conch shell must remain under the care of the *muru*, and be kept in one place in the *horiomu*. Drums may be taken outside with the consent of the *muru*, but the conch shell may not be removed from the sacred ground under any circumstances. This regulation is observed during the initiation ceremonies also.

The two clans on one side of the *horiomu* may not speak to any of the three clans on the other side; the latter may not speak to the former whilst they are in the sacred precincts.

If the wife of a man gives another man food to take to her husband, he would not give it into his hand, but put it on the ground, and the husband of the woman would then pick it up.

The Karara Dance.—The *karara* dance is the most important part of the *taera* ceremonies. This portion of the programme is done in memory of those who have been dead several years. The word *karara* is the name of the large head-dresses, or rather masks, which were worn by the spirits during the dances, and which represented the heads of the shark and crocodile.

The *karara* opens about midday. There is an introductory bit of byplay just after the drums commence the overture. This is what is known as the *kupamo oboro* or spirit. The word *kupamo* means the natives of Kiwai Island, and is used by the coastal people as a mark of disrespect and inferiority. This *kupamo* spirit rushes from the *horiomu* with a small mask on his head, stone club, bow and arrows in his hands, beheading-knife and head-carrier hanging down his back, and runs half-way on the road towards the village, waving his arms about in a manner indicating that he has come from the west, and imitating the poling of a canoe. He then returns to the *horiomu*. This is done every day as a preliminary to the *karara* dancers appearing on the scene.

The women and children have been signalled to come and take up their usual places on the outside of the *horiomu*. The women have long grass petticoats reaching down to their ankles, and their bodies are adorned with croton leaves. A dance called *kokomi* is one in which men, women and children take part, the men dancing in the *horiomu*. Two

The *Taera* Ceremonies

men representing female spirits stand, one at each end of the two screens in the sacred ground, and act as leaders for the women and children. These are regarded as the most expert dancers, and are very popular. Whilst the *kokomi* dance is in full swing the masks of the two men wearing the *karara* head-dresses are seen above the screens. The M.C. blows the conch shell, the dancing ceases, the people sit down and the two men emerge from behind the screens. A very quick step-dance is performed, which does not last long as the men are soon tired, when they return behind the screens. I have seen this dance done several times in private but cannot attempt to describe it. This is repeated twice and the *karara* dancers are finished for the day. During the intervals when the two men are resting, five spirits, one from each clan, named *imigi*, come upon the scene. They wear head-dresses of *warakara* leaves, but no bird of paradise feathers or those of the cassowary. They carry stone clubs, beheading-knives and head-carriers. Often they have young coco-nuts in the carriers representing human heads. These men do not dance; they are nothing but clowns. They go round stealing food, robbing gardens and frightening women and bairns. They continually, by gesture, inform the women that they are hungry. Food is sent to them by children. When the clowns see the youngsters coming towards them with food they run forward, and the children put the refreshments down on the ground and run away home. These men are said to prowl round night and day in relays. When one lot is tired, off come their dresses, which are immediately donned by five others. They act in a very indelicate manner at times.

Another class of performers is called *sariamo*. These may also be called clowns. Their bodies and legs are decorated in such a way with leaves that they appear white. They come on to the stage dragging a lot of skinned young coco-nuts fastened to the end of a long rope; all bend double like a number of old cripples. The women are said to weep when the poor unfortunate spirits come on the scene. When the *sariamo* appear for the last time near the end of the *taera* one of these men represents an old woman coming along with a heap of firewood on his head. The men cry out: " Poor old woman, having to carry such a heavy load of wood. Where are the young women that the old woman has to do this? Why cannot the young women give an old one a little firewood? " The old man on taking his departure puts his hand to his forehead, looks at the women, sighs deeply, then departs, staggering under his supposed heavy burden.

For five days the Doriomo and Gaidai clans dance the *karara* three times every evening, and all the performers already mentioned also take their part. The *kokomi* is danced daily by the men, women and children. At the end of the five days the *karara* head-dresses, the drums and all the food from the *dodo* on the Doriomo side in the sacred ground are handed over to the three clans and remain in their care until they have danced their *karara* for the dead, which generally lasts five days. The *muru* or M.C. and the conch shell do not pass into the hands of the three clans but are kept in charge of the Doriomo clan.

When the three clans have completed their part of the pro-gramme the drums and *karara* head-dresses are returned

The *Taera* Ceremonies

to the care of the Doriomo people. The *karara* is danced for two days more, during which period several new turns appear.

The Taera draws to a close.—The *karara* spirits inform the *imigi*, who are also called orphan spirits, that they had better get off to their home in the west. They accordingly depart into the woods, throw away their dresses and return by a roundabout way to the *horiomu*. Other dancers in like manner mysteriously disappear.

The Kepeduwai Oboro, or the Shooting Spirits.—An attempt is now made to deceive the women and children by the departure of the spirits to the distant west. It must be remembered that the men-folks have not been sleeping at home during the time the ceremonies have been in progress, but in the *horiomu*. They have seen their families at times when they themselves have not been in dancing costume. Now if the men dancers for the dead, whom the women and children believe to be real spirits, were to be absent from home for a short time the village would be denuded of men and the deception unmasked. To avoid this, natives from neighbouring villages are secretly brought into the *horiomu*, who assume the costumes of the dancers and show themselves in public. The first thing these visitors do is to fasten a rope to the branches of a tree near the *horiomu* and pull on this with all their might, thus causing the branches to shake, the home men making a whistling noise, which in the village sounds as if people were weeping. The women and children are quietly informed that the branches shake because the men weep with grief at their projected departure from the village.

The old men instruct the women that they are to give the departing spirits food for the long journey back and, in order that they may not be unnecessarily delayed on their way home, that the food should be cooked.

The Mawata men appear in the village without dancing costumes and show themselves, unostentatiously of course, to their kith and kin, and point out that there are a lot of the spirits to be provided with food. The food is cooked, rolled up in a small mat, tied round with a *bata* or plaited belt and taken by the males of the village to the spirits. The bodies of the latter are covered with light-coloured teased coco-nut leaves, and their heads with leaves which hide their identity. They fall in one long line; each spirit carries a bow in his left hand, a bundle of arrows under the right arm, also the food looped over the shoulder with the *bata*, and an arrow held aloft in the right hand. The procession moves with slow and solemn step from the *horiomu* past the village, the men calling out good-bye as the spirits pass their houses on their way to the canoes, which are supposed to be hidden in a creek some distance away. So the long procession of sore-footed and crippled, limping spirits vanishes into the woods and makes the best of its way to its own home. So ends the dancing part of the *taera* held in memory of the long-dead.

CHAPTER XXI

THE *GAERA* CEREMONY

THE word *gaera* is used in three different senses. In the first place, it is the name of a large wooden framework, stand or stall, upon which food is stacked. In the second place, it is used to denote a peace ceremony. In the third, a yam festival and dance.

It will perhaps be an advantage briefly to describe the wooden structure named *gaera* and the manner in which it is built. A long pole is set upright in the ground, sometimes twenty feet above the surface of the earth. At a distance of some twelve feet from this pole a number of forked sticks, or bamboos, twelve or fifteen feet long, are put into the ground three or four feet apart, forming a circle round it. These forked sticks are lashed together by several rows of rattan cane. Other timbers are placed at right angles to the central post and the outer circle of forked sticks. These are fastened with cane, one end to the central post and the other end to the timbers forming the circle. Several tiers or rows are made one above the other. The top tier, called *todo*, remains a kind of platform, and is about two-thirds of the distance from the top of the central post. The number of tiers of course depends upon the wishes of the builders.

Kiwai legend says that the first *gaera* was constructed by a bird named *kamuka*, or the scrub hen. One day whilst the *kamuka* was lying outside his own house a cassowary came along and trod on his feet. The bird said to the cassowary: "Why did you tread upon my feet? You are not a proper man. You never made any gardens. You always walk about the forest and eat the fruit on the trees." The cassowary answered: "Why do you hate me so much? You are only a small boy, whilst I am the son of a chief." The *kamuka* replied: "I am a man, and know how to make a garden." The cassowary then said: "All right, you just go to work and make a big show of food for me to see." The bird answered: "Good. You lie down here. You don't know how to sit on the ground and must therefore lie down." The *kamuka* then went into the forest and called his friends together, and with their assistance brought great quantities of yams, bananas, coco-nuts and other foods to the house. They then set to work and built a *gaera*, placing the food upon every tier from the bottom to the top. The *kamuka* gave some of the food to the cassowary. He did not eat or masticate it, but simply swallowed it down whole whilst lying on the ground. He kept his eyes continually on the *gaera* and the food there. When the work of stacking fruits of the garden on the framework of the *gaera* was finished, the *kamuka* said to the cassowary: "You are not a proper man like me. You are like a pig or wallaby. You swallow your food and do not chew it." The cassowary became very angry at these words. He arose, looked at the *kamuka*, who was standing on the side of the ground near the river, then kicked the *gaera* with his foot. It fell to the ground. (The name of the place is Bauda, now called the Maikasa river.) The cassowary then went off into the forest. The *kamuka* said: "My bad friend has left me." He then stretched out his wings and said to his followers: "You stay here. I leave the food for you." He flew away and settled on a *warakara* tree and called out: "*Kepoka, kio, ku, ku, ku, ku!*" Those men are now sitting in the bush and have been since that day when they helped to bring in the food; their names are Motoraigo, Daporaigo and Wasiraigo.

The Gaera, or Peace-Making Ceremony.—The *gaera* has no connection in any shape or form with the *muguru* or initiation ceremonies.

The *gaera*, which is made in the interest of peace, is a very interesting ceremony, which may be called one of reconciliation. It is held under some such circumstances as the following. One man has done an injury to another and a violent quarrel ensues. In such a case the men-folk would naturally take the side of the member of their own clan, and the trouble would spread; then the women-folk would begin to take up cudgels on behalf of their own clan, and soon there is a feud between two different clans. Trouble of this kind has been known to last for months and even years in the native community, just as such things have done even in civilized, or supposedly civilized, countries. After one such quarrel, which may have severed lifelong friendships, has been carried on for some time, the father or elder brother of the injured party may intervene, and suggest that the son or brother make a garden for a *gaera*. This would be made at the very first opportunity, and when the food is ready for being taken out of the ground arrangements for holding a *gaera* would be made without delay. Every person in the village knows what is on foot. When the inspection of the gardens (*giradaro*) is made, the owner of each garden must reveal the secret to the men of the village. When the elders go past a plot planted for the *gaera*, the maker of that particular garden would call out : "*Gaera!*" The person for whom it is being made is then filled with shame.

The central post of the *gaera* is a fixture in the village and remains in the same position until decay sets in, when it is removed and replaced. The framework for the *gaera* ceremony would be built by the young man making it, and his friends. All the able-bodied men of his own clan would flock to his assistance, and in a very short time the stall would be completed.

Karea is made on the ground in the village and not in the *darimo* or men's club. The father of the man making the ceremony generally conducts the *karea*. He takes a basin of *gamada*, and leaves of the same plant, dips the latter into the former, lifts his hand to the level of his face, then shakes the leaves, the fluid falling in spray upon the ground, and says : "To-morrow my boy [gives the name] will make *gaera. Karea goi* (good luck to him)." This is repeated several times.

Large quantities of *gamada* are made for consumption by the clan running the function. When their mouths get very sore by constantly chewing the root, other friends are called in who most willingly assist. The old and middle-aged men spend the night drinking and smoking. The ceremony lasts about eighteen days or more. It must not be concluded that the ritual is carried on incessantly for this length of time. On the contrary, the performances rarely begin before three P.M. and may be curtailed any day, except

The *Gaera* Ceremony

on the last two days of the series, when they must be carried out in full.

On the first day of the *gaera* ceremony the *kaikai oboro*, or the dance of the spirits with white feathers in memory of the recent dead, is performed. This takes place in the sacred ground and has been fully described in another chapter.

On the second day the person making the *gaera* goes to his garden with five empty baskets and fills them with food, then returns to the village and places all five within the sacred enclosure. There is one basket for each clan. These are left on the ground opposite to the place where the respective clans sit during any sacred ceremony. On the top of each basket of food a small bundle of grass arrows (*tea apera*) about twelve or fourteen inches long is placed.

Within the sacred precincts a forked stick is placed in the ground in a slanting position. To the fork of this stick is tied the end of a banana stalk (*sime wapo*), the bract (I am not quite sure that it is the bract), about twelve inches in length. The grass arrows are divided amongst the male members of each clan. Every man provides his own bow. At a given signal the men begin to fire the grass arrows into the banana bract. All remain sitting and sing:

> "*Manugu biariko,*
> *Manugu sawaiamo,*
> *Matima e, sawaia e.*"

There is no meaning in these words; there may have been once; if so, it has been lost.

When the grass arrows penetrate the banana bract the

audience shouts "*vi, vi, vi!*" The enthusiasm and shouting increase in intensity as the number of arrows finding the mark becomes greater. As soon as the grass arrows have all been fired the whole crowd of men return to the settlement and hand over the toy bows to the children, who then procure a supply of arrows for themselves and have a shooting game on their own account. The forked stick to which the banana bract was tied is left standing in the sacred ground, where it remains until the end of the ceremonies. The five baskets of food are carried into the village and divided between the families of the different clans.

Next day the women proceed to the gardens to obtain food for the men-folk and their children, whilst the men themselves go into the woods to procure long sticks, named *gugus*. These are brought into the village and painted red, white or black. Ornamental leaves are fastened to each stick. A piece of banana leaf is tied to the top, which appears as a flag when the stick is waved. These decorations being completed, the *gugus* are laid in a leaning position against the two screens, each clan using its own screen for this purpose.

There is now an interval for refreshments, after which the men dress for the next performance. All the men then go to the sacred ground, and each clan takes its own sticks or *gugus* from the screens. Some of these are so long that two men are required to carry them. A procession is formed which marches along the sea-beach. A halt is called from time to time, when the *gugus* are placed on the surface of the ground and moved backwards and forwards; meanwhile lively songs are sung. The procession moves on until the village is reached, where the women and children are

The *Gaera* Ceremony

assembled. The poles are again placed on the ground and moved to and fro as before, all standing and singing. There is no dancing or drumming. This is quite a festive occasion; some of the men amuse the women and children with clownish tricks, creating much amusement. At the conclusion of the programme the men return to the sacred ground and place the long poles in a leaning position against the screen, where they remain for the night. The whole of this performance is repeated next day, except the shooting of the arrows into the banana bract.

The next three days are devoted to a dance called *misamisa*. The men dress in the sacred ground at three P.M., proceed to the village and dance till six P.M.

The *gaera* framework or stall is now stacked with food. The person making the *gaera* places a part of his contribution on the top of the framework and part on the ground, the intervening spaces being filled with food supplied by members of the various clans. Then follows the *gaera* dance, which is continued all night. At daylight all the dancers disrobe and sit on the ground in anticipation of the coming scene. When all is quiet the person who has been wronged slowly mounts the wooden framework and stands upon the top tier or platform, called *todo*, and with bow and arrow in hand begins to address the assembly in a loud voice, and says: "Friends, I have been wronged by a man [here the name is spoken]. I want to make an end of this trouble to-day. I have made this feast for you." He then raises his bow, places the arrow on the bow-string, fires the arrow into the sea, and says: "I shall no more think about this quarrel. It is now finished." He then descends to the ground. The food is distributed. The portion which was put on the ground is given by the man to his former enemy, the rest is divided amongst the other members of the community.

A large earthen oven is then made, about fifteen feet long, two feet broad and eighteen inches deep, named *kurikuri*; this is filled with food, which when cooked is shared by all the inhabitants of the settlement.

The man who has done the wrong will make a garden ready for the following south-east season, when he will make another *gaera* and return the present of food which he has received, after which the feud is considered at an end. Only one *gaera* can be made during the year. Along the coast the *gaera* was only made for the purpose of settling a quarrel. It is now a thing of the past.

A dance named *anibibi*, which lasts three days, closes the ceremony; this dance is very disgusting and indelicate.

On the island of Kiwai in the Fly river a *gaera* is held yearly which is a yam festival. Small wood stands are erected round a central forked stick; yams are placed on the sticks and other kinds of vegetables on the stand.

CHAPTER XXII

HEADHUNTERS ON THE WARPATH

ORIGIN *of Head-Hunting among the Kiwais.*—Local Kiwai tradition says that head-hunting originated at Iasa, a village on the island of Kiwai, in the delta of the Fly river. The story is as follows.

There were two men living in the settlement named Gorobe and Namudu. They instituted a new ceremony named *mimia*, and it was whilst they were developing the ritual that they were joined by another man named Nabeamuro, who was somewhat of a giant and a very powerful fighter. The three men became very friendly, and the warrior taught his two new friends the science of war. They practised fighting daily, two against one, and soon the new recruits became skilled in the use of arms.

During the time that these instructions were being given a native arrived at Iasa from Waribodoro in Manoueti, a distance of about forty miles. He travelled by canoe. He soon became friendly with Gorobe and Namudu, but was unable to secure any respect whatever from Nabeamuro. This fact much distressed the two friends Gorobe and Namudu, who talked the matter over together and decided to speak to their colleague and if possible induce him to act civilly towards their guest; but their confrère would not be advised. This unsatisfactory state of affairs continued for some days and was at last ended by the great warrior slaying the stranger, after which he cut off his head and hung it on a forked stick (outside his house), which he put into the ground, where it remained one day. He then made an earthen oven called *moboro*, in which he placed the head for a time, after which he removed all the fleshy substance and produced the bony skull. When asked why he had killed the man, he replied: " I wanted to make a big name for myself and let all the people know that I am a great fighter." Needless to say his fame and prowess soon spread abroad through all the country round about, and he was feared by both friends and neighbours. Now the two men, Gorobe and Namudu, seeing that Nabeamuro had become much esteemed and had derived a considerable amount of influence from the fact that he possessed a human skull, decided to emulate his deeds, and forthwith began to collect heads. They also obtained much notoriety by their respective achievements and won many trophies.

Other members of the tribe living round about, hearing of the great honours and homage gained and received by the men of Iasa, followed in their footsteps, and began to hunt the bushmen who lived inland on the mainland, and soon became the possessors of a large number of skulls. Such is the history of the practice.

I have often spoken with headhunters and their sons and inquired their reasons for the indulgence in this somewhat unpleasant pastime. They advance the following reasons:—(1) they fight and take heads to avenge some act of theft from their gardens, or on account of an injury or murder committed by the enemies of their tribe; (2) to teach the enemy that punishment of a drastic character will follow evil-doing; (3) that skulls are taken as trophies; (4) that being in possession of a number of heads makes a man more important and gives him much influence in the counsels of his own tribe, and increases his reputation in the surrounding district.

War.—The Kiwais have three methods of waging war on land: firstly, by making a midnight raid upon a village and attacking at break of day; secondly, by waylaying men on a track or in the forest; thirdly, by attacking men whilst at work in the garden.

In making a raid upon a village there is no such thing as an attack in daylight if such can be avoided. The plan adopted is to make a surprise attack under cover of darkness whilst the settlement is peacefully sleeping. The men going out on such an expedition, should it be near at hand, would regulate their departure from home according to the distance they had to travel before reaching the object of their journey. The men assemble in their fighting outfit and march from the village in single file. There is no demonstration of any kind. The men will travel only as far as they consider it safe in daylight. Scouts are sent out to reconnoitre. In the old days the Mawata men used the natives of Masingara to lead them to bush villages which they themselves did not know. The party will halt and sleep a considerable distance from the place to be attacked. Spies bring in their reports, and upon these the movements of the force are determined. In the early morning the commander himself, with a few of the most experienced men, goes forward to spy out the nakedness of the land. If the information derived is unsatisfactory the attack may for the time being be abandoned.

Should the report, however, be satisfactory, the party will noiselessly advance toward their objective under the guidance of the men sent out to reconnoitre. When the village in the bush, which is composed of only a few houses built on the ground, and not on piles as among the Kiwais, is eventually sighted the men take cover again and wait until just before dawn. In crouching attitude they advance in single file, ears eagerly straining to pick up the slightest sound which may come from the slumbering enemy. It is astonishing how these men can wend their way through the forest in semi-darkness without breaking a twig or making the slightest noise. Before making the final move the commander again consults his scouts, and, if they decide to attack, the final dispositions are made, and all strategic positions occupied to cut off any retreat of the enemy. From the accounts I have heard from natives, one of which will be published in detail, the Kiwais are strategists of no mean order.

When the first streak of daylight flashes across the heavens the village is surrounded. In single file, as before, the men stealthily move forward to take up their respective positions. One party is allotted to each house. At a given signal the invaders endeavour to enter the houses without awakening the sleepers. If the doors are difficult to open the inmates are aroused and pandemonium reigns supreme. Should the men succeed in entering without disturbing the inhabitants, the conflict is not of long duration. The attackers leave their bows and arrows outside and get to work with a wood or stone club. A gentle tap on the head and there is not even a murmur, and as soon as " the victim ceases to breathe his head is removed." Not a soul is spared if it is possible to prevent one escaping. Even should some of the men be wakened at the commencement of hostilities they would not be able to offer much resistance, as men just aroused from sleep, and not knowing what is going on in the darkness, would be useless, or practically so. During the attack the fighting men can only distinguish their own side in the darkness by the uniform of white mud which has been plastered upon the body. There is also a disadvantage in this, as the white serves as a mark for the enemy to shoot at, or serves to locate the warriors whilst moving about, and helps the inhabitants to keep out of the way by hiding, or escaping from the house.

The head is removed by the bamboo knife cutting down to the vertebræ and then turning the skull round on its axis until it is free. The rattan head-carrier is then passed through the mouth and under the lower jaw, one end being put through the looped rattan. This is tightly drawn into position ready for the journey home. The number of heads obtained depends upon the size of the village. Should the raid have been organized to avenge a murder committed by a bushman, the houses would be plundered, then burned to the ground, after which the gardens would be robbed and completely destroyed. If any of the attacking party should have been killed their bodies would be taken home for burial. The wounded, if any, would be carefully looked to before the party starts on their homeward march. Here the surgical implement, the ipa shell, may be of service in removing any arrows from the bodies of the attackers.

One very strange custom is practised when a victim is struck on the head with a club. The one dealing the blow calls out the name of his son, and says: " I am Waiba's father." A similar expression is also used when men spear dugong.

The victors who advanced so noiselessly and silently to the field of conflict are now transformed into a mad, turbulent mob, singing, dancing and shouting like demented beings. With the loot obtained and the bleeding heads in their hands they set out for home.

The Return of the Braves.—The return of the victorious warriors is, for the first part of the journey home, rather subdued, but when they come in sight of the village there is a scene of the wildest enthusiasm. The women put on head-dresses, paint their faces and adorn their bodies with any other ornaments that may be at hand. Old men and women weep for joy on seeing their sons and husbands with fresh honours in their hands. The men who have not obtained a head lead the procession of head-hunters into the village. They sing and dance as they advance near the settlement:

> " *Anipapa degurora deguro,*
> *Siripapa degurora deguro.*"

The women sing one word only, " *godare, godare, godare,*" repeated again and again, dancing meanwhile. The old men drum and the youths blow the conch shells in honour of the great victory. There is, however, one portion of the community that does not join in the celebrations—the children. These tremble with fear, and " sit unable to move," and terrified beyond what words can express at the ghastly sights revealed to their eyes.

I asked an old head hunter one day to describe the appearance of the warriors on their return home, and these are his words: " They looked fine with the bleeding heads in one hand and their weapons in the other. Their eyes were fierce, very red, and protruded from their orbits, just like those of a turtle which has been on its back three or four days exposed to the fiery heat of the sun."

A forked stick is placed in the ground opposite the house of each man who has obtained a head, which is hung upon the forked portion of the stick. The arms are all leaned against a fence in the middle of the village, after which the men remove all signs of the bloody conflict in which they have been engaged by bathing in the sea or the nearest creek. On their return the best food available is placed before them in their houses, and liberal portions of *gamada* served to all. A fire has meanwhile been lighted about a yard from each stick which is adorned by a head. This is kept burning for five days and nights to keep away flies, ants, and other pests. After a long rest the victory is celebrated by a great dance from three P.M. till dark, which is about six P.M. The fighting men come on to the dancing-ground first, carrying their trophies in their right hands and bows and arrows in the left. Those who have no heads follow behind with stone clubs, bows and arrows. The women come next with *eas*, or pieces of wood used as garden spades. Then follow the drummers, the young men and big boys. Five rings are formed by the dancers and orchestra.

The dancers walk round three times, then turn and walk

round three times in the opposite direction. This is called the *pipi* dance, and the *pipi* song is sung, to the accompaniment of a number of drums. They sing,

> "*Anibo sanibo
> Pipi ruai*,"

as they walk round the ring. This step is very slow. One foot is lifted about twelve inches from the ground and the

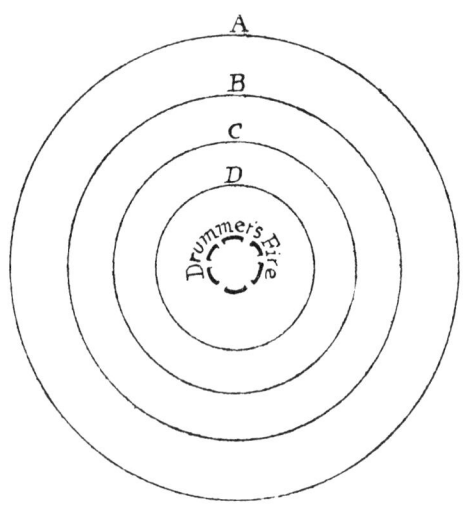

PLAN OF WAR DANCE

A denotes the position of the women. Each one carries two coco-nut shells full of water and dances behind her husband ready to give him a drink of water when required. B denotes the position of the men with human heads in their hands, and others carrying arms. C, circle of young men. D, circle of boys.

knee bent forward. The high state of nervous tension affects the voice, facial muscles and the whole bodily frame. The excitement begins to grow more and more as the drums beat out a louder note, followed by the violent blowing of the conch shells. After a time another war-song is sung:

> "*Ina sugupagana sugupagana,
> Ina sugupagana.*"

The singing becomes more animated, the step quicker and the dancing madder. The drummers beat with all their might; the decapitated heads are raised aloft in one hand and their weapons in the other. The men are shooting at some imaginary foe, whilst the women are digging their wooden spades into the imaginary bodies of the enemy by striking the ground with the sharp end of the spade. The climax is soon reached, when the song is changed:

>" *Aniboo saniboo*
> *Pipi ruai.*"

The drummers cannot get more speed on, the singing is at its loudest, the step at its quickest, the passions most violent. The whole crowd is riotous, frantic, mad.

At sundown the dance ceases until next afternoon. The heads are left hanging on the forked sticks. All arms are taken inside the men's club-house. *Gamada* is drunk in large quantities. The men who have been engaged in warfare are now at liberty to join their wives and families. The dance is carried on for five successive days in the coastal villages. The heads are carried daily by the owners when dancing. At the end of this period the heads are somewhat high. A *moboro* or oven is made in the ground. This is a hole about two feet deep; the circumference depends upon the number of heads to be treated. The hole having been dug, it is filled with firewood; upon the wood a number of stones are placed, if procurable, and the wood is lighted and burned. Whilst the embers are red-hot the fire is extinguished. The hot stones and burning charcoal are scraped together into a heap and then spread out over the bottom of the oven.

Leaves from the banana plant are laid upon these stones and hot embers, and the heads are laid upon the leaves. The bark of the *te* tree is then used to cover the whole oven. After a time the oven is opened up and each man removes his own treasure from it. These are immediately carried to the seaside, when the wet cleansing process is carried out. The muscular tissues are removed without any difficulty and thrown into the sea. The brain is washed out of the cranium by continually shaking the head under water. No stick is inserted into the foramen magnum as is done by the Dorro headhunters. The men who have done this often inform me that there is not much labour involved in the process. When the washing is completed the skulls are again hung upon the forked sticks and allowed to dry. After one day's drying they are all painted red with *were*: this is soil, which when burnt, becomes a scarlet-red. One croton leaf, split into two halves, is tied to the left and right zygomas respectively, and a piece of *iga*, twine made from the teased skins of coco-nuts, is placed between the teeth and passed through the nasal cavity. This serves as a cord to hang up the skull. No other decorations were placed upon the heads of enemies.

When the skulls have been washed the persons who have been engaged in the operations indulge in the luxury of a salt-water bath. Great attention is given to the cleansing of the teeth, nostrils and mouth. When the ablutions are satisfactorily performed the men are supplied with a quantity of perfumed leaves. With these they rub their bodies from head to foot. This is an act of purification.

A father who has been on a successful head-hunt and

returned with a coveted trophy, should he have a son five or six years of age, will take a small portion of the flesh from the head, about the size of a pea, and a drop of blood, mix these with a little sago, yam or taro, or some other vegetable, make into a kind of pill, and give to the young child. The concoction is called by the same name as the one given to the boys who are being initiated into the *gamabibi* craft; the composition is, of course, not exactly the same. This is said to make the boy *serawo nanito* (fierce for ever).

When a woman's husband has been killed and his head taken away by the enemy, the woman is not allowed to marry again until the death of her husband has been avenged and a head brought back from the offending tribe. Should a man from another clan go forth to take vengeance, and should he be successful in bringing back into the village a head from the shoulders of one of the enemy, he may take the widow to wife. Should some member of the woman's clan avenge the death of the husband, he is rewarded in one of two ways: if the woman has any children, she gives one, preferably a boy, to the relative; if she has no children, payment is made in kind—mats, cooking shells, arm shells, necklaces of dog's teeth and other valuables. After this payment has been made the widow may marry any whom she pleases.

Women and War.—I have often heard it said by Europeans that the women of the Kiwai tribe would not marry a man unless he had won some honour on the field of battle, and that in the old days men went from the Fly river to Tureture and Mawata and purchased heads with canoes and other produce, and that these heads were carried off to the Fly and the owners were looked upon as warriors, and that they could easily procure the favours of women after such an exploit.

I have spoken to old women upon this subject and asked what the women in bygone times looked for in a man they wished to marry. In every case the answer has been the same: first, that he must be good-looking; second, that he must be a good gardener and dancer. When questioned upon the possession of skulls, they say that the young women did not put much emphasis upon this, but that their fathers, brothers and the male members of the clan did. Some of the old men I have consulted confirm this statement.

When two men have been instrumental in capturing and decapitating an enemy the skull is divided, one man taking the upper and lower jaws and the other man the rest of the skull. The former is considered the more valuable of the two.

A careful record is kept of the number of heads taken by one individual. Each warrior, though he has no knowledge of writing, keeps a faithful record of his successes. For every head taken a notch is cut near the handle on the beheading-knife. I have before me as I am writing the son of a renowned head-hunter, Adagi, who is in possession of his father's old beheading-knife. He will neither sell nor barter it. I asked why he wished to keep it and here is his reply: " I want to give that beheading-knife to my boy, so that he may know what a great man his grandfather was. I have not got the heads he took to show him, but the marks my father made on the knife are there and are a witness that he cut off a lot of heads. It would not be much use my telling the boy what his grandfather had done. He might not

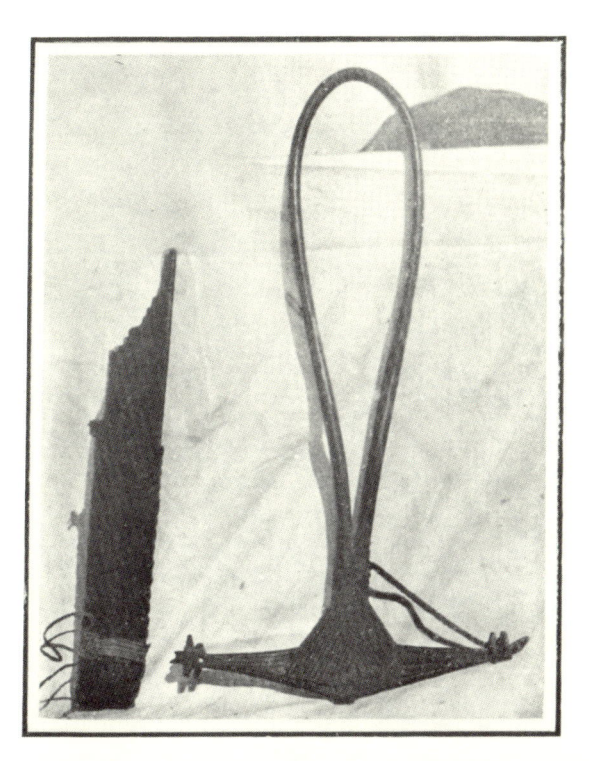

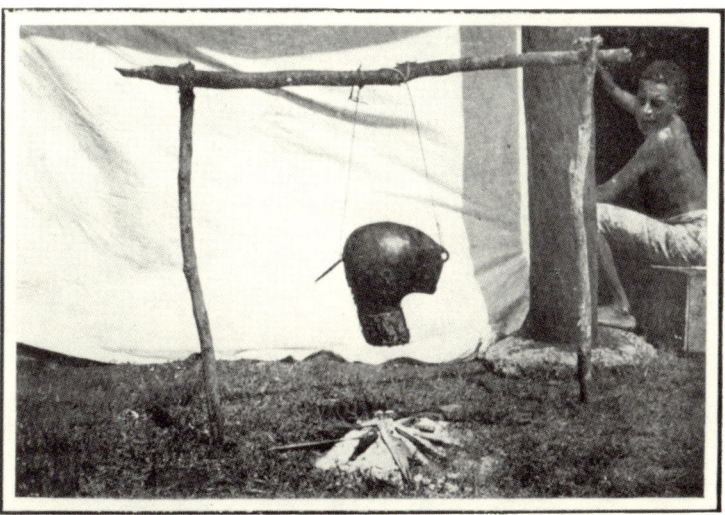

OLD HEAD KNIFE AND HEAD CARRIER.
The notches record the number of heads taken. There are 15 in this case.
DRYING A HEAD.
This shows the method of drying the head after it has been stuffed. The fire is on the ground beneath the head.

believe me, but if I give him the knife, and he sees the notches, he will believe." I made no further effort to purchase the treasure.

In the higher regions of the Fly river a splendidly made cuirass is worn. I have not, however, any definite information of these people although I have one of these in my possession.

Naval War.—When men go on an expedition by canoe a certain number of women are carried simply as cooks for the men. Should there be an engagement before the attacking party get ashore the women are kept concealed inside the canoes. The Wabuda people in the delta of the Fly have the greatest reputation in the district for fighting at sea. If any canoes from Kiwai were seen crossing over to the mainland, the Wabuda men put to sea and often captured both canoes and crews. In an engagement at sea the first thing aimed at is to secure a commanding position by cutting off the retreat of the enemy, and when that manœuvre is accomplished the bowmen aim at the men steering the different canoes. When these men are out of action, even though others step into their places, a big advantage has been gained and the greater force generally comes off victorious. The victims are beheaded and their bodies mutilated and thrown into the sea.

Many years ago the three villages of Parama, Sui and Sumai, with their combined fleets, went up the creek named Imioro, between Sui and Daware. They left their canoes some distance from the village at sundown and sent out scouts, who returned and reported that the bushmen were engaged in some initiatory ceremonies. At break of day the combined forces of the three villages surrounded the bushmen's camp and not a soul got away. I have heard the descendants of these villages boast of this great achievement and the number of heads they took home.

Canoes have often made journeys of some two or three hundreds of miles from home, women accompanying the expedition.

The days of fighting in the Fly delta and along the coast are now happily ended between Daru and the Dutch boundary. But farther up the Fly and in the regions of the Bamu and Turama rivers the fighting is still carried on. The Government is, however, rapidly putting an end to the head-hunting expeditions.

The following account was dictated in the Kiwai language and written by one of my boys. The translation is as literal as it is possible to make it:

" My name is Duwani. Many years ago I went to a village named Iasa, on Kiwai Island, to purchase a canoe. There were three other men with me, Tabaia, Noisai and Adagi. We had been there three days when the Iasa men said to me: ' You must stay here a few days longer as we are going out to fight, and when we come back you shall have a canoe.' They launched all their canoes, and when they were getting ready to go into them one of the men said to me: ' Are you a woman that you want to stay in the village? Why cannot you come and help us to fight?' We four Mawata men then joined the party. We went up the river with the tide to a village called Kubira. When we got there some men said: ' Let us go and kill the people at Kowabu.' Others said: ' No, let us go and kill the men of Doropodai because they have killed some of our own people. We must pay them back.' The Kubira folks went out and caught a lot of fish with nets. We ate the fish with sago and other vegetables. When the evening meal was finished Adagi got fever and did not take part in the fight. Next morning we set out for the village of Doropodai, which was then in the bush. They had been driven from their old village some time before by the Wabuda fighting men. We slept on the top of a small hill some distance from the village we were going to fight. Before daybreak a few men went out to look round the Doropodai camp. When they came back we talked and then divided into two companies. One company went to the right of the village and one to the left. The Doropodai people saw some of us and then ran away. Some of them fired arrows at us and we fired back. I shot two people, one man and one woman. My friend Noisai hit them both on the head with a stone club and I cut off their heads and carried them back to Kubira and from there to Iasa. I gave the Iasa people my two heads and they gave me a good canoe.

"Daida the Iasa policeman also took part in the fight and got the head of one woman.

"Sogoi, another Iasa policeman, was present and got the head of a man."

Both constables were considerate enough to remove their uniforms before entering the ranks of the fighters.

CHAPTER XXIII

SORCERY

ACCORDING to one mythical narrative related by the Kiwai people the foundation of sorcery dates back to the time of a man named Maruu, who lived at Manuwete and was the owner of the first pig known to mankind. Briefly, the story is as follows.

There was a ball of sago lying on the ground in the forest near the branch of a large *warakara* tree which had been blown down by the wind. Maruu stood on the branch with a coco-nut in his hand, which he skinned, and threw the skin on the top of the sago ball. He broke open the nut, took an ipa shell and cut two crescent-shaped pieces of coco-nut, each half-an-inch broad, and threw them near the ball of sago; the calyx of the nut, together with the thin end of the bract, about five inches long, were also added to the heap. He then left the woods and returned to his home. Next morning he again went into the forest and on his arrival at the *warakara* tree he heard three grunts. He then looked round to find the cause of the noises and was much surprised to see that the things he had left on the ground the night before had been transformed into a pig. The ball of sago became the body of the animal, the two pieces of crescent-shaped nut the tusks, the calyx the snout, the coco-nut skin the bristles, and the bract the tail. Maruu addressed the pig and said: " I am your father, you belong to me."

Sorcery

The next day Maruu told some of the boys to bring the pig into the house, but they were unable to catch it because it was so wild and fierce. One man, by name Duruba, took a bow and arrow and shot it. The owner was very angry. He filled a hollow reed with blood, and took one rib-bone from the left side of the thorax and sharpened one end of it. The animal was placed on a platform in the woods and a great dance was held. At four P.M. the pig was taken inside the house (*darimo*), Maruu leading the procession, followed by the dancers, whilst the pig-carriers brought up the rear. It was laid upon the *dodo* (platform) in the middle of the house. The carriers and the party who had caught the pig were given permission to eat it, but were told not to give any part of the meat to the old men and women. Some of the girls were permitted to partake of the flesh because it was not *muguru* time on their side of the village. After the feast Maruu addressed the dancers and said: " You have killed this pig, eaten it and spoiled its life. By and by you will all die." The dance was resumed, and whilst the conch shells and drums were at the loudest and the dancing furious the *darimo* or men's club-house fell down where a different party were making *muguru* in another house. This clearly proved that the latter *muguru* was not the proper thing, but that the one of Maruu was the *muguruia*, the true *muguru*. What more could be desired for proof of this?

The man who had cut up the animal made a request to the people to whom Maruu had given the pig that he might be permitted to take its skin, ribs and snout, which was immediately granted. Maruu informed him that these things were *giware nuunumabu,* or things for producing sickness.

The Sorcerer.—The sorcerer is found in every Kiwai village without exception. His influence is great and the whole community stands in awe of him. He is a professor of magic and the natives have unbounded faith in his art and in the methods employed by him. He professes to have the power to cause sickness and death. He also claims to be able to counteract the evil forces he has set at work, and to restore a sick man to health. I have a sorcerer before me as I write who assures me that he at least does not claim to have any power over spirits. He claims that the charms which he carries are so powerful that once he sets them in motion death will follow unless he interposes. He informs me that the only outfit he carries consists of a pig's skin, which he has cooked in the fire, pieces of pig's ribs, and part of the snout.

I have gleaned the following information from him as to why he practises this black magic. If another person has a very big garden and an abundant harvest and does not send him a portion of the produce he gets angry, and watches his opportunity for inflicting punishment upon the person now regarded as an enemy. The sorcerer will prowl round his garden and if possible get possession of the gardener's wood spade (*ea*) and rub it with a piece of the pig's skin he carries about with him. When the gardener comes and takes up the spade he feels sick, goes home and begins to languish. The name of the sorcerer, or rather his identity, is often made known in dreams. On the following day one or more relatives may call upon the sorcerer for an explanation of his action in causing one of their family to be grievously stricken with some unknown sickness. The sorcerer of course will deny the charge, but if pressed will admit

Sorcery

having committed the deed, and give his reason—namely, that he caught a lot of fish last week and gave the sorcerer none, or that he has heaps of food in the garden and gives a quantity away, but never a bit to the worker of magic. The latter must therefore be placated. He is promised that if he will restore the sick one he will not be forgotten in future. The sorcerer then takes a small portion of food, such as a banana or a piece of sago, talks to it for a few seconds in a soothing manner, and finally gives it to the patient. The magic-man stands by for a few minutes, then asks the sick person if he is better, and the answer is in the affirmative. Quantities of food will be sent on regularly after this, or a portion of the garden may be given over to the dispenser of medicine.

Another method employed by the sorcerer is to rub his hands with the pig's skin, go to the house of the person who has offended him, walk under the floor and with his hand rub the board upon which the enemy sleeps, and immediately the man comes to lie down on his bed he is stricken with sickness. Instead of rubbing the plank, he may stroke the *saro* (long post) near which the man to be punished lies at night. The post is stroked only one way—downwards, which means death. Should the sorcerer be persuaded to remove the evil spell, he returns to the post and strokes it in the opposite direction—that is, upwards—which signifies that the sick man will get up and live. This is not the only way the evil magic is counteracted. Sometimes it is done by stamping the heel violently on the ground and muttering a lot of words which no one understands. The sorcerer always makes a point of calling round and asking the sick person if he is feeling better. Suggestion may play a good part in helping the patient to recover.

A third mode of causing death or sickness is by placing a small piece of the pig's skin inside food and giving it to the person disliked. If the sorcerer should be angry he will say to a man: "This is your last day; you will not see the sun rise to-morrow." It seems impossible to believe that such a curse pronounced upon a man will cause him to sicken and die, but so great is the fear of the sorcerer and his charms that unless the curse be counteracted the condemned man will die. He gives up all hope and simply passes away.

I will briefly relate two or three examples of the actions of sorcerers upon their victims, to show the belief that the natives have in the power of the worker of magic to cure complaints.

In one of the coastal villages, which is supposed to be the most advanced in the west, a young man was taken ill after the sorcerer had been seen to rub the plank over which the young man slept. An elder brother of the sick man called upon the magic-worker and charged him with causing the sickness. This was not denied. He simply replied: "Your brother speared a dugong last week and did not give me any." The elder brother replied: "If you will cure him I will give you the very first dugong that I spear." "All right," was the reply, "I will cure him; don't mention my name or I will kill you." The man recovered and a whole dugong was paid for the service rendered. That sorcerer is feared, yet terribly hated.

An example showing the natives' belief in the healing powers of the sorcerer may be interesting.

Sorcery

Some years ago a little fellow who acted as chief cook for me, both afloat and ashore, informed me that his father was very ill with fever, and asked permission to go to see him. Knowing the father well, I sent ten grains of quinine by the boy. On his return to my house he reported that he had given his father the medicine. The following day I sent the boy home to see how his father was. He was away about an hour. He informed me that his father was quite well and taking a little exercise. I then asked: "Did your father take the quinine?" He replied: "No, sir; the *giware dubu* [sorcerer] made him better. He took a kangaroo-skin and a bundle of grass out of father's back; he got better at once." I then inquired where the kangaroo-skin and bundle of grass were. The lad replied: "He threw them over the fence near the house; I did not see them, but mother did." I then asked: "Do you believe that story?" He answered, speaking very quietly: "My mother told me, sir." I left it at that. I could not undermine the boy's faith in the word of his mother. He had been with me four years, had travelled much, and I did not think he could swallow such a statement.

The information of the sorcerer's methods of working as outlined above has been given me by sorcerers themselves. These, however, are not by any means the only ones practised. Some men have more elaborate outfits than others. I have heard of sorcerers on Kiwai Island who have gone to the grave of a newly buried corpse, scraped the earth away from the thorax and cut off the finger-nails and a portion of hair, and added these to the collection of pig's skin and bones. Others again have a collection of small stones which are said to be first rubbed with the skin of the pig and then thrown about at night-time upon the house where the undesirable person lives. When they are thrown from the hand of the sorcerer he calls the name of the person he wishes to kill, and asks the stones to carry sickness to the particular man or woman named.

I have not found a single instance amongst the Kiwais where a sorcerer has obtained a particular portion of a living person's body, such as hair or nails, or anything connected with a person, with a view to injuring or causing the death of that individual.

The sorcerer, though he is feared by all the community without a single exception, does not always get things his own way. I know a man who threatened to kill a sorcerer who was suspected of having caused the daughter of the man to be grievously sick. Fortunately the child got better. The following historical case may be of interest.

A Sumai man named Gabua went to work on a diving-boat in Torres Straits. He was returned home before his contract of service was completed on account of ill health. In due course he arrived at Daru. At the time of his arrival the Sumai sorcerer happened to be in Daru, and upon hearing that Gabua was aboard a lugger in the harbour went off to see him, and, as was only natural, shook hands with him. After being paid off before a Government officer, Gabua went aboard again and told one of his friends that he was much worse, and that he thought it was because the sorcerer, named Pairio, had touched his hand. In the course of a few days Gabua arrived at his native village. He went ashore and told his family and friends that Pairio had touched his hand.

The following day Gabua died, but before passing away asserted that Pairio had caused his sickness, and asked those near him to shoot the said sorcerer. One man named Ataio called a few of the older men together, and they decided, quite unanimously, that, as many women and children had died recently (Pairio had long been suspected and hated), these being followed by the death of Gabua so soon after his arrival home, it was time Pairio was brought to justice.

On the morning of Gabua's death the sorcerer had been seen going in the direction of his garden. He was followed by at least six, if not more, of those who had sat in judgment and condemned him. They found him in his garden tying up bananas, then, getting into position, every man fired an arrow, some of which pierced his arms and legs; his body was untouched. Looking up he saw his assailants and said he wanted to talk. They agreed to listen. He then informed his hearers that he had bewitched all the villages on Kiwai Island and many others and that soon the inhabitants would all be dead. He was asked if his words were true, and upon his saying " Yes," one named Kamura lifted his bow and sent an arrow which entered his lungs on the left side. He died immediately and was buried by his family.

There is another kind of magic much more terrible than that, which is termed *giware*. This I believe has come from the inland tribes behind Mawata and has been practised along the coast for many years. It is also well known in the Fly river. It is called *mauwamo*. There is a great difference between the two kinds of sorcery, *giware* and *mauwamo*.

Briefly stated, the former works out in the open. The agent can be seen dancing under a person's house, rubbing the board upon which a person sleeps with his hand. Everybody knows that he carries death charms in his little bag slung over his left shoulder. When a man is sick the sorcerer, for a small consideration, will recall the spell and show his compassion with the stricken man and his relatives. If the magic is not counteracted the patient may die a lingering death.

The *mauwamo* man, on the other hand, always works in the dark. He may be known, and is known, but no one can see what he is doing. He carries about his instruments of death in a little bag. When once a man is marked out for death there is no possibility of the sentence being counteracted. Death is relentless, swift and sure. There is no compassion, no mercy. His fees are said to be much higher than those of the ordinary practitioner or sorcerer. I have referred elsewhere to one Saisami being killed by a shark in Torres Straits last year. This was put down to the action of some *mauwamo* man.

Whilst the ordinary sorcerer appears to work by charms alone, the *mauwamo* man is able to incarnate himself in the bodies of sharks, snakes, crocodiles, pigs and cassowaries. These animals are said to perform whatever he wills should be done. He also invokes the aid of the spirits which inhabit the forest to assist him in any nefarious scheme he has on hand. One informant tells me that he has one point in common with the spirit medium—he chews a certain kind of wood, the nature of which is unknown, and this enables him to capture the spirit of any enemy; the death of the body naturally follows the seizure. He will make *karea* by himself, or call in one or two other professors of the craft

Sorcery

to be present whilst he makes it. He takes a basin of *gamada*, a coco-nut and a stick, then calls upon the spirit of the one he intends to kill and asks it to come inside the *gamada*. This is sprinkled, and the name of the victim spoken aloud. The coco-nut is afterwards broken with the stick and the water allowed to run on the ground. The flesh of the nut is then eaten, after which the victim meets an early death. He is said to carry about with him certain charms, consisting of the tail, or part of it, of a kangaroo and a piece of dried human flesh which has been cut from the thigh of a dead man.

The above particulars of the working of the *mauwamo* men are all second-hand. I have endeavoured time and again to get information from those actually engaged in this method of black magic but have not obtained one particle from them.

Both the ordinary sorcerer and the *mauwamo* men teach their sons the secrets of the trade. It is, however, possible for an outsider to acquire these on payment of a knife and tomahawk.

The most distinguished sorcerer I have seen and met was Magaga of Wabuda. I first came across him in his own village in 1908. I anchored off the village at seven P.M. Some of my crew, hearing the drumming and singing ashore, informed me that some of the *muguru* ceremonies were taking place, so I refrained from going ashore in the moonlight, lest my presence should cause trouble. At seven A.M. next morning I went ashore with three of my crew. Several young men in their paint and feathers came to the beach and helped us to land. I heard a voice talking very loudly, and looking round saw Magaga standing on the veranda of the men's club-house, which was about three hundred and fifty feet in length. He was gesticulating and swinging his arms in dramatic fashion, and called the village boys away. They promptly obeyed his call. His only garment consisted of a bit of grass tied round the biceps muscle of his left arm. His Jewish nose was covered with red paint, or rather red mud, which had been daubed on without any idea of artistic decoration. He greeted me when I reached the house with the words: "Get back to your canoe, we don't want you here." I humoured the man by walking a short distance from the house where he was and then turned round. I motioned him to come to me, holding up a stick of tobacco. This soothed his ruffled feelings. He came to me and I gave him the tobacco. In a very short time I had him aboard the *Ada* (my boat) to dinner. I gave him a plate of rice with a little tinned meat, but he refused to touch them. I presented him with a piece of cloth to put round his loins, but he evidently thought it beneath his dignity to wear it. He stayed about an hour aboard, examining the ship, then became fidgety and wanted to get ashore. I was anxious to gain his friendship, and as he was going over the side of the vessel a few large biscuits were handed to him. These he dropped over the side of the dinghy into the sea as he went ashore. During the afternoon I paid the village another visit and found Magaga again on the veranda of the house. I had a small mirror in my bag which the old man had seen on board. I showed it to him again and presented it to him. It seemed to soften the poor man's heart. He was as vain as ever a girl was, when standing before that small mirror. I believe he really admired himself. The result of this little present was far-reaching. He took me into the club-house, an honour which I had not expected. I have referred to the carvings on some of the huge pillars in another chapter. The house was decorated in a festive manner with coloured leaves from the croton-trees, and large coco-nut leaves were hanging round the central post where the ceremony was to take place. I was not permitted to look inside this enclosure, nor did I attempt to do so.

Kiwai Superstitions.—(1) If there is a sick man in a village and another person dreams that a canoe has sunk or split open at sea, the sick man will die.

(2) If a man is sick and a second person dreams that a third person has speared a dugong from a *narato*, and that the animal got away with the *amu* or line, the sick person will die.

(3) Should a dugong spear break in the hand of a man standing on a *narato* out at sea whilst he is attempting to spear the animal, he will surely die.

(4) If a person dreams that another man has killed a man, woman or child in battle, the latter will be sure to kill a dugong of the same sex when he next goes out fishing.

(5) If a man in a dream sees his own body covered with excreta, he will be sure to kill an enemy on the next expedition. The excreta is a sign of blood.

(6) If a man dreams that his neighbour's wife is dancing with a long grass petticoat and the usual cassowary-feather head-dress, the husband of that woman will spear many turtle.

(7) In the north-east turtle-time all the sprouting coco-nuts are painted red; should a man be able to fill a canoe with sprouting nuts, without borrowing from a neighbour, he will fill his canoe with turtle on the following fishing trip.

(8) If a man has made a pig trap in the bush and then dreams that a house has fallen down in the night-time, it is a sure sign that the pig trap has fallen and that the animal has been caught.

(9) Should a man dream that a piece of rope has got round his legs or body, he will die after being bitten by a snake.

(10) When a party of hunters are out with dogs and a man dreams that he or some other person has killed one or more bushmen in battle, the hunting party will bring back many pigs, wallabies and cassowaries.

(11) If a man dreams that he has collected a lot of food and stacked it in a certain place, that food will be consumed by the people who will attend his own funeral as mourners.

(12) If a number of men should set out to visit a certain village and have to cross a creek or pool of water, and one of the party should see his own shadow in the water with a head carried in his mouth, the whole company would return with haste, as the shadow was a sign that their own heads would soon be decapitated and placed in head-carriers.

(13) If at night-time, after sundown, pieces of wood, stones or mud should begin to fly about in a house and hit one of the inhabitants, that person will die owing to the fact that his spirit is discontented and has thrown things about.

(14) When the sun and moon sink below the horizon,

Sorcery

they simply pass through the earth and come up on the other side next day.

(15) If a man in a dream should see a canoe come from the west, Adiri, and the spirit come ashore, any sick man, woman or child in the village would die. The spirit from the canoe would take the spirit of the sick person and both would go to Adiri.

(16) If a person dreams that one of his teeth in front comes out of the mouth, a brother or sister will die. If he dreams that one of the molar teeth has come out, some person in another family will pass away.

(17) If a man dreams that the village has been destroyed by fire, it is thought that some great sickness will soon fall upon the people.

(18) If when the moon is at full a cloud should come over part of it, the village nearest the clouded part will have sickness and death in their ranks.

(19) If a man dreams that another person has an arrow in his back that person is doomed.

(20) If a dog barks at night continually, a sick person in the village will die. If the owner of a dog dies, that dog will not bark again.

CHAPTER XXIV

KIWAI IDEAS OF THE SPIRIT WORLD

IT is no easy matter to set forth the ideas of the Kiwai people concerning the spirit world. They have ideas, and many of them, but these are most indefinite, amazing, perplexing and illogical. It is indeed most difficult to find out what they do and what they do not believe. They have, however, very definite ideas regarding some things in the spirit world.

It is a universally accepted belief that man is a spiritual being, and that there are three distinct spirits dwelling in each person: the *urio*, the *uriona*, and the *oboro*.

The Urio.—The *urio* is that part of the man which thinks and wills; the conscious mental activity. It is not a fixture in the human being. It can and does leave the body in sleep and in times of sickness. The natives say: " The *urio* runs away when a man's body gets sick, and wanders round in the forest, or walks about in the garden of the person to whom it belongs." When the illness is over the *urio* may return and enter the body of its own accord, or it may be brought back by one specially gifted in seeing and handling spirits, in which case the spirit is placed against the back of the sick person, and when it has entered the body he makes a quick recovery.

The *urio* leaves the body in sleep and goes a long distance away. No native cares to waken another lest the *urio* should be angry because it has to return to the body before it is ready to do so. When a man opens his eyes after sleep it is a sure sign that the spirit, which has been wandering round, has returned to the body.

The Uriona.—The meaning of the word *urio* is the spirit which can leave the body and return whenever it wills to do so. The suffix *na* means thing or things. *Uriona* is therefore the thing or things of the spirit. A picture, a photograph, or the shadow of a person in water is called *uriona*. It is something more than a picture or shadow. I think it is what we call life, animate existence. When a person sleeps, the *uriona* does not leave the body but remains in it; but when death comes both the *urio* and the *uriona* die at the same time as the body. A tree is said to have a *uriona* when standing, but when it falls to the ground it has not.

A short time ago I had a bushman in my house from Togo. He had never seen a looking-glass. When he stood in front of a large one and for the first time in his life saw the picture of himself and of his own face, he had no idea what it was he was looking at. It was only when another native, whom he knew, came and stood by his side that he became restless on seeing his own and his friend's form in the glass. The new-comer used the word *uriona*, whereupon the bushman bolted from the room with dispatch. It took a considerable time to convince him that there was no black magic at work, and to get him to stand in front of the mirror again. To give him confidence I stood by his side. He held up his hand, moved his fingers about, made horrible grimaces, put out his tongue again and again, laughed and showed his teeth, and appeared to enjoy himself, but he was far from comfortable until he got away from the glass.

Some years after James Chalmers was murdered at Goaribari a number of natives from that island were brought to Daru to be signed on for plantation work. The recruiter of these men sent them to church on Sunday morning. Whilst I was giving out the first hymn I noticed that they were very restless, but before I had read through one verse there was an awful panic, followed by a stampede. Some rushed out at one door, some at another, and a number sprang up on the seats and jumped through the windows of the church (which are about five feet from the ground), and cleared off as fast as they could run.

Just before the stampede I noticed one of the men pointing to something over the top of my head. It was a large photo of Chalmers. They had recognized that it was the man they had killed, or rather they thought that it was Chalmers' *uriona* that had mysteriously returned; hence the disturbance. It must have seemed uncanny to them to find the spirit of the man on the wall years after his death.

The *oboro* is the spirit which lives after the body dies. It is intangible, without substance, something which cannot be handled except by persons who have a particular power of dealing with spirits. Natives describe the *oboro* as "a white light like that of white fire." It is a facsimile of the person to whom it belonged. It is the same height and breadth, and has the same characteristics.

After death the *oboro* wanders round the settlement for a few days and may often be seen after dark. It is very cunning, sly, ill-disposed, and is greatly feared. Unless it is treated well and appeased, trouble and misfortune will speedily overtake the near relatives. It is for this reason that food is placed on the grave. I think, however, it would be more correct to say that it is fear plus affection which prompts this action.

Spirits have been known to touch people and sickness has immediately followed. The hand of the *oboro* is cold, whilst that of the *urio* is hot.

I have often been in villages when spirits of the dead have been reported to be walking about. Consternation and panic seize all the women and children, who rush off into their houses as quickly as possible. It is always the men who see these spirits and create such scares. I have often heard them boast that they have done these things.

Spirits of Ancestors.—The Kiwais are all firm believers in the existence of their ancestors' spirits, that these take an interest in their daily lives, and that they are able to help or mar their undertakings. In all their ceremonies—for fighting, hunting, fishing, gardening—offerings are made and toasts drunk to their ancestors, who are earnestly and solemnly entreated to come to their aid on the projected enterprise. There is never a garden site chosen, a garden fence built, a yam planted or any fishing expedition undertaken without these spirits being called upon to bless and prosper the enterprise.

Divination.—When a man knows that food is being taken from his garden he is naturally anxious to find out who is the offender. He will then take his father's skull and place it near his own head when sleeping. If the identity of the thief is not made known to him in a dream, he will place a stick alongside the skull the following night, and will tell it in unmistakable language that unless the truth is revealed he will smash it with a stick. If the spirit will not give the desired information willingly, coercion will be applied to the skull to compel the spirit to do so.

Mediums.—By the word medium I mean a person who has special powers of seeing spirits, handling them, and being able to forecast events from the actions of the said spirits. These mediums exist in every community and every word of theirs is implicitly believed.

A native named Kaiku and his son Samae, natives of Mabadauwane, are said to possess this power, and both have a considerable reputation as spirit mediums. The father derived his ability from his ancestors and has transmitted it to his son. It is said that the ancestors acquired their power first through the instrumentality of dreams. A spirit appeared to one of them in a dream and commanded him to go into the bush in the early morning, when a special tree would be pointed out to him, called spirit-wood. He was to cut off a branch; with part of this he was to rub himself all over; another part he was to chew, then spit on the ground; after which he would be able to see and handle the spirits of others.

Should any spirit be refractory, and try to evade the medium by running away, the chewing of the wood and the spitting process must be repeated several times. If after doing this the spirit be perverse, and resist capture, the medium must return home and inform relatives that the omen is fatal. The owner of the spirit will die.

When a person is sick in a village the medium is called in and the above ritual is performed.

A short time ago a young man named Saisami, of Mabadauwane, was taken by a shark whilst swimming some fifty miles from home. A few days after his death was reported in the settlement Kaiku used the spirit-wood and had the pleasure of seeing Saisami's spirit sitting on a stone near the village.

Sometimes a spirit may not run away but may prevent itself being taken. In that case the medium returns home and says to the next-of-kin : " I have seen the spirit of your child and it did not jump. You had better look out." This message is a warning that death may be expected at any moment.

A most interesting case was related to me quite recently concerning the man Samae. There was a man in the village nigh unto death. The distressed relatives sought the aid of the medium. The latter went out into the bush and procured some of the spirit-wood, but did not discover the spirit of the sick man. He then walked the road leading to the patient's garden, chewed another mouthful of wood, spat upon the ground and found the spirit immediately.

Now it happened at that particular time that the medium had a kind of broom, which is obtained from the coco-nut tree. This he had trailed in the mud, and of course it was dirty. On seeing the sick man's spirit he struck it with the dirty broom across the lumbar region, and commanded it to return to its rightful owner without delay. Now by some strange coincidence, at the very time this happened, which was after dark, the sick man felt a pain across his loins.

He informed those sitting round of this fact, and upon their looking at the place indicated, there were the muddy marks of the broom, corresponding to those which had been made by the medium upon the spirit. The spirit, after being chastised, returned home, entered the body and left the dirty marks upon the sufferer's skin. The patient made a quick recovery. My informant said: "There is no doubt about the muddy marks upon the body. I saw them."

Another instance where mediums are said to be able to forecast events may be given. A man is sick. His wife calls in the medium to bring the wandering spirit back to her husband. A little after dark the medium finds the spirit. Should the latter's legs be encircled by a snake, or the fangs of the snake be fixed in the muscles of the body, and should the medium be able to remove the snake, the invalid will recover. If, however, he is unable to do this, the omen is most unfavourable and an early death may be expected.

It is not necessary that a person should be sick before the medium can see the spirit of that individual. The medium often sees spirits menaced by snakes, alligators and other dreadful things, and tries to rescue them from the death-dealing creatures.

It is interesting to note the manner in which the spirits are carried about by the mediums. For this purpose each medium carries about with him when engaged on this class of work a long wicker-work glove for covering the wrist, a gauntlet. It is carried in the left hand, and with the right the medium holds the spirit and then puts it into the gauntlet. He then takes it and places it against the back of the sick man; the spirit enters his body, and the invalid makes a quick recovery.

The spirit of a woman about to become confined, named *boto urio*, may be seen sitting on the veranda of the house. The medium is called. He may catch the spirit in his gauntlet or drive it away with his broom. When the spirit enters the woman's body the baby is immediately born. Should the spirit whilst sitting on the veranda bleed at the nostrils, the omen is bad and the woman will die.

Telepathy.—My dictionary says that telepathy is " the sympathetic affection of one mind or person by another at a distance, through a supposed emotional influence and without any direct communication by the senses." It is a common belief in the Fly river district that such sympathetic affection really does exist. In proof of which they assert that if one of their clan dies some distance from home, at the very moment when his spirit leaves the body a feeling of unrest comes upon the spirits of the other members of the clan, their bodies become weak and this weakness is felt for twenty-four hours. The natives call this spirit-sympathy or compassion.

State after Death.—There is no settled idea regarding the future state, nor of the place where the spirits are supposed to go, beyond the fact that it is towards the west.

Earthquakes.—In 1922 we had several earth tremors, followed by an earthquake. This was not of a violent character, but just enough to make one feel a trifle uncomfortable. This caused great consternation in the district. The natives reported that the water in the swamps " shook on the surface as if it were boiling." Generally speaking, the cause was attributed to evil spirits, but not so in every place. The head men of Kowaku held a lengthy council meeting to consider the matter and determine the cause. Their verdict was that "the earthquake was caused by the pigs in the village grunting too much, and in order that this may not occur again all the pigs must be killed." This order in council was duly carried out, and there has not been another earthquake in the district since.

In another village a native was recovering from a long illness. The head men decided that the earthquake had been caused by the man's spirit wandering too much. He died that night, but I do not think it was a natural death.

General Ideas.—The Kiwais do not believe in the natural causes of misfortune, sickness or death. These are the work of evil spirits, who are ever striving to bring disaster upon them. Their souls are dominated by an awful overhanging fear of the unknown. This sense of fear, this something, they know not what, is a terrible reality and makes life a burden. Their one aim is to propitiate these unseen forces, to obtain their favours, that good crops may be produced, bumper harvests, and success in their fishing and hunting ventures; and also that they may be kept free from sickness and disease.

CHAPTER XXV

PSYCHOLOGY OF NATIVE DANCING

"DANCING is the universal human expression, by movements of the limbs and body, of a sense of rhythm which is implanted among the primitive instincts of the animal world. The rhythmic principles of motion extend throughout the universe, governing the lapse of waves, the flow of tides, the reverberations of light and sound, and the movements of celestial bodies; and in the human organism it manifests itself in the automatic pulses and flexions of the blood and tissues. Dancing is merely the voluntary application of the rhythmic principle, when excitement has induced an abnormally rapid oxidization of brain tissue, to the physical exertion by which the overcharged brain is relieved. This is primitive dancing; and it embraces all movements of the limbs and body expressive of joy or grief, all pantomimic representations of incidents in the lives of the dancers, all performances in which movements of the body are employed to excite the passions of hatred or love, pity or revenge, or to arouse the warlike instincts, and all ceremonies in which such movements express homage or worship, or are used as religious exercises. Although music is not an essential part of dancing, it almost invariably accompanies it, even in the crudest form of rhythm beaten out on a drum" (*Ency. Brit.*).

In this chapter I purpose to set forth, in a simple manner,

some of the methods employed by natives to produce certain mental states amongst the spectators at dances which may be called religious exercises.

The coastal Kiwai dances may be roughly divided into four classes: (1) religious dances; (2) war dances; (3) initiation dances; (4) social dances, which are merely for amusement.

Religious Dances.—The dance in memory of the recent dead, which took place once a month during the south-east season of the year, has been described in a previous chapter. When the natives were asked the reasons why this dance, which was the most important of all the native ceremonies, took place once a month, the following three reasons were given: (1) *wade dogo gido* (for a good harvest); (2) *misiro kirobo gido* (for good luck or good fortune in fishing); (3) *samo gido* (for joy).

It will be advantageous at this point briefly to state the beliefs held by the natives concerning the spirit world. The whole tribe of Kiwais formerly believed, as many do at the present time, that the spirits of their dead had the power to produce a bumper harvest, to give success to all kinds of fishing, especially for dugong and turtle, or to cause the reverse to happen—to blight their gardens and cause misfortune during fishing operations.

In the chapter on the dance in memory of the recent dead it has been stated that the women and children firmly believed that the dancers representing the spirits of the dead were actually the *real spirits* of their departed relatives and friends. The men, however, did not share that belief; they knew that the whole thing was a piece of deception, but did their utmost to encourage the belief held by the women and children. Yet these same men firmly believed that the spirits of their ancestors were present at all their dances, and also at their gardening operations and their fishing, though unseen by them, and that they rejoiced at the honour done to their memory by the dancers and the sacrificial gifts of food.

Addison in *The Spectator* of 14th March 1711 seems to have had ideas of the spirit world not far removed from those held by the Kiwai Papuans. He says: " For my own part, I am apt to join in the opinion with those who believe that all the regions of nature swarm with spirits, and that we have multitudes of spectators on all our actions, when we think ourselves most alone; but instead of terrifying myself with such a notion, I am wonderfully pleased to think that I am always engaged with such an innumerable society in searching out the wonders of creation, and joining in the same consort of praise and adoration."

Milton has finely described this mixed communion of men and spirits in Paradise, and had doubtless his eye upon a verse in old Hesiod, which is almost word for word the same with his third line in the following passage:—

> ". . . Nor think, though men were none,
> That heaven would want spectators, God want praise;
> Millions of spiritual creatures walk the earth
> Unseen, both when we wake and when we sleep;
> All these with ceaseless praise His works behold
> Both day and night. How oft from the steep
> Of echoeing hill or thicket have we heard
> Celestial voices to the midnight air,
> Sole, or responsive each to other's note,

> Singing their great Creator ? Oft in bands,
> While they keep watch, or nightly rounding walk,
> With heavenly touch of instrumental sounds,
> In full harmonic number joined, their songs
> Divide the night, and lift our thoughts to heaven."
>
> *Paradise Lost*, iv. 675-688.

The large quantity of food which was given to the men who danced as representative spirits during the festivals was considered *tarena* (sacred). It might perhaps be regarded as a sacrifice made to the spirits of the dead, who were pleased with the great generosity of their relatives and with the elaborate costumes worn by the spirit dancers; who rejoiced in the knowledge that they were not forgotten, and that their favours in having produced a good harvest were treasured in grateful hearts.

It was a firm conviction in the mind of every Kiwai native that if they did not show their respect and gratitude to the spirits of their dead by gifts of food the spirits would be displeased and misfortune would fall upon their gardens and their fishing would be unsuccessful. One old man said to me: " If no food were provided for a spirit, no preparations made for a dance in its honour, the spirit who was present and saw others honoured would return to Adiri disappointed and angry. It would say: ' My boy did nothing for me; all right, I will do nothing for him.' " The native idea seems to have been : the greater the amount of food presented to the spirit of the dead, the greater the pains taken in dressing for the dance, the greater would be the joy of the spirit, and the greater the favours that would be bestowed upon the givers of the food and upon the performers in the dance.

Psychology of Native Dancing

If any man were to neglect his duty to the memory of the dead, he offended not only the departed spirit, but offended against public custom and public opinion. Such an offence never passed unnoticed. The offender would be reminded of it sooner or later. If he should happen to have a little unpleasantness with a member of his own clan, he would be reminded of his neglect, and told that the supply of food given to the spirits of his ancestors was very meagre. Then the one who had failed in his sacred duty would be filled with shame, and would immediately take steps to rectify his misconduct.

The giving of the food to the spirits, which gratified and pleased them, also gave great pleasure to the givers of the food, and also to the spirit dancers who ate it. Thus the departed spirits, who had returned to their old homes for the time being, rejoiced and made merry with the living members of the tribe or community.

After each of the monthly dances held in memory of the dead the *huwo*, or teased coco-nut leaves used as a covering for the body by the various performers, together with the *makamaka*, or leg ornaments, and croton leaves which had been used as ornaments, were always buried in the gardens or along the side of a river or swamp, that the gardens might be more productive, and a great quantity of fish procured. Thus every effort was made to keep on good terms with the departed spirits and secure their goodwill, so that when they were called upon they would hear and grant the requests of the suppliants.

Doctor Allen Menzies in his *History of Religion* says: "Every sacrifice is also a festival. If this be the case it is unnecessary to spend much time in considering a number of theories formerly regarded with favour as to the original meaning and intention of sacrifice. The view that it is originally simply a bribe to the deity to induce him to afford some needed help receives a good deal of countenance from primitive expressions. '*Do ut des*': 'I give to thee that thou mayest give to me'; 'Here is butter, give us cows'; 'By gifts are the gods persuaded, by gifts great kings.' Was early sacrifice then simply a business transaction, in which man bringing a prayer to the deity brought a gift too, as he was accustomed to do to the great ones of the earth, in order that the deity might be well disposed toward him and grant his petition? Even if this were the case, if sacrifices were offered with the direct and almost avowed intention of getting good value for it, yet if it takes the form of a meal, it is lifted above the most sordid form of bribery. There is a difference between slipping money into a man's hand and asking him to dinner, even if the object aimed at be in both cases the same; and when the invitations are numerous and formal, there must be a moral, not an immoral, relation between the two parties. Where the sacrifice is a meal, intercourse is sought for; a certain sympathy exists between the worshipper and the worshipped; they stand to each other not in the relation of briber and bribed, buyer and seller, but in that of patron and client, or father and son."

I think that the above quotation represents the case of the Kiwais and their gifts to the spirits of their dead in a far better way than I could have stated it.

It has already been pointed out that the women were duped and easily imposed upon by the male members of the community. The women accepted the statement without question that the dancers were real spirits who had journeyed all the way from Adiri to visit them. The men had to keep up this deception, and in order to do so they had to resort to much trickery and fraud, the recent discovery of which by the women had, I believe, a lot to do with the decline and death of the ceremony. That, however, is a matter which does not come in here.

Attention and how it was pre-adjusted.—It was whilst talking over the dance in memory of the recent dead with a few old men, all of whom had taken an active part in many of the dances in their younger days, that I first saw something of the definite working of the native mind in the ritual of the ceremonies. This dance, or the preliminary part of it, began before sunrise. This seemed to me somewhat purposeless, and I told the old men so. One replied: " It's our custom and it was our fathers'." I made some remark about it being too early, and suggested that the people would not like being disturbed before daylight. They smiled at my simplicity; then old Duwani the headhunter said: " We began early to let the women know that the spirits of their dead were going to come, so that they might get ready to see them; the women have plenty to do; they have to blacken their bodies, put on the long grass petticoats, and go to the gardens for food for the spirits."

Now if this statement be correct, and it seems to me quite reasonable, it looks as if the early start or the initial part of the ceremony was enacted with the object of causing the women and children to fix their minds upon, or think about, the spirits of their recent dead. It was a preliminary announcement, and it is only natural that after the intimation the women who had recently been bereaved would be on the tiptoe of expectation.

The minds of the women would be occupied with one idea—the arrival of their expected visitors. Their attention would be pre-adjusted. Sully says : " The fixing of attention is rendered easy and rapid or the reverse by the preceding state of the attention."

Now when the native women attended the dance their attention would be easily secured.

Another method employed to fix the attention of the spectators was the manner in which a new spirit was brought into the dancing arena. By a new spirit is meant one which had not previously appeared in the death dance. Such an one came on the stage in company with a number of old spirits. The latter stood round forming the "psychical fringe," whilst the former danced. When I inquired the reason why only one new spirit danced at a time and not the whole of them, the reply was: "You can watch only one thing at a time, and if a lot of new spirits danced together you would not know which belonged to you." The point aimed at here seems to be that if there be only one object to look at the whole attention will be directed to that object. In other words, he meant to say that a person can attend to one thing more easily than he can to two or three things. Sully writes : " The smaller the number of objects on which the attention is concentrated the more will each receive." If there be only one object the whole of the attention will be focused upon it and a strong mental impression produced.

The amount of attention would also be increased by the

skill of the performing representative spirits, whose one ambition would be to attract and keep the attention of the onlookers by their dexterity and ability.

Suggestion.—By their pantomimic display, in which the natives are very clever, they are able to impart a notion or idea in an indirect and unobtrusive manner. To illustrate this I will give a few examples. When the spirits were assembling for the death dance it was customary for those who had been dead a long time to be seen coming from the burial ground with their bodies covered with white clay, suggesting the idea that the bodies had been buried for a considerable length of time. On the other hand, the spirits of the recent dead did not have any clay upon them, conveying the idea that they had not been in the grave long enough for the soil to adhere to their bodies or spirits.

The spirit of a man who had been taken by a crocodile was seen emerging from the water at the very spot where he was seized by the reptile, or where he was last seen alive. This spirit was observed crouching in the water with its head just above the surface as the sun came above the horizon. The old men, who were standing round for the purpose, did not fail to draw the attention of the women and children to the apparition in the river or sea. As soon as a crowd had assembled, the figure rose, came ashore and went into the sacred dancing enclosure.

The manner in which the spirits of children were brought on the stage is rather pathetic. The spirit of a child could not be expected to know the way from the land of the departed. A guide was deemed necessary, as the way was long and the child would get lost if allowed to travel alone. An old spirit was selected to lead the child. A piece of string was tied round his waist, the other end was held by the hand of the wee bairn, so that there was no chance of its missing the way. The experienced spirit led and the child followed behind.

Women spirits were always represented by men dancers. They were attired in long grass petticoats reaching down to their ankles, and were thus easily recognized as women spirits.

Men spirits were dressed and armed as if going forth to war. The faces of both men and women spirits were covered so that their identity could not be discovered.

These skilful actors and born imitators were able to mimic any defects or idiosyncrasies of the dead persons they represented. Take the case of a dancer assuming the likeness or character of a dead warrior. All the fighting gear of the latter was placed on the ground in the dancing enclosure. The dancer during his performance picked up each of these implements in turn and exhibited them to the spectators. The stone club was held aloft and shaken in the direction in which the deceased had obtained his trophies of human heads. The knife was used to imitate the act of beheading an enemy. The head was put into a carrier and waved above the head of the performer. The dugong harpoon was taken up, and the dancer, turning towards the sea in the direction of the deceased's favourite reef, harpooned an imaginary dugong.

In another dance called the *oromo rubi oboro*—namely, the dance of the spirits of the sea-beach—the acting was delightful and full of suggestion. The first time I witnessed this performance, which is over twenty years ago, I recognized

Psychology of Native Dancing

four out of the six things represented by the actors. The first performer represented a crocodile swimming in the water. Now if any person had previously seen one of these reptiles in its native element, lifting its head just above the surface of the water then submerging it again, and repeatedly doing the same thing, he would not have had difficulty in recognizing what the native was suggesting. When I saw this performance, it brought back to my mind a crocodile which I had seen a few weeks before off the village of Auti in the Fly river and all the incidents connected with it, and the attempt of my boy to shoot it. This was the first time I had seen a crocodile outside a zoological garden.

A second dance suggested a cassowary. This was both clever and highly amusing. The actor imitated the walking of the bird to perfection. The somewhat peculiar manner in which it places its feet on the ground was suggested by the movements of the hands. The way the bird swallows its food was particularly well done. The best part, however, was the imitation of the bird looking into the branches of an imaginary tree to see if there were any fruit upon it. When the survey was finished and considered satisfactory, the performer kicked the tree, causing the fruit to fall to the earth, after which the bird walked round inspecting the amount which had fallen to the ground.

Another figure represented a fish-hawk with outstretched wings floating majestically over the sea, waiting its opportunity to pounce upon and seize any fish which might come to the surface.

A dog scraping the ground with its hind feet was also well done.

The two items on the programme which I failed to recognize (they were explained to me afterwards) were the imitation of a king-fish and a shark, depicted rushing through the water chasing their prey. This, however, is a digression and has been inserted here merely to show the ability of the natives to express their meaning by actions without words.

With regard to the death dance, enough has been said, I think, to prove that the Kiwai men in their dances are able to convey ideas and notions by suggestion and imitation.

Association of Ideas by Similarity.—I have related in the chapter on Death and Burial the manner in which a corpse was measured to obtain the length of the grave required. For the sake of my argument it will be necessary to repeat briefly the method employed, which was as follows. A person died; a long stick was placed alongside the body and a notch made upon it corresponding to the length of the corpse. The stick was then laid upon the ground, where it was intended the body should be buried, and two wooden pegs were put into the earth, marking the size of the grave needed. The marked stick was then carefully removed to one of the houses.

At a later date a solemn and impressive ceremony was held to select a person to represent the spirit of the departed in the next dance in memory of the dead. The men assembled in the club-house and sat in a line. An old man then took the notched stick and advanced toward the sitting company. The first man in the line stood up. The old man then placed the stick alongside the standing figure; if he were taller or shorter than the notch he sat down in silence.

The first man whose height corresponded with the notch on the stick was appointed to dance as the spirit of the one recently dead.

I suspected the reason of this, but to make sure I asked the old men the following question: " Supposing I were dead, could not Mr So-and-so [I mentioned the name of a man much taller than the writer] dance as my spirit? " They all smiled and looked a little surprised at such an absurd question. One of them replied: " No, you could not have a tall man dancing as the spirit of a short one, nor could you have a short man dancing as the spirit of a tall one." Another said: " That would be *karatai* [silly]; if you did so people would not know the spirits of their own dead."

I do not think there can be any doubt in this case of what is in the mind of the native or what he desires to do. The point is to get a man the same height as the deceased to dance as his spirit, that the similarity of the dancer will suggest and bring before the minds of the spectators the image of the person represented.

The question will probably arise in the mind of the reader, as it did in mine, as to how they would get over the difficulty of a man dancing as the spirit of a young person, if one of similar height were not available. I accordingly put the question to them. This, however, did not present any difficulty to the imaginative minds of the coastal Kiwais. The solution of the problem was as follows. A week or so before the dance was to be held in which the child spirit would make its first appearance, a few male relatives, one at a time, had a little quiet talk with the mother upon the subject, and each one suggested to her that the child's spirit would probably have grown much taller since it went to the place of departed spirits. In this way the mother's mind was prepared, by suggestion, for seeing a spirit somewhat taller than what she would otherwise have expected.

Thus the women and children, spectators at the dance, with their attention pre-adjusted, seeing the pantomimic display by actors similar in height to their recent dead, vainly believed that the objects before them were the real spirits of their loved ones. So great was the impression produced upon their minds that they often said: "That is my child," or "That is my husband."

Map for "Among Papuan Headhunters."

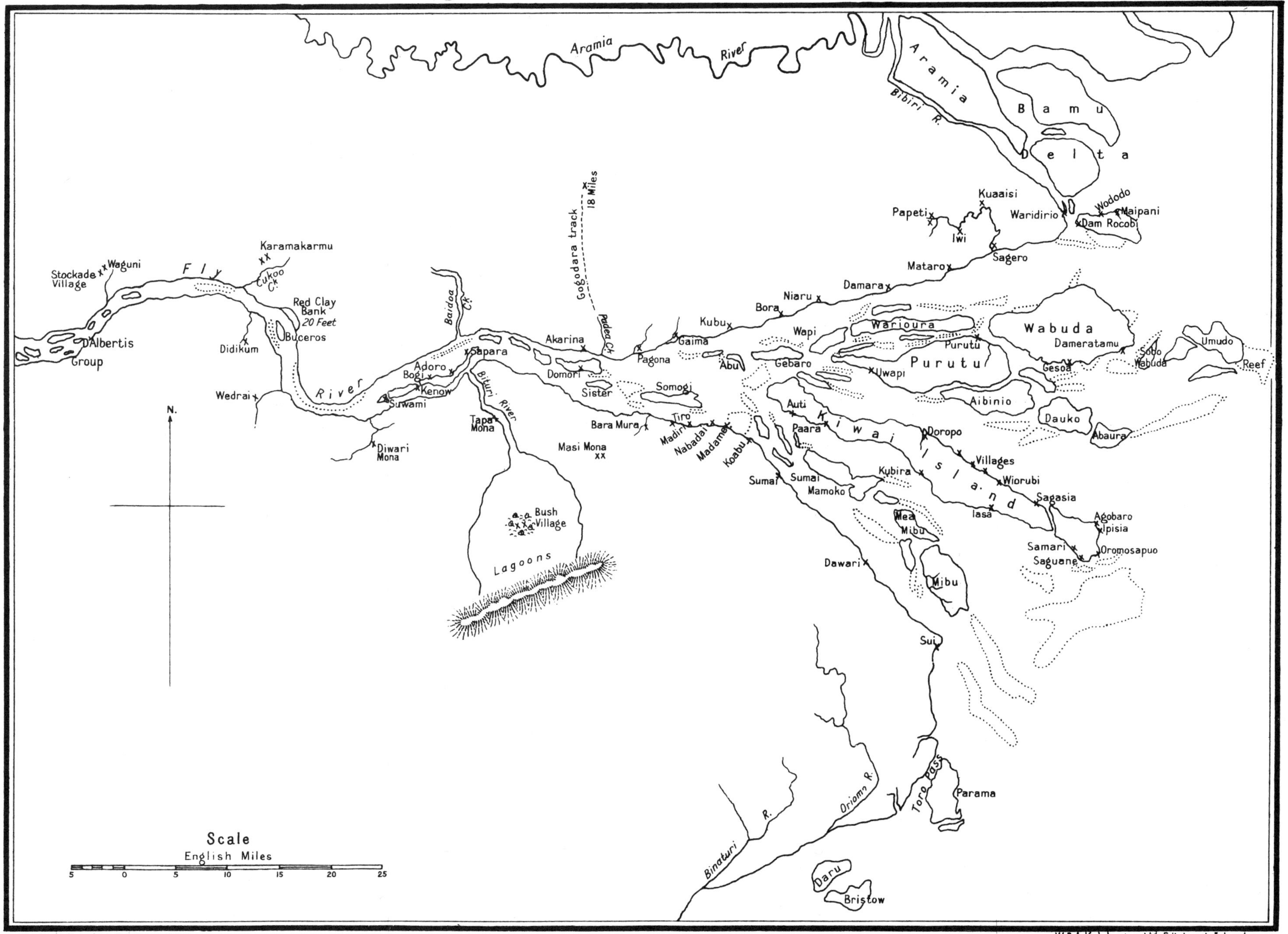

Seeley Service & Co., Ltd.

W. & A. K. Johnston Ltd Edinburgh & London

INDEX

ADAGI's story, 139
Adigo, wristlet, 236
Agu, plan of, 99
Ancestors, spirits of, 110, 293
Animals of district, 24
Arapoo, 102
Art, 26, 27
Awaro, 115

BEAUTY, no appreciation of, 79
Beheading—
  Knife, 272
  Method of, 265
Birds, 24
Birth customs, 28
Bisare or pill, 214
Bull-roarer, *madubu*—
  Origin of, 201
  Use of, 94, 101, 203, 204, 206
Burial—
  Distinguished person, 169
  Feast, 172
  Only child, 169
  Special cases, 167

CANOES—
  Decoration of, 114
  Making, 112

Central post, 88
Ceremonies—
  Canoe-making, 109
  Death and burial, 165
  Departed spirits, 178
  Dugong-fishing, 130-131, 136
  End of mourning, 72
  Harvest, 98
  House-building, 83, 89
  Initiation, 189, 201, 205, 208, 219
  Marriage, 47
  Memorial, 334
  Peace-making, 255
  Return from war, 266
  Shooting spirits, 251
  Taera, 241
  Taro, 101
  Turtle-fishing, 118, 121, 124, 125
  War, 217
  Wete, 38
  Yam harvest, 98
  Yam-planting, 94
Charms—
  Dugong-fishing, 134
  House, 83, 88, 90
  Taro, 104
  Turtle-fishing, 118
  Yam, 93, 97
Childbirth, 62

Index

Club-house—
  Building of, 82
  Plan of, 86
Coco-nut, 55
Conch shell, 136, 209
Cradles, 29

DANCES—
  Anibibi, 260
  Bow, 232
  Children's, 143
  Kaikai oboro or spirit dance, 175-188
  Karara, 248
  Madia, 42
  Marriage, 47
  Misamisa, 259
  Peace-making, 260
  Pipi, 268
  Rat, 41
  Religious, 300
  Suggestion in, 307
  Taero, 241
  War, 267
  Wabea, 217
  Wete, 40, 47
Dancing, psychology of native, 298
Darimo or club-house, 83, 86
Death customs, 66, 165
Dishonesty, 77
Divination, 293
Dori head-dress, 45
Dugong—
  Ceremonies after fishing, 137
  Charms, 134
  Discription of, 128
  Fishing ceremonies, 130
  Methods of, 134
  Spearing platform, 132
  Tale of fishing, 139
Dyes, 63

EAR-LOBE customs, 33
Earthquakes, 297
Eating the dead, 174
Education, 34, 35

FAIRIES, goblins, 110
Feasts—
  Aropoo, 102
  Burial, 172
  Canoe-making, 108
  Horiomu, 178
  House-building, 108
Fence-making, 93
Fibres, 64
Fireplace, 87
Fish, 24
Floors, 85
Fly River, estimates of speed, depth, volume, etc., 17
Flying-foxes, 98
Food of natives, 54-57

Gamada, 89
Games—
  Aniopu, 142
  Ball, 144
  Bows and arrows, 147
  Cat's-cradle, 162
  Dancing, 143
  Dog and pig, 158
  Epoo kokoio, 143
  Flying-fox, 148
  Hide-and-seek, 163

Index

Hockey, 152
Hopping, 161
Mud-pies, 145
Nuku koroio, 146, 150
Sailing models, 143
Shooting grass, 145
Swinging, 164
Tig, 159, 160
Tops, 144
Water game, 155
Winding game, 161
Gardens—
  Charms for, 93
  Inspection of, 190
  Making of, 94
Gesture language, 91
Gifts to dead, 302
Giware, a form of magic, 283
Gora, dancing instrument, 236

HARPOON, 129
Head-hunting—
  Methods of, 265
  Origin of, 261
  Reasons for, 262
  Return from, 266
Heads, preserving of, 269
Home life, 62
Horiomu or sacred dancing-ground, 178-180
Hospitality of natives, 26
House-building, 82
Hunting, 116-117

Ibure bean, 88
Ideas, general, of Kiwais, 298
Initiate, *kowea mere*, 189

Initiation ceremonies—
  First, 189
  Second, 201
  Third, 205
  Gamabibi muguru, 208
  Mimia abere, 219
  Taera, 241
Inspection of gardens, *giradaro*, 190

Kaikai, 181
Kamuka or scrub hen, 253
Karea or good-luck ceremony, 89
Kiwai people, 25
Kokokoko spirit, 90
Kubai, 119-122

Mabusi, 104
Maigidubu, 96, 102
Makamaka or leglets, 185
Marriage, 45-51
Mat-making, 57
Mauwamo, 283
Mediums, 294
Memorial ceremony or *uruba muguru*, 334
Mirror, effect of, 291
Momogo, 87
Motomoto, 114
Mourning costume, the removal of, 72

NAMING of children, 28
Natives, characteristics of, 25, 26, 27, 64, 76
Needles, 58

Oboro spirit, 292
Ororaorora, 102, 110, 215

Index

Outriggers, details of, 114
Patora or platform on boat, 115
Pests, 24
Piercing nose and ears, 31, 32
Pipi head dance, 89
Polygamy, 50
Proposals of marriage, 48
Purification after war, 270

REMARRYING of widows, 70
Reptiles, 24

SAGO-MAKING, 59
Sailing, methods of, 116
Saro or central post, 88
Scenery of Fly river, 21
Sea, ritual at, 121
Seasons—
  Description of, 19
  Native, 105
Sharpening of stone axes, 112
Sorcery—
  Methods, 279
  Origin, 278
  Sorcerers, 27, 278
  Types, 283
Spirits—
  Ancestral, 110, 118, 176, 177, 293
  Dance, 175
  Earth, 102, 110, 215
  Types, 290-292
  World of, 290
State after death, 297
Suggestion in dances, 307
Superstitions, 287

TARO, 101
Telepathy, 297
Thatch, 86
Tools, 82
Tops, spinning, 144
Tree-felling for canoes, 108-111
Turtle-fishing—
  Canoes returning empty, 125
  Ceremonies before, 118
  First turtle ceremonies, 124
  Methods of, 123

Urio spirit, 290
Uriona, 291
Uruba maguru or memorial ceremony, 334

Wapo or harpoon handle, 129
War—
  Land, 261
  Sea, 273
Warakara, 180
Water-bottles, 117
Wete ceremony, 38
Widows, 66
Women—
  Character, 64
  Childbirth, 62
  Day's work of, 52
  Exchange of, 48
  Marriage, 45
Woto, planting-stick, 95

YAM—
  Gardens, 92
  Harvest, 98